TEACHER'S EDITION 4

English
No Problem!

Kathryn Quinones
Office of Adult and Continuing Education
New York City Department of Education, NY

Donna Korol
Office of Adult and Continuing Education
New York City Department of Education, NY

D1441694

New Readers Press

English—No Problem! ®
English—No Problem! Level 4 Teacher's Edition
ISBN 1-56420-354-9

Copyright © 2004 New Readers Press
New Readers Press
Division of ProLiteracy Worldwide
1320 Jamesville Avenue, Syracuse, New York 13210
www.newreaderspress.com

Printed in the United States of America
9 8 7 6 5 4 3 2

All proceeds from the sale of New Readers Press materials
support literacy programs in the United States and worldwide.

Acquisitions Editor: Paula L. Schlusberg
Developer: Mendoza and Associates
Project Director: Roseanne Mendoza
Project Editor: Pat Harrington-Wydell
Content Editor: Rose DeNeve
Production Director: Heather Witt-Badoud
Designer: Kimbrly Koennecke
Cover Design: Kimbrly Koennecke
Cover Photography: Robert Mescavage Photography

Authors

Kathryn Quinones
Office of Adult and
  Continuing Education
New York City Department
  of Education

Donna Korol
Office of Adult and
  Continuing Education
New York City Department
  of Education

Contributors

National Council Members

Audrey Abed, *San Marcos Even Start Program, San Marcos, TX*

Myra K. Baum, *New York City Board of Education (retired), New York, NY*

Kathryn Hamilton, *Elk Grove Adult and Community Education, Sacramento, CA*

Brigitte Marshall, *Oakland Adult Education Programs, Oakland, CA*

Teri McLean, *Florida Human Resources Development Center, Gainesville, FL*

Alan Seaman, *Wheaton College, Wheaton, IL*

Reviewers

Sabrina Budasi-Martin, *William Rainey Harper College, Palatine, IL*

Linda Davis-Pluta, *Oakton Community College, Des Plaines, IL*

Paticia DeHesus-Lopez *Center for Continuing Education, Texas A&M University, Kingsville, TX*

Gail Feinstein Forman, *San Diego City College, San Diego, CA*

Carolyn Harding, *Marshall High School Adult Program, Falls Church, VA*

Trish Kerns, *Old Marshall Adult Education Center, Sacramento City Unified SchoolDistrict, Sacramento, CA*

Debe Pack-Garcia, *Manteca Adult School, Humbolt, CA*

Lydia Omori, *William Rainey Harper College, Palatine, IL*

Pamela Patterson, *Seminole Community College, Sanford, FL*

Catherine Porter, *Adult Learning Resource Center, Des Plaines, IL*

Jean Rose, *ABC Adult School, Cerritos, CA*

Eric Rosenbaum, *Bronx Community College Adult Program, Bronx, NY*

Laurie Shapero, *Miami-Dade Community College, Miami, FL*

Terry Shearer, *Norht Harris College Community Education, Houston, TX*

Abigail Tom, *Durham Technical Community College, Chapel Hill, NC*

Darla Wickard, *North Harris College Community Education, Houston, TX*

Pilot Teachers

Connie Bateman, *Gerber Adult Education Center, Sacramento, CA*

Jennifer Bell, *William Rainey Harper College, Palatine, IL*

Marguerite Bock, *Chula Vista Adult School, Chula Vista, CA*

Giza Braun, *National City Adult School, National City, CA*

Sabrina Budasi-Martin, *William Rainey Harper College, Palatine, IL*

Wong-Ling Chew, *Citizens Advice Bureau, Bronx, NY*

Renee Collins, *Elk Grove Adult and Community Education, Sacramento, CA*

Rosette Dawson, *North Harris College Community Education, Houston, TX*

Kathleen Edel, *Elk Grove Adult and Community Education, Sacramento, CA*

Margaret Erwin, *Elk Grove Adult and Community Education, Sacramento, CA*

Teresa L. Gonzalez, *North Harris College Community Education, Houston, TX*

Fernando L. Herbert, *Bronx Adult School, Bronx, NY*

Carolyn Killean, *North Harris College Community Education, Houston, TX*

Elizabeth Minicz, *William Rainey Harper College, Palatine, IL*

Larry Moore, *Long Beach Adult School, Long Beach, CA*

Kathryn Powell, *William Rainey Harper College, Palatine, IL*

Alan Reiff, *NYC Board of Education, Adult and Continuing Education, Bronx, NY*
Brenda M. Rodriguez, *San Marcos Even Start, San Marcos, TX*
Juan Carlos Rodriguez, *San Marcos Even Start, San Marcos, TX*
Joan Siff, *NYC Board of Education, Adult and Continuing Education, Bronx, NY*
Susie Simon, *Long Beach Adult School, Long Beach, CA*
Gina Tauber, *North Harris College, Houston, TX*
Diane Villanueva, *Elk Grove Adult and Community Education, Sacramento, CA*
Dona Wayment, *Elk Grove Adult and Community Education, Sacramento, CA*
Weihua Wen, *NYC Board of Education, Adult and Continuing Education, Bronx, NY*
Darla Wickard, *North Harris College Community Education, Houston, TX*
Judy Wurtz, *Sweetwater Union High School District, Chula Vista, CA*

Focus Group Participants
Leslie Jo Adams, *Laguna Niguel, CA*
Fiona Armstrong, *New York City Board of Education, New York, NY*
Myra K. Baum, *New York City Board of Education (retired), New York, NY*
Gretchen Bitterlin, *San Diego Unified School District, San Diego, CA*
Patricia DeHesus-Lopez, *Center for Continuing Education, Texas A&M University, Kingsville, TX*
Diana Della Costa, *Worksite ESOL Programs, Kissimmee, FL*
Frankie Dovel, *Orange County Public Schools, VESOL Program, Orlando, FL*
Marianne Dryden, *Region 1 Education Service Center, Edinburgh, TX*
Richard Firsten, *Lindsey Hopkins Technical Center, Miami, FL*
Pamela S. Forbes, *Bartlett High School, Elgin, IL*
Kathryn Hamilton, *Elk Grove Adult and Community Education, Sacramento, CA*
Trish Kerns, *Old Marshall Adult Education Center, Sacramento City Unified School District, Sacramento, CA*
Suzanne Leibman, *The College of Lake County, Grayslake, IL*
Patty Long, *Old Marshall Adult Education Center, Sacramento City Unified School District, Sacramento, CA*
Brigitte Marshall, *Oakland Adult Education Programs, Oakland, CA*
Bet Messmer, *Santa Clara Adult School, Santa Clara, CA*
Patricia Mooney, *New York State Board of Education, Albany, NY*
Lee Ann Moore, *Salinas Adult School, Salinas, CA*
Lynne Nicodemus, *San Juan Adult School, Carmichael, CA*
Pamela Patterson, *Seminole Community College, Sanford, FL*
Eric Rosenbaum, *Bronx Community College, Bronx, NY*
Linda Sasser, *Alhambra District Office, Alhambra, CA*
Federico Salas, *North Harris College Community Education, Houston, TX*
Alan Seaman, *Wheaton College, Wheaton, IL*
Kathleen Slattery, *Salinas Adult School, Salinas, CA*
Carol Speigl, *Center for Continuing Education, Texas A&M University, Kingsville, TX*
Edie Uber, *Santa Clara Adult School, Santa Clara, CA*
Lise Wanage, *CASAS, Phoenix, AZ*

Contents

Unit 1   Taking the First Step 10

◆ Vocabulary: Goal-setting words • Problem-solving words
◆ Language: Compare present perfect and simple past (review) • Compare present perfect and past perfect
◆ Pronunciation: Intonation with statements • Intonation with *yes/no* questions
◆ Culture: Changing jobs

Unit 2   Selling Your Skills 24

◆ Vocabulary: Interview words • Words for feelings
◆ Language: Conditional contrary to fact • Indirect speech
◆ Pronunciation: Sentence stress • Vowel sounds in *say, said, says*
◆ Culture: Expected behavior in the workplace

Unit 3   Getting Help 38

◆ Vocabulary: Words for offering and asking for help • Words for talking about difficult issues
◆ Language: Objects of prepositions • Prepositional phrases
◆ Pronunciation: *Of* after a word ending in a consonant • Holding over final consonants
◆ Culture: Getting professional help

Scope and Sequence

Unit Number and Title	Global Unit Theme (across all levels)	Unit Topic/Skill	Lesson-Specific Life Skills	Vocabulary	Language
Unit 1 Taking the First Step	Life stages: personal growth and goal setting	Looking to the future	L1: Clarify your personal goals L2: Think about your past experiences L3: Talk about job or career goals	Goal-setting words Problem-solving words	Compare present perfect and simple past Compare present perfect and past perfect
Unit 2 Selling Your Skills	Making connections	Presenting your skills	L1: Talk about your skills L2: Talk about how to act in an interview L3: Understand how to use problem-solving skills to get a better job	Interview words Words for feelings	Conditional contrary to fact Indirect speech
Unit 3 Getting Help	Taking care of yourself	Getting and giving guidance and support	L1: Get advice from others L2: Practice getting information about important issues L3: Find information on an organization	Words for offering and asking for help Words for talking about difficult issues	Objects of prepositions Prepositional phrases
Unit 4 On Your Own	Personal finance	Making important decisions	L1: Find information to support an opinion L2: Understand how to fill out complex forms L3: Be able to check your home and workplace for safety	Words about small businesses Words related to safety	Connecting ideas with *so, because,* and *although* *Who, which,* and *that* in adjectival clauses
Unit 5 Think before You Buy!	Consumer awareness	Becoming an educated consumer	L1: Analyze a product you want to buy L2: Practice doing research to make good purchasing decisions L3: Read and analyze a section from a textbook	Words that consumers need	Present and past participles used as adjectives Embedded questions

Pronunciation	Culture	Tasks and Unit Project	EFF Skill/Common Activity (The basic communication skills— read with understanding, convey ideas in writing, speak so others can understand, listen actively, and observe critically— are taught in every unit.)	SCANS Skills (The basic skills of reading, writing, listening, and speaking are taught in every unit.)	Technology
Intonation with statements Intonation with *yes/no* questions	Changing jobs	T1: Make a plan for your future T2: Make a time line T3: Plan and take action UP: Write a letter to yourself from the future	Plan Reflect and evaluate	Manage human resources Self-management	Search the Internet for career information
Sentence stress Vowel sounds in *say, said,* and *says*	Expected behavior in the workplace	T1: Asking the right questions T2: Make a list of US social and business customs T3: Present a collage of your skills and achievements UP: Make a personal achievement record	Cooperate with others	Creative thinking	Use a computer to design a cover page for your achievement record; use a computer to write and design a brochure
Of after a word ending in a consonant Holding over final consonants	Getting professional help	T1: Start a resource guide T2: Gathering and using informational publications T3: Gather more information on an organization UP: Make a resource guide	Guide others	Interpret and communicate information Self-esteem	Find your organization's web site and gather more information
-tion ending Reductions with *have*	Independence as a cultural value	T1: Debate an issue T2: Interview a small business owner T3: Safety check UP: Create a business	Solve problems and make decisions	Acquire and evaluate information Understand systems	
Stress in compound nouns	Technology and progress	T1: Do an informal product analysis T2: Research and rate a product T3: Create an original product ad UP: Create a class consumer guide	Solve problems and make decisions Use information and communications technology	Information: Acquire and evaluate information Decision making	Make a cover design for the class consumer guide using computer graphics and type; make a table on the computer

Scope and Sequence

Unit Number and Title	Global Unit Theme (across all levels)	Unit Topic/Skill	Lesson-Specific Life Skills	Vocabulary	Language
Unit 6 Protecting Your Rights	Protecting your legal rights	Understanding your rights	L1: Understand how a contract protects your rights L2: Learn how to take legal action L3: Learn more about your rights and what happens in court	Legal terms	Adverbs of time with the past perfect Special problems with prepositions, articles, gerunds, and infinitives
Unit 7 Participating in Your Community	Participating in your new country and community	Becoming an active community participant	L1: Discuss voting procedures L2: Identify basic responsibilities of government L3: Learn how to be a more active community member	Language for participating in a democracy	Present and past participles used as adjectives Past participles of irregular verbs
Unit 8 It's Never Too Late	Lifelong learning	Finding your learning style	L1: Learn how to find educational resources L2: Listen actively L3: Practice giving a short speech	Words for giving a speech Words about ways to learn	Past continuous Past perfect continuous
Unit 9 Celebrating Success	Celebrating success	Getting the job you want	L1: Start a resume L2: Prepare a work history L3: Prepare for a job interview	Words for resumes Words for job interviews	Passive voice in simple present (review) Verb tenses (review)

Pronunciation	Culture	Tasks and Unit Project	EFF Skill/Common Activity (The basic communication skills—read with understanding, convey ideas in writing, speak so others can understand, listen actively, and observe critically—are taught in every unit.)	SCANS Skills (The basic skills of reading, writing, listening, and speaking are taught in every unit.)	Technology
Consonant blends	Written and verbal contracts	T1: Make a class list of legal terms T2: Listen to a recorded message T3: Present your argument UP: Create a personal legal glossary	Advocate and influence Resolve conflict and negotiate	Understand systems	Videotape a television show with a court scene to watch in class; record yourself and your teacher on a cassette recorder
Disappearing /h/ of function words	Tradition of self-reliance and community involvement	T1: Registering to vote T2: Stay informed T3: Write about an issue UP: Make a Community Resource Guide	Take responsibility for learning	Acquire and evaluate information	Type and print a community resource guide on the computer; find a state government web site on the Internet
Disappearing sounds and syllables	Learning at any age	T1: Make a resource guide T2: Listen actively to a speaker T3: Write a speech UP: Find your personal learning style	Take responsibility for learning	Know how to learn Responsibility	Use a computer to publish a summary of and questions on a speech about lifelong learning
Diphthongs Syllable stress	Personal qualities admired in the US	T1: Prepare to write a resume T2: Start a work history T3: Prepare for a job interview UP: Prepare a resume	Plan	Manage human resources Self-management	Do Internet research at the web site of a large company

About This Series

Meeting Adult Learners' Needs with *English—No Problem!*

English—No Problem! is a theme-based, performance-based series focused on developing critical thinking and cultural awareness and on building language and life skills. Designed for adult and young adult English language learners, the series addresses themes and issues meaningful to adults in the United States.

English—No Problem! is appropriate for and respectful of adult learners. These are some key features:
- interactive, communicative, participatory approach
- rich, authentic language
- problem-posing methodology
- project-based units and task-based lessons
- goal setting embedded in each unit and lesson
- units organized around themes of adult relevance
- contextualized, inductive grammar
- student materials designed to fit into lesson plans
- performance assessment, including tools for learner self-evaluation

Series Themes

Across the series, units have the following themes:
- Life Stages: Personal Growth and Goal Setting
- Making Connections
- Taking Care of Yourself
- Personal Finance
- Consumer Awareness
- Protecting Your Legal Rights
- Participating in Your New Country and Community
- Lifelong Learning
- Celebrating Success

At each level, these themes are narrowed to subthemes that are level-appropriate in content and language.

English—No Problem! Series Components

Five levels make up the series:
- literacy
- level 1 (low beginning)
- level 2 (high beginning)
- level 3 (low intermediate)
- level 4 (high intermediate)

The series includes the following components.

Student Book

A full-color student book is the core of each level of *English—No Problem!* Literacy skills, vocabulary, grammar, reading, writing, listening, speaking, and SCANS-type skills are taught and practiced.

Teacher's Edition

Each teacher's edition includes these tools:
- general suggestions for using the series
- scope and sequence charts for the level
- lesson-specific teacher notes with reduced student book pages
- complete scripts for all listening activities and Pronunciation Targets in the student book

Workbook

A workbook provides contextualized practice in the skills taught at each level. Activities relate to the student book stories. Workbook activities are especially useful for learners working individually.

 This icon in the teacher's edition indicates where workbook activities can be assigned.

Reproducible Masters

The reproducible masters include photocopiable materials for the level. Some masters are unit-specific, such as contextualized vocabulary and grammar activities, games, and activities focusing on higher-level thinking skills. Others are generic graphic organizers. Still other masters can be used by teachers, peers, and learners themselves to assess the work done in each unit.

Each masters book also includes scripts for all listening activities in the masters. (Note: These activities are not included on the *English—No Problem!* audio recordings.)

 This icon in the teacher's edition indicates where reproducible masters can be used.

Audio Recording

Available on CD and cassette, each level's audio component includes listening passages, listening activities, and Pronunciation Targets from the student book.

This icon in the student book and teacher's edition indicates that the audio recording includes material for that activity.

Lesson-Plan Builder

This free, web-based *Lesson-Plan Builder* allows teachers to create and save customized lesson plans, related graphic organizers, and selected assessment masters. Goals, vocabulary lists, and other elements are already in the template for each lesson. Teachers then add their own notes to customize their plans.

They can also create original graphic organizers using generic templates.

When a lesson plan is finished, the customized materials can be printed and stored in PDF form.

This icon in the teacher's edition refers teachers to the *Lesson-Plan Builder,* found at www.enp.newreaderspress.com.

Vocabulary Cards

For literacy, level 1, and level 2, all vocabulary from the Picture Dictionaries and Vocabulary boxes in the student books is also presented on reproducible flash cards. At the literacy level, the cards also include capital letters, lowercase letters, and numerals.

Placement Tool

The Placement Test student booklet includes items that measure exit skills for each level of the series so that learners can start work in the appropriate student book. The teacher's guide includes a listening script, as well as guidelines for administering the test to a group, for giving an optional oral test, and for interpreting scores.

Hot Topics in ESL

These online professional development articles by adult ESL experts focus on key issues and instructional techniques embodied in *English—No Problem!,* providing background information to enhance effective use of the materials. They are available online at www.enp.newreaderspress.com.

Addressing the Standards

English—No Problem! has been correlated from the earliest stages of development with national standards for adult education and ESL, including the NRS (National Reporting System), EFF (Equipped for the Future), SCANS (Secretary's Commission on Achieving Necessary Skills), CASAS (Comprehensive Adult Student Assessment System) competencies, BEST (Basic English Skills Test), and SPLs (Student Performance Levels). The series also reflects state standards from New York, California, and Florida.

About the Student Books

Each unit in the student books includes a two-page unit opener followed by three lessons (two at the literacy level). A cumulative unit project concludes each unit. Every unit addresses all four language skills—listening, speaking, reading, and writing. Each lesson focuses on characters operating in one of the three EFF-defined adult roles—parent/family member at home, worker at school or work, or citizen/community member in the larger community.

Unit Opener Pages

Unit Goals The vocabulary, language, pronunciation, and culture goals set forth in the unit opener correlate to a variety of state and national standards.

Opening Question and Photo The opening question, photo, and caption introduce the unit protagonists and engage learners affectively in issues the unit explores.

Think and Talk This feature of levels 1–4 presents questions based on classic steps in problem-posing methodology, adjusted and simplified as needed.

What's Your Opinion? In levels 1–4, this deliberately controversial question often appears after Think and Talk or on the first page of a lesson. It is designed to encourage lively teacher-directed discussion, even among learners with limited vocabulary.

Picture Dictionary or Vocabulary Box This feature introduces important unit vocabulary and concepts.

Gather Your Thoughts In levels 1–4, this activity helps learners relate the unit theme to their own lives. They record their thoughts in a graphic organizer, following a model provided.

What's the Problem? This activity, which follows Gather Your Thoughts, encourages learners to practice another step in problem posing. They identify a possible problem and apply the issue to their own lives.

Setting Goals This feature of levels 1–4 is the first step of a unit's self-evaluation strand. Learners choose from a list of language and life goals and add their own goal to the list. The goals are related to the lesson activities and tasks and to the unit project. After completing a unit, learners revisit these goals in Check Your Progress, the last page of each workbook unit.

First Lesson Page

While the unit opener sets up an issue or problem, the lessons involve learners in seeking solutions while simultaneously developing language competencies.

Lesson Goals and EFF Role The lesson opener lists language, culture, and life-skill goals and identifies the EFF role depicted in that lesson.

Pre-Reading or Pre-Listening Question This question prepares learners to seek solutions to the issues presented in the reading or listening passage or lesson graphic that follows.

Reading or Listening Tip At levels 1–4, this feature presents comprehension and analysis strategies used by good listeners and readers.

Lesson Stimulus Each lesson starts with a reading passage (a picture story at the literacy level), a listening passage, or a lesson graphic. A photo on the page sets the situation for a listening passage. Each listening passage is included in the audio recording, and scripts are provided at the end of the student book and the teacher's edition. A lesson graphic may be a schedule, chart, diagram, graph, time line, or similar item. The questions that follow each lesson stimulus focus on comprehension and analysis.

Remaining Lesson Pages

Picture Dictionary, Vocabulary Box, and Idiom Watch These features present the active lesson vocabulary. At lower levels, pictures often help convey meaning. Vocabulary boxes for the literacy level also include letters and numbers. At levels 3 and 4, idioms are included in every unit.

Class, Group, or Partner Chat This interactive feature provides a model miniconversation. The model sets up a real-life exchange that encourages use of the lesson vocabulary and grammatical structures. Learners ask highly structured and controlled questions and record classmates' responses in a graphic organizer.

Grammar Talk At levels 1–4, the target grammatical structure is presented in several examples. Following the examples is a short explanation or question that guides learners to come up with a rule on their own. At the literacy level, language boxes highlight basic grammatical structures without formal teaching.

Pronunciation Target In this feature of levels 1–4, learners answer questions that lead them to discover pronunciation rules for themselves.

Chat Follow-Ups Learners use information they recorded during the Chat activity. They write patterned sentences, using lesson vocabulary and structures.

In the US This feature is a short cultural reading or brief explanation of some aspect of US culture.

Compare Cultures At levels 1–4, this follow-up to In the US asks learners to compare the custom or situation in the US to similar ones in their home countries.

Activities A, B, C, etc. These practice activities, most of them interactive, apply what has been learned in the lesson so far.

Lesson Tasks Each lesson concludes with a task that encourages learners to apply the skills taught and practiced earlier. Many tasks involve pair or group work, as well as follow-up presentations to the class.

Challenge Reading

At level 4, a two-page reading follows the lessons. This feature helps learners develop skills that prepare them for longer readings they will encounter in future study or higher-level jobs.

Unit Project

Each unit concludes with a final project in which learners apply all or many of the skills they acquired in the unit. The project consists of carefully structured and sequenced individual, pair, and group activities. These projects also help develop important higher-level skills such as planning, organizing, collaborating, and presenting.

Additional Features

The following minifeatures appear as needed at different levels:

One Step Up These extensions of an activity, task, or unit project allow learners to work at a slightly higher skill level. This feature is especially useful when classes include learners at multiple levels.

Attention Boxes These unlabeled boxes highlight words and structures that are not taught explicitly in the lesson, but that learners may need. Teachers are encouraged to point out these words and structures and to offer any explanations that learners require.

Remember? These boxes present, in abbreviated form, previously introduced vocabulary and language structures.

Writing Extension This feature encourages learners to do additional writing. It is usually a practical rather than an academic activity.

Technology Extra This extension gives learners guidelines for doing part of an activity, task, or project using such technology as computers, photocopiers, and audio and video recorders.

Assessment

Assessment is completely integrated into *English—No Problem!* This arrangement facilitates evaluation of class progress and provides a systematic way to set up learner portfolios. The pieces used for assessment are listed below. You may use all of them or select those that suit your needs.

Check Your Progress

Found on the last page of each workbook unit, this self-check is tied to the goals learners set for themselves in the student book unit opener. Learners rate their progress in life and language skills.

Unit Checkup/Review

For each unit, the reproducible masters include a two-page Unit Checkup/Review. You can use this instrument before each unit as a pretest or after each unit to assess mastery. If it is used both before and after, the score differential indicates a learner's progress.

Rubrics for Oral and Written Communication

The reproducible masters include a general rubric for speaking and one for writing (Masters 10 and 11). You can use these forms to score and track learner performance on the unit tasks and projects. Copy the rubric for each learner, circle performance scores, and include the results in the learner's portfolio.

Forms for Evaluating Projects or Tasks

For three projects, the reproducible masters include a form on which you can evaluate learner performance. Make a copy for each learner, record your assessment, and add the form to the learner's portfolio.

Peer Assessment

Peer assessment helps learners focus on the purpose of an activity. Encourage learners to be positive in their assessments of each other. For example, ask them to say one thing they liked about a presentation and one thing they did not understand. Use the Peer Assessment Form (Master 15 in the reproducible masters) when learners are practicing for a performance. Peer assessment is best used to evaluate groups rather than individuals and rehearsals rather than performances.

Self-Assessment

Self-assessment is a way for learners to measure their progress. Use the self-check masters (Masters 12 and 13 in the reproducible masters) at the beginning of Unit 1 and at the ends of Units 3, 6, and 9. Then save them in learners' portfolios.

Ongoing Assessment

These minirubrics and guidelines for specific activities and tasks in the student book are integrated into the teacher notes. They often focus on assessing one particular language or life-skill function. You can include the pieces you evaluate in learners' portfolios. After using these resources systematically for a few units, you will probably develop similar ways of assessing learners' progress on other parts of the unit.

Teaching Effectively with English—No Problem! Level 4

The following general suggestions for using level 4 of English—No Problem! can enhance your teaching.

Before beginning a unit, prepare yourself in this way:
- Read the entire set of unit notes.
- Gather the materials needed for the unit.
- Familiarize yourself with the student book and workbook pages.
- Prepare copies of masters needed for the unit.

Materials

The notes for each unit include a list of specific materials. These lists do not include the following, which are recommended for all or most units:
- large sheets of paper (butcher or flip-chart)
- magazines, newspapers, catalogs (to cut up)
- art supplies (scissors, glue, tape, colored pencils, markers, colored and plain paper, etc.)
- a "Treasure Chest" box or other container of prizes (new pencils, pens, erasers, rulers, stickers, hard candy, small candy bars, key chains, and things collected at conferences or found at dollar stores)

Grouping

Working in groups increases learner participation and builds teamwork skills important in the workplace.

Learners can be grouped randomly. Four or five on a team allows for a good level of participation. For increased individual accountability, assign roles to group members. These commonly include
- group leader, who directs the group's activities
- recorder, who writes group responses
- reporter, who reports the group's responses to the whole class
- timekeeper, who lets everyone know how much time is left for an activity

Groups and roles within groups can be changed as needed.

Talking about the Photos

Contextualized color photos are used as starting points for many unit activities. Talking about the photos with learners is a good way to assess prior knowledge and productive vocabulary. For every photo, follow one or more of these suggestions:
- Encourage learners to cover the caption and focus exclusively on the photo at first.
- Ask general questions about what learners see: Who are the people in the photo? What is their relationship? Can you say anything about their ages, jobs, or nationalities? Where are they? What's happening? What do you think is going to happen next? Encourage learners to explain their answers. Ask for both descriptive and interpretive answers. Respond to all answers neutrally. Probe for more detail by

asking questions such as: What makes you say that? What else do you see?

- As learners name items in the photo, write new vocabulary on the board or an overhead transparency.
- If a photo has a lot of detail, groups can compete to list the most items or write the most sentences about it. Make this more challenging by showing the photo for 30 seconds and asking the groups to work from memory.

Reading Titles and Captions

Focusing on titles and captions helps learners create a context for the unit or lesson.

Unit and Lesson Titles Discuss vocabulary that appears in titles, and ask learners to talk about how the titles relate to the lessons. In some cases, you can ask learners to predict what will happen in the story.

Captions Use the captions to discuss the characters and the story. Ask questions like these: Do you know anyone like this or in this situation? What do you think the character will do?

Identifying and Analyzing Problems

The questions in What's the Problem? set up the central issue for the unit. Directions in the student book are purposely open-ended. Learners may think about the questions individually or discuss them with a partner or group. If they discuss the questions, ask volunteers to share ideas from their small groups. Then follow up with a class discussion.

Setting Goals

Do some or all of the following:
- Ask volunteers to read the goals they added aloud. Validate all answers by listening neutrally and asking for details. List these goals on the board or an overhead transparency.
- Form groups according to first-choice goals. Ask learners in each group to discuss why they made the choice they did. Have a recorder in each group take notes. A group reporter can tell the class the reasons for the group's choice. Ask: Did any of you change your mind after talking with the group?
- Rank the goals by counting the number of learners who picked each one as a first choice. This activity allows you to discuss concepts such as majority, fractions, and proportions.

Listening Comprehension

One lesson in each unit is driven by a listening passage, such as a recorded phone message, conversation, speech, or commercial announcement.

Ideally, you will have access to a cassette or CD player and will be able to use the *English—No Problem!* audio recording. This recording allows learners to hear a variety of native-speaker and non-native-speaker voices. For teachers who need or prefer to read the audio portions, scripts for the listening passages are printed on pages 136–140 of the student book. Complete scripts for the passages and for all student book listening activities are on pages 136–143 of this book.

In presenting the listening passages, the following sequence is recommended:
- Review the directions.
- As learners listen to the audio the first time, have them take brief notes on what they hear. Model simple note taking to demonstrate that they do not have to write every word or worry about correct spelling.
- Play the audio or read the listening script as often as learners want.
- If the passage is long, play a short section and ask questions about what they heard.

Provide listening practice in each class. Dictate pairs of words. Have learners dictate sentences to one another. Play bingo, listen to audiotapes, and listen to music tapes and sing along.

From time to time identify problem words to work on (e.g., fit/feet; woman/women) in this way:
- Number the words (*bit* = 1) (*beat* = 2)
- Say a word, and ask learners to indicate the number of the word they heard.
- Repeat several times with similar words.
- Have volunteers read the words.

Reading Comprehension

The readings in *English—No Problem!* are designed to be as useful as possible to adult English language learners. They are modeled on practical documents that adults want and need to read in everyday life. The reading lessons present the strategies and skills needed to successfully navigate such documents.

Attention Boxes The words in these unlabeled boxes are not active vocabulary, but learners will need them to understand the passage. When possible, demonstrate each word by pointing or miming. Pronounce each word, and elicit a definition.

Reading Tips Each tip focuses on a reading strategy, for example, scanning for specific information or predicting content. Help learners apply these strategies to other student book and workbook readings.

In-Class Reading Follow some or all of these suggestions when learners read in class:

- Ask learners to read the passage silently first. They can mark any problem words, but they should not open their dictionaries at this point.
- Read the passage aloud so that learners can hear correct pronunciation of the words.
- Encourage learners to answer comprehension questions before dealing with new vocabulary.
- Review problem vocabulary, and ask learners to read the passage aloud in pairs or in groups.

Comprehension Questions Have learners answer the questions in groups. Set a time limit. You may wish to give each group a different question to work on.

A recorder writes the response with group input. Group members check the answers and make corrections before a reporter reads them to the class. Have volunteers write the answers on the board or an overhead transparency. After each response, ask: Does anyone want to add to this answer?

Introducing Vocabulary

Read the words aloud and have learners repeat them after you. Then do the following:
- Elicit definitions and sample sentences for words that learners already know.
- Have learners write their own sentences in pairs. Collect the sentences, or ask volunteers to write one of theirs on the board or an overhead transparency. Focus on the meaning of the vocabulary word rather than on grammar.
- Write vocabulary words on the board or an overhead transparency. Say each word aloud. Have learners tell where to put stress marks. Clap out the words, emphasizing stressed syllables.
- Ask for the number of syllables in each word. Write the number next to each word.
- Write the headings *Noun, Verb,* and *Adjective* on the board or an overhead transparency. Ask learners to categorize the vocabulary words. Some words will fall into more than one category.
- Learners can use their dictionaries to build word families, such as *achieve/achievement.*

Reinforcing Vocabulary

The words in the Vocabulary boxes are used often in the student book and the workbook. These activities can provide further reinforcement:
- Collect and post a running list of unit vocabulary words on a large sheet of paper. Refer to it for bingo games, pair dictations, alphabetization, cloze sentences, syllable stress, and pronunciation lessons. After completing a unit, continue to post the com-prehensive list so that all active vocabulary for the term is eventually displayed.
- Ask learners to locate the words in the unit and read the sentences in which they find the words.
- Put each term on a large flash card. Use the cards throughout the unit to review meaning, pronunciation, and form.
- Use story writing to reinforce both meaning and use of vocabulary. First create a sample story that uses your own set of five words. Write the words on the board or an overhead transparency. Tell learners the story, or write it on the board or transparency. Then give each group a set of five words and a large piece of paper. Some words may appear in more than one set, or you can include words from previous units. Ask the group to create a story using all of its words. Emphasize that although the story can be silly, it should make sense. It is not necessary to put a vocabulary word in every sentence.
- Help learners develop the skill of deducing the meaning of a new word from context. Encourage them to speculate about the meaning of a word, discuss it, and then confirm by looking it up in a dictionary.

Word Search From time to time conduct a word search. In this activity, learners find a vocabulary word in their book and tell others where it is located (e.g., "The word *portfolio* is in Unit 1, on page 14, paragraph 3.").

Possible Homework Assignment Ask learners to use one of the vocabulary words five times in conversation outside class. In the next session, have them report on when and how they used the word. This activity can become part of the class routine each time new vocabulary is introduced.

Writing Skills

At this level, learners are developing their paragraph-writing skills. The writing activities in the book emphasize supporting main ideas with related details and using correct paragraph form. Do not try to correct every mistake in your learners' writing. Learners need to be aware of the *focus* of the writing activity, and your corrections should help them focus.

Writing well involves both fluency and accuracy. To help learners develop fluency, have them write often, but do not always collect and correct their writing. Rather, ask them sometimes to share their writing in groups and respond to the content. This helps them learn to communicate ideas effectively.

Partner/Group Chats

While learners are conversing in pairs or groups, circulate; join as many conversations as possible. Pair fluent learners with learners who have more difficulty.

Role-Plays

When learners role-play, encourage them to think about the beginning and end of the conversation. Put commonly used phrases on the board so that they can use them for greeting, introducing, thanking, and saying good-bye. Discuss the level of formality appropriate for the situation. After learners finish, ask volunteers to perform role-plays for the class.

For telephone role-plays, position learners back-to-back to better simulate phone use.

Grammar

The student book deliberately uses only essential grammatical terminology. Each Grammar Talk section includes example sentences and questions to help learners arrive at the grammar concept deductively.

Introduce a grammar point this way:
- Have learners read Grammar Talk silently. Ask for volunteers to summarize.
- Read the sentences to learners. Ask learners to repeat.
- When Grammar Talk includes questions, have learners discuss the answers.
- Elicit more example sentences, and write them on the board or an overhead transparency.
- Discuss any specific issues related to the grammar point, and answer learners' questions.

Pronunciation

Many adult ESL series give scant attention to pronunciation, but *English—No Problem!* gives it proper emphasis within an array of integrated skills.

Try to include a 10-minute pronunciation lesson in each class meeting. Use lessons in the text, or conduct your own lesson as the need or desire arises. Vary your lessons to incorporate different components of pronunciation: sentence stress, syllable stress, intonation, and vowel sounds.

Stress Word and sentence stress, which are so important for good English pronunciation, are often overlooked by learners themselves, who tend to focus on challenging sounds.

When teaching a new word, elicit the stress and number of syllables from learners. Use chants or songs to practice stress and rhythm. When learners are preparing to role-play, have them exaggerate syllable length and intonation. (Hiiiii! How've you beeeen lately?) Demonstrate how drawn-out syllables and question intonation can signal friendliness as well as provide important clues to meaning.

Reductions Closely tied to sentence and word stress is the issue of reduced vowel sounds. Most unstressed vowels in English have the schwa ("uh") sound. When learners stress an unstressed vowel, it interferes with the rhythm of their speech. When teaching a new word, point out which vowels have reduced pronunciation.

Unit Project

Prepare learners for the unit project at the beginning of each unit. During the introduction, tell them what they will be doing at the end of the unit. Highlight information and materials that may be needed for the project as they come up in the unit.

Technology Skills

Some learners may have no computer skills whatsoever, while others may be able to work proficiently with computers. Encourage all learners, whatever their skill level, to do the Technology Extras in the student book. Let them know that they can practice English at many ESL web sites and in ESL chat rooms. A trip to a library or community center may help those without computers or computer skills to get started. Provide focus with a small project or a few questions, such as these:
- Find out three things that happened the day you were born.
- What's the weather in your hometown today?
- Find a recipe for one of your national dishes.

Customizable Graphic Organizers

The teacher notes indicate when to use one of the Customizable Graphic Organizers in the reproducible masters. Gather Your Thoughts in each unit opener and the Class/Group/Partner Chats almost always can be done using one of these forms. Use the following procedure to customize these masters:
- Make one copy of the Customizable Graphic Organizer (chart, idea map, etc.) appropriate for the activity you are doing.
- Fill in the heads as shown in the student book.
- Duplicate enough copies for each learner or group and distribute them.

After learners complete their graphic organizers, draw a chart on the board or an overhead transparency. Fill in the headings. Ask learners to read answers from their sheets. Write the answers on the chart.

Tried-and-True Techniques and Games for High Intermediate Learners

Use these lively activities as needed to reinforce previous instruction and to create a dynamic learning environment.

Listening and Writing Activity

This writing activity also helps learners listen for main ideas:

- Tell learners that you are going to read a story or paragraph. Explain that they will need to remember the content without taking notes.
- Use a simple story or paragraph with familiar vocabulary. Read it aloud at a normal speed twice.
- Ask groups to discuss what they remember.
- Read the story or paragraph a third time.
- Give each group a large sheet of paper and ask them to re-create the story. Stress that it is not important to use the exact words you did. The purpose is to capture the content.

Using Photos and Art

From time to time, conduct minilessons in visual literacy. Bring in art prints, news photos, or ads. Ask learners to study them silently for several minutes and then list orally or in writing what they see. Encourage them to look for more and more detail. In groups or pairs, have them take turns telling what they see in the picture. When they report back to the class, maintain neutrality. Probe for details and deeper interpretations by asking questions like these: Why do you think that? What else can you say about the picture? Why do you think this picture was taken (painted)? How does it make you feel?

Jigsaw Reading

Jigsaws help learners practice all language skills and require real communication. This type of activity can be done with any piece of text that can be divided into four sections. Choose text with previously learned vocabulary. Jigsaws work best when completed in one session. You may also find that they work best when used at the end of a unit.

Follow these steps:

- Prepare questions or a task that requires learners to synthesize information from all sections of the text (e.g., read about four people and decide which you would hire, read about four apartments and decide which you would rent, read about someone's life and identify the most important, happiest, and saddest events).

- Model a jigsaw with learners, walking them through each step.
- Put one section of the text in each corner of the room. Put learners in groups of four. Each person from a group goes to a different corner of the room to read the information there. (If your class does not divide evenly into groups of four, put five learners in some groups. Have two learners look at the same information in those groups.)
- Have each person learn the information in his or her corner. Then have learners return to their original groups to share the information. Learners should not take notes until they are back in their groups.
- Once learners return to their groups, they can complete the task or answer the questions together.

One/Two Question Interview

This is a good way to get everyone energized and speaking. Each pair of learners has a question to ask as many other learners as possible. Partners take turns: one asks the question, and the other records the response. Allow a set time for the interviews. An advantage of the one/two question interview is that pairs need both to ask their questions and to answer questions from others. This generates a lot of language. Insist on English for this activity.

Password

Make vocabulary cards for the unit vocabulary words. Divide the class into teams. Hold a card over the head of a learner on the first team so that the rest of the team can read the card. Team members then describe the word using definitions or examples; if anyone uses native language, the team loses its turn.

If the learner guesses the word within 30 seconds, the team gets a point and the word card is removed from play. If the learner can not guess the word in the allotted time, the card is put back in the middle of the deck and the second team takes a turn. The game is over when all the cards are gone; the team with the most points wins.

Concentration

Make flash cards for the unit vocabulary words with the definition on one card and the word on another. Model the steps below:

- Keeping words and definitions separate, learners arrange the cards in rows, facedown on the table.
- Taking turns, learners turn over one word card and one definition card.

- If the cards do not match, the learner turns them facedown again *in the same place.* A learner who finds a matching pair keeps the cards.

When all cards are matched, the learner with the most matches wins.

Bingo

Use the generic bingo card (Master 1 in the reproducible masters) to review vocabulary for a unit. Duplicate the master and distribute one copy to each learner. Write unit vocabulary words on the board or an overhead transparency. (You will need 25 words.) Ask learners to choose words randomly and write a word in each square. Circulate to be sure they understand that they should write the words in random order.

Give each learner a pile of markers—dried beans, paper clips, pennies, or small squares of card stock. Then call out the words in random order. The first learner to mark a row of five words down, across, or diagonally calls "Bingo!" and wins. Ask winners to read out the words they have marked and tell you the meanings.

Once learners understand the game well, ask a learner to call out the words.

Flyswatter

This game can be played in front of the class with two flyswatters.

Write unit vocabulary words on an overhead transparency, spreading them out so they are spaced around the glass. Divide the class into two teams. One member of each team holds a flyswatter and stands near the projector screen.

Read a definition. The first learner to hit the correct word on the screen earns a point for the team. Then the flyswatter is passed to another team member. Team members can help by yelling answers, but learners may hit the screen only once. They are not allowed to change their minds and try a new word.

Flyswatter can also be played to reinforce spelling (you read a word and learners hit the correct spelling) or grammar (you read a sentence with a missing word and learners hit the correct word).

Question Exchange

Use this activity to practice a grammar point.

Write questions using the grammar point. The questions should be ones learners can answer from their own experience (e.g., "Where did you go last weekend?" to practice the past tense). Write each question on an index card and give a card to each learner. (It is all right for some learners to have the same questions.)

Learners stand up and find a partner. Partners then ask each other the questions they are holding. When they finish talking, they exchange questions; then each finds a new partner to answer the new question. Encourage learners to talk about their experiences. For a follow-up activity, ask each learner to write on the board or an overhead transparency one memorable thing he or she discovered about another learner. Then have all learners together correct the sentences.

Unit 1: Taking the First Step

Materials for the Unit

- Old family photos
- Customizable Masters 3 and 5
- Generic Assessment Masters 11–14
- Unit Masters 16–21

Self-Assessment

Give each learner a copy of Generic Assessment Masters 12 and 13 (Speaking and Listening Self-Checks and Writing and Reading Self-Checks) as they begin this unit. Go over the items together. Add the completed forms to each learner's portfolio.

Taking the First Step

Read the title; then review the four unit objectives listed below it.

- Follow the suggestions on p. 5 for talking about the title.
- Explain that in this unit learners will be celebrating their roots and looking to the future.
- Tell learners about a relative who influenced and encouraged you. Show family pictures.

Question

Read the question below the arrow.

- Use the question to open a discussion of learners' cultures and family accomplishments.
- Ask volunteers to answer the question.
- Have partners tell each other their stories.
- Use the US and world maps on student book pp. 141 and 142 to locate key events that learners discuss.

Extension

Assign a free-writing exercise on the topic "Important Things I Learned from ___" (family member). Have learners write for 3–5 minutes.

Photo

Ask these questions:

- Can you guess the part of the world the women come from? Can you guess the country?

- What is their relationship? Why do you think so?

Caption

Read the speech and thought bubbles in the picture. Ask a learner to read the caption aloud.

- Brainstorm a definition of the word *goal*. Elicit examples of goals.
- The caption and thought bubble introduce the possibility of obstacles to achieving goals. In this case, we see Patria's fear and lack of confidence.
- Ask learners, "Why do you think Patria is not sure that she can reach her goals?"

Think and Talk

Follow the suggestions on p. 6 for comprehension questions.

Extension

Play an observation game. Ask groups to compete to list as many items in the picture as they can.

Answers

1. Answers will vary.
2. Possible answers: Patria is proud of her. She is afraid she can't do all her grandmother did.
3. Answers will vary. Encourage discussion.

Vocabulary

Follow the suggestions on p. 6 for introducing and reinforcing vocabulary words.

Tell learners the vocabulary focus is goal setting.

- Ask learners to write all the words in their notebooks and circle the ones they do not know.
- Brainstorm with learners the meanings of words they circled. Have learners verify meanings in a dictionary.
- Have learners work in small groups to create sentences with all the vocabulary words.
- Ask a volunteer from each group to write a sentence using a vocabulary word on the board or an overhead transparency. Continue until each word has been used in a sentence.

Gather Your Thoughts

- Have each group identify the one thing they see as key to reaching goals. Ask learners for reasons to support their opinions.
- List on the board or an overhead transparency the factors that the groups chose. Take a vote to show what learners think are the first, second, and third most important.

What's the Problem?

Follow the suggestions on p. 5 for identifying and analyzing problems.

- Review each factor in reaching success, including learners' additions from "something else."
- Ask learners what barriers or challenges might arise in trying to reach goals.
- Discuss *luck*. Ask, "What could be bad about depending on luck all of the time?" Have learners give examples.
- On a large sheet of paper, draw a two-column chart. Write the heads *People who reach their goals are* and *People who reach*

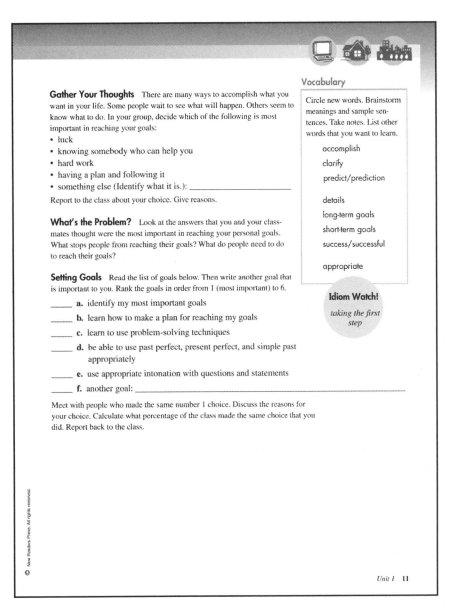

Gather Your Thoughts   There are many ways to accomplish what you want in your life. Some people wait to see what will happen. Others seem to know what to do. In your group, decide which of the following is most important in reaching your goals:

- luck
- knowing somebody who can help you
- hard work
- having a plan and following it
- something else (Identify what it is.): _____

Report to the class about your choice. Give reasons.

What's the Problem?   Look at the answers that you and your classmates thought were the most important in reaching your personal goals. What stops people from reaching their goals? What do people need to do to reach their goals?

Setting Goals   Read the list of goals below. Then write another goal that is important to you. Rank the goals in order from 1 (most important) to 6.

_____ **a.** identify my most important goals

_____ **b.** learn how to make a plan for reaching my goals

_____ **c.** learn to use problem-solving techniques

_____ **d.** be able to use past perfect, present perfect, and simple past appropriately

_____ **e.** use appropriate intonation with questions and statements

_____ **f.** another goal: _____

Meet with people who made the same number 1 choice. Discuss the reasons for your choice. Calculate what percentage of the class made the same choice that you did. Report back to the class.

Vocabulary

Circle new words. Brainstorm meanings and sample sentences. Take notes. List other words that you want to learn.

accomplish

clarify

predict/prediction

details

long-term goals

short-term goals

success/successful

appropriate

Idiom Watch!

taking the first step

Unit 1   **11**

their goals do at the top of the columns. Under the heads, list characteristics of people who reach their goals.

<u>Extension</u>
Post the list. Leave it up throughout the course. Refer back to it whenever you find links to these ideas in other units.

Setting Goals

Follow the suggestions on p. 5 for setting goals.

Lesson 1: Planning for Success 🌐

Read the lesson title aloud. Then present the lesson objectives to learners.

- Tell learners that in this lesson they will clarify their personal goals.
- Explain that *clarify* means *to make something easier to understand.*

Question

Read the introductory question.

- Use the question to open a discussion of learners' attitudes toward goal setting. Explore with them the relative importance of planning and goal setting in their home cultures.
- To help clarify thinking and prioritizing, brainstorm examples of important goals and dreams.

Photo

Have learners study the picture. Then ask these questions:

- How is this picture different from the one on p. 10?
- How is it similar?
- Why do you think they have taken things out of the closet?

Explain to learners that working on a project with someone can provide time for conversation.

- Ask learners to tell stories of working with another person.
- After each story ask, "Did you learn anything that you did not know before?"

Listening Tip

Read the tip aloud.

- Tell learners that giving people your full attention when they speak is called *focused listening.*
- Ask learners to practice focused listening at home.

<u>Extension</u>

Ask, "How can listening carefully help you to learn a new language?" (helps someone learn native pronunciation, correct use of idioms, cultural thought patterns).

LESSON 1   Community

Planning for Success

- Clarify your personal goals
- Compare present perfect with simple past

How did coming to the US affect your dreams and goals?

- Listening Tip 🎧 A good way to understand what you hear is to practice focused listening—listening for a specific type of information. One way to focus your listening is to take notes. Listen to Patria and her grandmother talk. Give them your full attention. Listen for what they say about their dreams. Write a few words to help you remember what you hear. The listening script is on page 136.

botanical garden
botanist
diploma
herbs

Idiom Watch!
a dream come true
dead-end job
take a chance

Patria and her grandmother are talking about their dreams.

Talk or Write
1. Patria's grandmother had dreams. What were they? What are Patria's dreams?
2. How did the grandmother's dreams change? Why did they change?
3. How can dreams be helpful in reaching goals? In addition to dreaming, what else does Patria say you need to do?
4. What is one goal you dream of reaching? What plan do you have for reaching that goal?

12 *Unit 1 Lesson 1*

🎧 Play the audio or read the listening script on p. 136. Follow the suggestions on p. 5 for listening comprehension.

Talk or Write

This exercise helps learners practice focused listening.

- Tell learners the questions are about dreams and ways to achieve them.
- Distinguish between dreams you have while awake *(daydreams)* and dreams you have while asleep. Ask, "Which kind are Patria and her grandmother talking about?"

<u>Possible Answers</u>
1. Patria's grandmother dreamed of becoming a nurse. Patria dreams of being a botanist.
2. The grandmother changed her dream when she got married and had children. She found a new dream in the US.
3. Dreams can help you see your long-term goals, but in addition, you need to keep planning and working hard.
4. Answers will vary.

Vocabulary

Follow the suggestions on p. 6 for introducing and reinforcing the vocabulary words.

Partner Chat

Use Customizable Master 5 (Idea Map). Follow the suggestions on p. 7 for customizing and duplicating the master. Make a copy for each learner.

- Model the discussion by telling learners about people who, after reaching their goals, found the reality better than they anticipated. Then describe someone who found the reality the same as or worse than they expected.
- Have partners tell one another about a goal they achieved and how the reality met or failed to meet their expectations.
- Ask learners to practice focused listening by completing the idea map for their partners.

Tell learners to save their completed idea maps to use in Activity B.

Grammar Talk

Follow the suggestions on p. 7 for introducing the grammar point.

- Have learners find the verbs in each sentence. Point out that the *past tense* sentences use the *simple past* form of the verb and the *present perfect* sentences use *have* + participle.
- Use the questions to write rules for using the *simple past* and *present perfect.*

Answers

- The *past tense* sentences use the *simple past* form of the verb, and the *present perfect* sentences use *have* + participle.
- The *simple past* talks about an action completed at a specific time in the past.
- The *present perfect* talks about something that happened at an

unspecific time in the past and is continuing.

- A *past participle* is used with *have* or *has* in the present perfect.

Use Unit Master 16 (Grammar: Review of the Present Perfect) now or at any time during the rest of the unit.

Activity A

This activity provides a contrast between the two target tenses.

- After partners ask and answer the questions, have each partner create one additional *Have you ever . . .* question to ask the other. Tell learners to write the question and answer in their notebooks.

- Have each pair of learners stand at the front of the room. Each partner takes a turn asking his or her new question.
- After a partner answers, have the other partner ask *Wh-* questions (e.g., What happened? What did you do? Where did you go? What did you like? What did you not like?).
- Write the questions and answers on the board or a transparency.

 Assign Workbook pp. 4–5.

Partner Chat Talk with a partner. Ask these questions:
- Have you ever achieved an important goal by first dreaming and then making specific plans? What was it?
- In what ways has the reality been better or worse than your dream?

Record your partner's answers on an idea map like the one below.
- In the left circle, write one or more ways the reality has been better than your partner dreamed.
- In the right circle, write one or more ways the reality has been worse than your partner dreamed.
- In the middle circle, record one or more things that have happened exactly as your partner dreamed and planned them.

Achieving My Dream — Better — Exactly the Same — Worse

Vocabulary

Circle new words. Brainstorm meanings and sample sentences. Take notes. List other words that you want to learn.

achieve

dream

imagine

reality

Grammar Talk: Comparing Simple Past with Present Perfect

Simple Past	Present Perfect
Grandmother's husband **gave** her a music box.	Grandmother **has listened** to the music for 50 years.
Patria **studied** hard in high school.	Patria **has dreamed** of going to college since then.

Compare the simple past sentences with the present perfect sentences. How are the verbs different? Which verbs talk about something that happened at a specific time in the past? Which talk about something that happened at an unspecified time or times in the past and is continuing? With your class, write a rule for using simple past. Write another rule for using present perfect. What verb form is used with have *or* has *in the present perfect?*

Activity A With a partner, ask and answer questions about things you have done. Have you ever asked an older family member to tell you about his or her life? Have you ever looked at photos with an older family member? Have you ever dreamed of improving your life? With your partner, write one or two questions to ask other group members.

Have you ever asked an older family member to tell you about his or her life?

Yes, I have.

Who did you ask? What did that person tell you?

I asked my uncle to tell me how he came to this country.

Unit 1 Lesson 1 **13**

Unit 1 *Lesson 1* 13

Activity B

Use the Partner Chat idea map to practice using the *present perfect*. Have learners answer the questions orally with a partner before writing them.

Activity C

Recognize that some learners may not want to close their eyes and fantasize about the future. If learners are receptive, play some soft music during this controlled fantasy.

- If employment is not a priority of many group members, change the topic to "my dream home" or another appropriate topic.
- Instruct learners to listen in a relaxed way to the questions and to answer the questions in their imagination. Remind them that although they may be thinking in their first language, they will use English to tell the group about their dream job.
- Read slowly, leaving time for thought between questions.

If time permits, embellish and add sensory details to ask questions like these:

- Is your workplace large or small?
- What color are the walls?
- Is there a window? What do you see out the window?
- Is it noisy or quiet?
- What is the climate like? Warm? Cool?
- What language are people around you speaking?
- What are you wearing?

Ask for volunteers to model answers for the large group. Then break learners into small groups.

- Tell each learner to spend one or two minutes telling the group about his or her dream job, using the questions in the text as a guide.
- Circulate from group to group. Listen and encourage.

Activity B **Partner Chat Follow-Up** Look at your Partner Chat idea map from page 13. In your notebook, answer these questions about your goals and your partner's goals.
- What important goal have you achieved by dreaming and planning? What about your partner?
- In which ways has the outcome of your goal been better than expected? What about your partner's goal?
- In which ways has the outcome of your goal been worse than expected? What about your partner's goal?

Activity C Try dreaming about your future for a few moments. Sit comfortably and close your eyes. Relax for a moment. Try to focus your mind. Your teacher will read these questions to you.
- It is 10 years from now. You have your dream job. You are at your workplace. What kind of place is it? An office? Hospital? Store? Someplace else?
- What are you doing?
- Are you alone or with other people? If you are with others, are you the boss or an employee? What are the other people doing?
- Where are you living? What is your city or community like?

Now tell a partner about your dream job. Try to imagine yourself at the job. Add more details if you want.

I am in California. The weather is warm and sunny.

One Step Up
In your notebook, write a short paragraph about your dream job. Include a main idea and supporting details. Tell why you are happy in the job.

 TASK 1: Make a Plan for Your Future

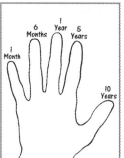

As a first step to planning, set some long- and short-term goals. Draw an outline of your hand on a piece of paper.
- At the top of your little finger, write "1 Month." On the finger, write something that you would like to achieve in one month.
- At the top of your ring finger, write "6 Months." On the finger, write something that you would like to achieve in six months.
- At the top of your middle finger write "1 Year." On the finger, write something that you would like to achieve in one year.
- At the top of your index finger, write "5 Years." On the finger, write something that you would like to achieve in five years.
- At the top of your thumb write "10 Years." On the thumb, write something that you would like to achieve in 10 years.

Work fast. Let your feelings guide you. Tell your group about some of your goals.

After everyone has had a chance to speak, bring the whole group together. Elicit reactions to the exercise with questions like these:

- How is an exercise like this useful in learning English?
- Were you comfortable?
- Did your mind wander?
- Would you enjoy doing this kind of exercise again?

One Step Up

Have learners write a short paragraph in their notebooks about their dream job.

Task 1

Tell learners to do the activity quickly and let their feelings guide them.

- As homework, ask learners to assign themselves one simple thing they can do to move closer to their goals. Tell them they will report back to the group with the results.
- Encourage learners to embellish their hand charts with pictures or drawings and put them in a file folder to refer to later.

Lesson 2: Learning from the Past 🌐

Read the title and point out the lesson objectives listed below it.
- Tell learners this lesson will help them use their own experiences and those of others to help them reach their goals.
- In addition, they will learn how to learn successfully. They will also make a time line of their lives.
- Ask learners what *learn how to learn* might mean. Ask, "Do you believe that a person can really *learn how to learn* better?"

Question

Read the introductory question aloud. If learners have difficulty answering, remind them of their earlier descriptions of talks with older people.

Photo

Ask these questions:
- Why was this picture included?
- Which pictures would you include in a time line of your life? Why?

Have learners read the caption. Ask, "Why did Patria make a time line of her grandmother's life?"

Reading Tip

Read the tip aloud; then follow these steps:
- To develop the target skill of reading time lines, draw a simple time line on the board or an overhead transparency.
- Plot events of the school year or the year's holidays as examples.

Learners who have not previously worked with time lines may find them difficult to read at first.
- Help them scan the time line and point to key events.
- Ask detail questions (e.g., When did she get married? What year was her daughter born?).

Talk or Write

In this exercise learners learn to read a time line.

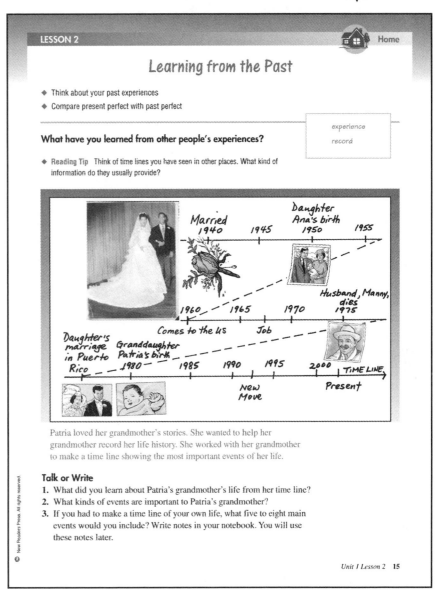

LESSON 2   🏠 Home

Learning from the Past

- ◆ Think about your past experiences
- ◆ Compare present perfect with past perfect

experience record

What have you learned from other people's experiences?

◆ **Reading Tip** Think of time lines you have seen in other places. What kind of information do they usually provide?

Married 1940 — 1945 — Daughter Ana's birth 1950 — 1955

1960 — 1965 — 1970 — Husband, Manny, dies 1975

Comes to the US — Job

Daughter's marriage in Puerto Rico — Granddaughter Patria's birth 1980 — 1985 — 1990 — 1995 — 2000 TIME LINE

New Move — Present

Patria loved her grandmother's stories. She wanted to help her grandmother record her life history. She worked with her grandmother to make a time line showing the most important events of her life.

Talk or Write
1. What did you learn about Patria's grandmother's life from her time line?
2. What kinds of events are important to Patria's grandmother?
3. If you had to make a time line of your own life, what five to eight main events would you include? Write notes in your notebook. You will use these notes later.

Unit 1 Lesson 2 **15**

Follow the suggestions on p. 6 for comprehension questions.
- Have learners work in pairs to answer questions 1 and 2.
- Question 3 can be answered individually or in pairs, with one partner helping the other think of events and dates.
- Ask about other ways time lines can be useful (e.g., in history books to show sequence of events).

Possible Answers
1. After learners give obvious factual information (dates of marriage, immigration, etc.), ask what they can say about the grandmother's life from the time line (e.g., She worked and raised a family. She emigrated after she had been married for 20 years.). Her birth date is not included. Why?
2. Answers will vary. Determine which are based on factual information and which on opinion by asking learners, "How do you know that?"
3. Model answers with events from your own life or that of a celebrity.

Vocabulary

Follow the suggestions on p. 6 for introducing and reinforcing the vocabulary words.

Brainstorm meanings with learners. Then have learners verify them in a dictionary.

Pronunciation Target

Introduce *intonation* by asking individuals to speak in their native languages.

- Ask listeners if they know what language they are hearing. Would they be able to tell without knowing what country the speaker was from? How?
- Explain that one way to recognize a language is by listening to *intonation.* Some languages have steady rhythm and *intonation,* but others do not. Ask, "How does English sound to you?"

🎧 Play the audio or read the sentences in the student book. Ask learners if they can hear and describe the "music," or *intonation pattern,* of the questions.

- Many people believe English speakers raise their voices at the end of all types of questions. To show this is not so, ask *Wh-* questions for contrast.
- Review examples of *yes/no* questions. In small groups, have learners ask and answer questions of this type. Assign a listener in each group to listen for correct intonation.

Class Chat

📑 Use Customizable Master 3 (3-Column Chart). Follow the suggestions on p. 7 for customizing and duplicating the master. Make a copy for each learner.

This chat includes intonation practice with *yes/no* questions and the past perfect.

Pronunciation Target • Intonation with *Yes/No* Questions

🎧 *Intonation is the rising and falling tone of your voice. Good intonation makes speech sound more interesting and easier to understand. Listen to your teacher or the audio.*

Have you ever been to a baseball ⬆ game?
Have they arrived ⬆ yet?

What did you hear? Generally when the expected answer in English is yes *or* no, *the speaker's voice goes up a little at the end of a question.*

Vocabulary

Circle new words. Brainstorm meanings and sample sentences. Take notes. List other words that you want to learn.

event

experience

dare

fulfill

Class Chat With a partner, choose one question from the list below. Take turns asking at least 10 people in your class the question. Ask them to explain their answers. Record names and answers on a chart like the one below. Make your voice go up at the end of questions.

1. Had you studied English before you came to the US?
2. Had you driven a car before you turned 16?
3. Had you met the teacher before you started this class?
4. Had you seen a baseball game before you came to the US?

One Step Up

If you get a *no* answer to question 1, 2, or 4, ask if the person has done that activity yet.

One-Question Interview

Your Question: _____

Name	Answer	Student said?

Grammar Talk: Compare Present Perfect and Past Perfect

Present Perfect	**Past Perfect**
I **have learned** that mistakes are necessary in life.	I **had made** many mistakes before I dared to ask for help.
He **has accomplished** his goal.	He **had accomplished** his goal before he came to the US.
They **have worked** here for six weeks.	I **had worked** for six weeks when my boss called me into his office.

Compare the present perfect sentences with the past perfect sentences. Think about when the action takes place. The present perfect sentences show action occurring at an indefinite time in the past or action that continues on into the present. The past perfect sentences show action completed before another event in the past.

16 *Unit 1 Lesson 2*

- Review short answers with *yes/no* questions briefly.
- Tell each pair of learners to select one question and write it at the top of their chart.
- Next, have partners walk around and take turns asking the question of as many other learners as possible. Tell the partner not asking the question to record the answers.
- As far as possible, keep the activity short and lively.

One Step Up

Repeat the activity with *present perfect* questions using *yet.*

Grammar Talk

Follow the suggestions on p. 7 for introducing the grammar point.

- Have learners read the sentences. Ask, "What is the difference between the two actions?"
- Elicit rules for using *have* + participle and *had* + participle.

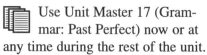 Use Unit Master 17 (Grammar: Past Perfect) now or at any time during the rest of the unit.

 Assign Workbook pp. 6–7.

Activity A

Have learners use their charts from the Class Chat to write sentences in their notebooks.

Activity B

- Tell learners to think of specific older people and what they have learned from them.
- As learners share their sentences, have group members make suggestions for improving use of the past perfect.

Activity C

Review the format of an informal letter before learners write a draft.

Activity D

This warm-up will prepare learners to take the activity out of class.

- Invite a guest to class for an interview. The guest can be another teacher, an administrator, or a friend or relative of a learner.
- Help each group prepare questions about goal setting, making a plan, and overcoming obstacles.
- Assign an interviewer, note-taker, and reporter in each group.
- After the interview, ask reporters to present to the class.

Task 2

Tell learners to complete this task using the life events they listed for the Talk or Write exercise (p. 15).

- Encourage learners to illustrate their time lines with photos, drawings, postcards, newspaper clippings, and other documents.
- Create a time line of your own life as well and present it first. Illustrate it with the old family photos you brought to use in this unit.
- Model the grammar points.

Ongoing Assessment

While learners work on this activity, circulate to check whether they understood the directions. Then consider their performance on these features:

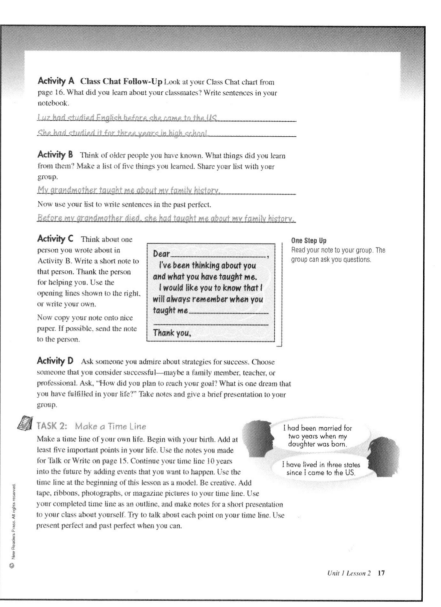

Activity A Class Chat Follow-Up Look at your Class Chat chart from page 16. What did you learn about your classmates? Write sentences in your notebook.

Luz had studied English before she came to the US.

She had studied it for three years in high school.

Activity B Think of older people you have known. What things did you learn from them? Make a list of five things you learned. Share your list with your group.

My grandmother taught me about my family history.

Now use your list to write sentences in the past perfect.

Before my grandmother died, she had taught me about my family history.

Activity C Think about one person you wrote about in Activity B. Write a short note to that person. Thank the person for helping you. Use the opening lines shown to the right, or write your own.

Now copy your note onto nice paper. If possible, send the note to the person.

> Dear_____,
> I've been thinking about you and what you have taught me. I would like you to know that I will always remember when you taught me_____
>
> Thank you,

One Step Up
Read your note to your group. The group can ask you questions.

Activity D Ask someone you admire about strategies for success. Choose someone that you consider successful—maybe a family member, teacher, or professional. Ask, "How did you plan to reach your goal? What is one dream that you have fulfilled in your life?" Take notes and give a brief presentation to your group.

TASK 2: Make a Time Line

Make a time line of your own life. Begin with your birth. Add at least five important points in your life. Use the notes you made for Talk or Write on page 15. Continue your time line 10 years into the future by adding events that you want to happen. Use the time line at the beginning of this lesson as a model. Be creative. Add tape, ribbons, photographs, or magazine pictures to your time line. Use your completed time line as an outline, and make notes for a short presentation to your class about yourself. Try to talk about each point on your time line. Use present perfect and past perfect when you can.

> I had been married for two years when my daughter was born.

> I have lived in three states since I came to the US.

Unit 1 Lesson 2   **17**

a. General detail and completeness of time line
  0 = time line out of sequence/not labeled
  1 = time line in sequence, labels incomplete or unclear
  2 = time line clear, accurately sequenced, and labeled

b. General quality of reading and following directions
  0 = time line not understandable
  1 = time line partially formed, directions not fully understood
  2 = completed time line reflects understanding of directions given

c. Use of language functions (present/past perfect) in presentation
  0 = no use of past/present perfect
  1 = use of past/present perfect with some problems
  2 = clear and appropriate use of language but not perfect

Use Unit Master 18 (Life Skill: Setting Goals and Deciding What to Do) now or at any time during the rest of the unit.

Lesson 3: Living Up to Your Potential

LESSON 3 — Work/School

Living Up to Your Potential

- Talk about job or career goals
- Learn about changing jobs in the US

stuck
frustrated
guide
peppermint
spearmint

Do you need perfect English to reach your goals?

- **Reading Tip** Good readers use their experience and knowledge to evaluate what they read. Read about Patria's goals and plans. Use your own experience and knowledge to decide if you agree or disagree with what she says.

I was in the Garden yesterday during my break. A guide was talking to a group of children. He gave them incorrect information about the plants. He said that spearmint and peppermint are the same. I wanted to say something, but my English is not good enough. I felt so frustrated! Why is English so difficult?

Idiom Watch!
live up to
take action

I am ready to take action to achieve my goals. My short-term goal is to become a guide at the Garden. I think I would like that job for a few years. My long-term goal is the goal I've always had — to become a botanist. Can I ever reach that goal? Is it possible for me to go to college? I need perfect English, don't I?

My grandmother taught me to love and understand plants and to use them to make people healthy. Even when I was a little girl, I had dreamed of becoming a botanist. I wanted to study botany in the university in Puerto Rico. Then we came to the US. Now I'm stuck working here in the cafeteria because I can't speak English well!

That's not right! Should I say something?

Patria has worked at the cafeteria in the Botanical Garden for two years. Jack, her co-worker, attends college. He and Patria write short letters to help her practice English. Here are paragraphs from some of Patria's letters.

Talk or Write

1. Patria wrote, "I am ready to take action to achieve my goals." Do you think she is really ready?
2. Patria did not say anything to the guide. She wrote, "My English is not good enough." Was that a good reason? Why or why not?
3. Patria wrote: "Why is English so difficult?" Do you agree that English is a difficult language? Why or why not?
4. Patria wrote to Jack, "Is it possible for me to go to college? I need perfect English, don't I?" Do you agree with her? Why or why not?

18 *Unit 1 Lesson 3*

© New Readers Press. All rights reserved.

Read the lesson title aloud. Then present the lesson objectives to learners.

- Tell learners in this lesson they will talk about their job or career goals and make a plan for achieving those goals.
- Write the word *potential* on the board or a transparency. Point out that it comes from a Latin word meaning *power.* Ask, "What does *living up to your potential* mean to you?"

Question

This question may reveal attitudes and insecurities about language ability. Be supportive as learners try to answer.

- Ask learners why they decided to learn English.
- Ask learners if they know anyone with poor English skills who has achieved personal and professional goals.

Photo

- Ask learners *Wh-* questions to elicit details about the photo (e.g., Who is this? Where is she? What do you see?).
- Draw out prior knowledge by asking questions like these:

  Have you ever been to a botanical garden? Where?

  What did you see there?
- Brainstorm a definition of *frustrated.* After learners check dictionaries, ask them to predict why Patria feels *frustrated.*
- If learners do not suggest it, tell them it can be frustrating to know you could do a certain job—and do it well—if only you had better English skills. Ask learners if they have ever felt this kind of frustration.

Reading Tip

Read the tip aloud.

- Assign a reading piece to each group. Then have each member tell whether they agree or disagree with what Patria has written and why.
- Ask volunteers from each group to express their opinions and support them with personal experience.

Talk or Write

In this exercise, learners use their own experience to evaluate what they read.

- Have learners work in pairs. Assign each pair a question.
- Tell the pairs to determine first whether the question asks for facts or opinions. (All the questions ask for opinions.) Then have them take turns answering their question.

Bring all learners together again and ask these questions:

- Did you agree on the answer?
- Did you agree on whether the question asked for fact or opinion?

Have one learner from each pair present their answers to the class. If partners do not agree on an answer, have each partner present his or her opinion and the reasons for it.

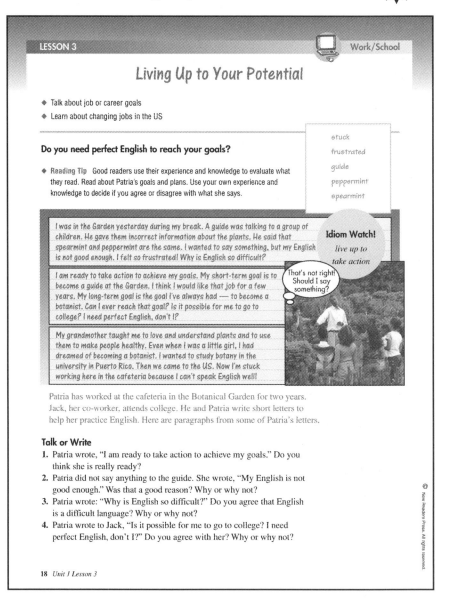

Vocabulary

Follow the suggestions on p. 6 for introducing and reinforcing the vocabulary words.

- Note the base form *stick* and the participle *stuck* in the word list. Then point out the informal use of *stuck* in the second sentence of In the US.
- Ask learners if they know other pairs of irregular verbs that sound alike (e.g., *sink/sunk, build/built, lead/led, ring/rung*).

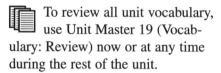 To review all unit vocabulary, use Unit Master 19 (Vocabulary: Review) now or at any time during the rest of the unit.

In the US

Extension

- Show learners sample questions from aptitude or personality tests.
- Ask, "Would you ever visit a career counselor to take an aptitude test? Why or why not?"

Compare Cultures

Ask these questions:

- Do you know people in the US who have changed jobs? What were their reasons?
- How do you feel about leaving a job for one you like better?
- How do you feel about changing jobs to make more money?

Put learners in groups according to country or culture to discuss the questions in the student book.

- Assign reporters to tell the class the results of the discussion.
- Ask, "Did people from the same country have the same opinions?"

Pronunciation Target

Play the audio or read the listening script on p. 136.

Learners may have difficulty hearing the rising and falling intonations. To assist them, do the following:

- As you play the audio or read the sentences, direct learners to look at the arrows in their books.
- Play the audio or read the sentences again. Ask, "Who can hear the intonation pattern?"
- Model the intonation pattern without exaggerating. Make statements about daily life, the weather, etc. Ask volunteers to try the pattern.
- Have learners practice in pairs, first with the model sentences and then with original ones.

Activity A

This activity uses goal setting to provide further intonation practice.

- As partners read their sentences to one another, listen and model by repeating each sentence in a natural voice. Some learners may find it easier to say the sentences than to read them.
- Ask partners questions about their goals. Encourage them to listen for the intonation pattern in the answers.

Technology Extra

Assign this as homework or make it the focus of a visit to a library.

 Assign Workbook pp. 8–9.

⭐ **In the US**   *Changing Jobs*

It's common for people in the US to change jobs and careers. If someone is feeling stuck in a job or frustrated with a career, that person may quit, go back to school, and try to find work in a different profession. People in the US sometimes take personality and aptitude tests to help them discover the best career for them. Career counselors offer these tests and recommend careers that fit people's interests, skills, and needs.

✏ **Compare Cultures**

Changing jobs and careers, reading books by career advisors, visiting career counselors, and taking personality and aptitude tests are common activities in the US, but not everywhere. Tell group members about experiences you or a family member have had changing jobs or finding a new career in another country. What was similar to what happens in the US? What was different? Which do you prefer?

Pronunciation Target • Intonation with Statements

🎧 *Intonation, the ↑ rising and ↓ falling of the speaker's voice, is one thing that makes English sound like English. When Americans talk, does the tone of their voices sound flat and steady, or does it seem to go up and down? Listen to your teacher or the audio.*

If you don't know where you're ↑ go ↓ ing, you'll probably never ↑ get ↓ there.
I like to visit the botanical ↑ gar ↓ den.
Ca ↑ reer counselors advise people on ca ↑ re ↓ ers.

Did you notice how the voice goes up and down at the end of phrases and sentences?

Activity A Write three statements about your goals. Trade papers with your partner. Read your partner's sentence out loud. Put an arrow for the up and down intonation at the end of your partner's sentences. Your partner will do the same with yours. Do you agree? Your teacher will listen to you read your sentences to each other.

Technology Extra
Search the Internet for information about a career that interests you. For example, look for career information at your state's Department of Labor web site. Write three useful facts from the information you read. Share your information with your group.

Vocabulary
Circle new words. Brainstorm meanings and sample sentences. Take notes. List other words that you want to learn.

aptitude
career
frustrated
personality
potential
profession
stick/stuck

Unit 1 Lesson 3 **19**

Activity B

Extension
- Have learners write one or two paragraphs with a topic sentence and supporting details on the topic "A Wonderful Job."
- As an alternative, learners could write on the topic "My Worst Job." This may bring out stories of exploitation and mistreatment of immigrants. Allow time for class members to share stories. Be supportive as you listen.

Learners can use Generic Assessment Master 14 (Writing Checklist and Error Correction Symbols) as they revise and edit their writing.

Activity C

- Outline and discuss a few interview basics (e.g., making eye contact with the interviewer, walking with confidence, waiting to be invited to sit, not leaning back in the chair, being prepared with answers to common questions).
- Help learners generate a list of simple interview questions (e.g., What is your name? What experience do you have? Why do you want this job?). Model a short interview with a volunteer.
- Break learners into groups of three and have them choose an interviewer, an applicant, and an observer that makes suggestions for improvement. Have them change roles until each has performed every role.
- Ask for volunteer groups to present to the class.

One Step Up

Write the "script" for one group's interview on the board or an overhead transparency. Have group members dictate as you write. Ask for corrections and improvements. Then have learners write their own scripts in their notebooks.

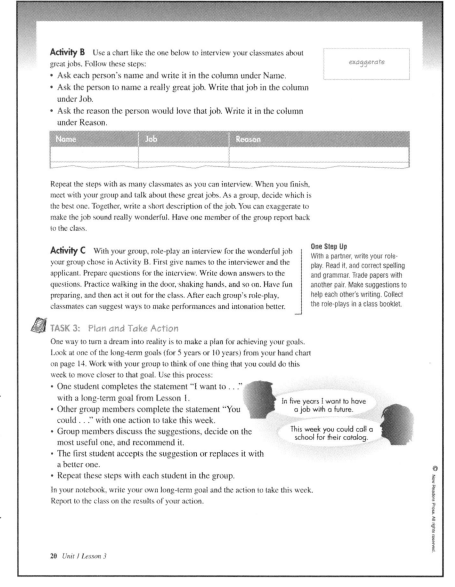

Activity B Use a chart like the one below to interview your classmates about great jobs. Follow these steps:
- Ask each person's name and write it in the column under Name.
- Ask the person to name a really great job. Write that job in the column under Job.
- Ask the reason the person would love that job. Write it in the column under Reason.

exaggerate

Name	Job	Reason

Repeat the steps with as many classmates as you can interview. When you finish, meet with your group and talk about these great jobs. As a group, decide which is the best one. Together, write a short description of the job. You can exaggerate to make the job sound really wonderful. Have one member of the group report back to the class.

Activity C With your group, role-play an interview for the wonderful job your group chose in Activity B. First give names to the interviewer and the applicant. Prepare questions for the interview. Write down answers to the questions. Practice walking in the door, shaking hands, and so on. Have fun preparing, and then act it out for the class. After each group's role-play, classmates can suggest ways to make performances and intonation better.

One Step Up
With a partner, write your role-play. Read it, and correct spelling and grammar. Trade papers with another pair. Make suggestions to help each other's writing. Collect the role-plays in a class booklet.

TASK 3: Plan and Take Action
One way to turn a dream into reality is to make a plan for achieving your goals. Look at one of the long-term goals (for 5 years or 10 years) from your hand chart on page 14. Work with your group to think of one thing that you could do this week to move closer to that goal. Use this process:
- One student completes the statement "I want to . . ." with a long-term goal from Lesson 1.
- Other group members complete the statement "You could . . ." with one action to take this week.
- Group members discuss the suggestions, decide on the most useful one, and recommend it.
- The first student accepts the suggestion or replaces it with a better one.
- Repeat these steps with each student in the group.

In your notebook, write your own long-term goal and the action to take this week. Report to the class on the results of your action.

In five years I want to have a job with a future.

This week you could call a school for their catalog.

Task 3

The objective of this task is to identify a practical, achievable action learners can take to move closer to a personal or professional goal.
- When learners finish, have each tell the class what action they plan to take and when.
- In a future class, ask volunteers to describe the action they took. This will encourage learners that have not taken action.

Review Unit Skills
See pp. 8–9 for suggestions on games and activities you can use to review the unit vocabulary and grammar.

- Collect and post a running list of unit vocabulary on a large sheet of paper. Refer to this unit list for bingo games, pair dictations, alphabetization, sentence completions, syllable stress, and pronunciation lessons.
- As you complete a unit, post the comprehensive list so that all active vocabulary for the term will eventually be displayed.

Unit 1 Challenge Reading

Reading Tip

Read the tip aloud with learners.

- Speakers of Romance languages may be able to guess the meaning of *social* from related words in their own languages.
- Tell learners that, although transferring meaning from one language to another is a useful skill, words that sound the same in different languages may not always mean the same.

Another useful skill is being able to guess, or predict, the meaning of a word from the way it is used. To convince any skeptics, do the following:

- Dictate the following passage or write it on the board or an overhead transparency. If dictating, help learners with spelling, but do not offer any definitions until the end.
- *The pedagogue came into the room carrying a large tome. She greeted her students, put on her glasses, opened the tome, and started reading. When she finished reading the first page, she closed the tome and asked, "Are there any questions about today's lesson?"*
- Prompt learners to guess that a *pedagogue* is a teacher and a *tome* is a book.
- Ask, "How did you guess the meaning of these completely new words?" Point out that the way these words were used (their *context*) gave clues to their meanings (e.g., The *pedagogue* greeted her students. She opened the *tome* and read.).
- Tell learners to list any words they guess as they read. When they finish, discuss the words they listed. Keep a tally of new words and how many learners guessed right.

◆ **Reading Tip** When you read, do you use a dictionary to look up every word that you don't know? If you do, you may read slowly, and this makes reading less enjoyable. You can often guess the meaning of a new word or new idiom by the way it's used in a sentence or a paragraph. This is called *finding meaning from context*. Look at the reading below for some examples. For example, what do you think the word *social* means in the first course description? Where do you think people would go for social dancing?

Personal Development Classes

Adults can take personal development classes through community colleges, religious organizations, and even public schools. Most personal development classes are inexpensive, and some are even free.

Some adult learners recently took personal development classes at a community college. They described their reasons for taking these classes and the skills that they learned:

Social Dancing I have never been satisfied with my dancing skills. I wanted to relax and become more sociable. I learned the most popular dances, including line dances and several types of Latin dances. The atmosphere was friendly and comfortable. I had been embarrassed to dance in public. Now, I've developed a lot of confidence. I am not afraid that people are laughing at me when I dance.

The Power of Your Will I have never been able to make up my mind about what to do with my life. I've had many ideas and plans, but few results. I wanted to learn how to set goals for myself. After taking this workshop, I understood the meaning of willpower. Having this ability to set goals for myself and stick to them is very important. Now each day I do at least one thing to move toward my goal.

Acting Since I was a child, I have aspired to be an actor. I had always wanted to find out if I really had the talent. In this course, I acted with other students in scenes from popular plays. I studied characters and did acting exercises. Our class presented a play at a senior citizens center. They loved it! I loved it too.

Buying Your Own Home I've often dreamed of buying my own home, but I was afraid I could never do it. I wanted to learn about the process of home buying. This course didn't give me every detail about buying a home, but it gave me essential information about how to become a homeowner.

Silent Reading

- Before reading, ask learners, "What does *personal development* mean to you?"
- Discuss the reasons people might take a course for personal, rather than professional, reasons. (Possible answers: for fun, to improve a skill, to prove something to themselves, to meet people, to do something active).
- After learners have read the article silently, ask, "Which personal development course would you register for?" Then, if possible, divide the class into groups according to which course they chose. If a group has only one member, have that person join the group of his or her second choice.
- Give groups a few minutes to discuss these questions: Why did you choose this course? What kind of personal development would you expect if you took the course?
- Have groups report back to the class.

Talk or Write

When possible, use the questions to stimulate further discussion.

Answers

1. Social dancing helped the writer develop self-confidence.
2. Each class changed the writer's attitude in some way. Discuss meanings of the word *attitude*. Ask learners to support their answers with evidence from the descriptions.
3. Answers will vary. For each new word, help learners identify the context that gives clues to its meaning.

Writing Task

Have learners organize their paragraphs using this pattern:
- Opinion in the first sentence
- Supporting facts in the body of the paragraph

Swimming for Beginners Although I have lived near beautiful beaches since I was a child, I was afraid to go into the water. For years, I had wanted to overcome my fear of water. The instructor taught me to relax my mind and my body in the water. I still haven't learned to be an Olympic swimmer, but I enjoy swimming now. I'm sure that everyone who takes this course will learn to swim—and learn to enjoy swimming!

Introduction to Computers I had never touched a computer before I took this course. I was afraid of computers because they looked so intimidating. This hands-on course, where we spent every minute in front of the computers, changed my attitude. I've already learned some basic programs, and I have my own e-mail account. I communicate with friends and relatives in my home country by e-mail. I also e-mail my new friends from computer class. I plan to continue taking computer classes. I'm sure my new skills will also help me find a better job.

How to Start Your Own Business I had worked in many jobs, but I'd never gotten along with my bosses. I wanted to work in a job without a boss. That's why I decided to start my own business. I knew that in my own business, I could be my own boss. This course taught me that starting your own business requires patience and hard work. It also gave me practical information about signing contracts and getting insurance.

Talk or Write

1. How did the person who wrote about Social Dancing change her life? Do you know of anyone whose life is better because of a personal development class? What happened?
2. Give one or more examples of classes that changed the writers' attitudes. How did each class change that writer's attitude?
3. List some words from the reading that were new to you. Share your list with a partner. What things in the reading helped you understand the new words?

Writing Task What do you think about personal development classes? Brainstorm ideas with your partner. Then, using your notes, write a paragraph about personal development classes. In your paragraph, state one of your opinions and give some facts to support it.

- Restatement of opinion in the final sentence(s)

Learners can use Generic Assessment Master 14 (Writing Checklist and Error Correction Symbols) as they edit their writing.

Unit 1 Project

Each learner writes a letter to him- or herself from a point in an imagined future.

Get Ready

Review the goals learners articulated in Task 1 and the time line they created for Task 2.

- Encourage learners to state goals based on their answers.
- Learners can draw new time lines, or they can continue the time lines they made in Task 2.

Do the Work

Use Unit Master 20 (Unit 1 Project: Form for an Informal Letter). Distribute one copy to each learner. Then follow these steps:

- Have learners select a specific point on their time line.
- Allow partners a few minutes to discuss the points they selected. Tell them to start by describing where they are and what they are doing.
- Explain to learners that they are going to imagine they are living in the future and are going to write to their present selves and give advice.

Model this activity by choosing a point on your own future time line and writing a simple letter to yourself.

- Use some of the details suggested in the student book.
- In the second paragraph, tell some of the steps you took to achieve your goal.
- In the third paragraph, give yourself advice on how to achieve your goal (e.g., You should not be discouraged. You should believe in yourself and know you will succeed.).

Then have learners write their own letters to themselves.

Extension

Write a group letter on the board or a large sheet of paper, using one learner's time line as a model.

UNIT 1 Project

Write a Letter to Yourself from the Future

Imagining your life in the future can help you plan and work to achieve your goals. Write a letter from yourself in the future to yourself in the present.

Get Ready

Start with the goals that you listed for Task 1, the time line that you made for Task 2, and the long-term goal and steps that you discussed for Task 3.

1. Draw another personal time line starting today and ending in 10 years. Include your short-term and long-term goals. Also include any good suggestions for steps you should take.
2. Cut out pictures from magazines to illustrate your future work, home, family, and community. Cut out want ads, information on courses, and other material that can help you take steps you plan.
3. Paste the cutouts to show where you want to be in 10 years and what you will do between now and then. You can also draw pictures.

Do the Work

Pick a specific time between now and 10 years from now on your personal time line. Write a three-paragraph letter to yourself from that time in the future. Follow these directions for your letter from the future you to the present you. Use the form your teacher gives you.

1. On the first line, write *Dear* [your first name].
2. Next, imagine you have achieved some of your goals. Write a draft of a paragraph about your new life. Use the illustrations from your time line to help you add details. Where are you? Home? Office? What kind of place do you live in? What is your family like? What are your hobbies? Write this paragraph in the present and present perfect tenses.
3. Now, write a draft of a paragraph about the steps that you took to achieve your goals up to that time. Write this paragraph in the past tense.
4. Next, write a draft of a paragraph with advice about the steps you should take to reach the rest of your goals by the end of the 10 years. Write in the present tense. Use the word *should*.

Present

Read your letter to a partner and listen to your partner read his or her letter. Show your letter to your teacher. Ask for suggestions to help your writing. Then revise your letter.

One Step Up
Write an answer from the present you to the future you.

Unit 1 Project **23**

Present

Ask partners to read their finished letters aloud to one another.

- Have learners polish their writing with a writing partner.
- Circulate among pairs. Answer questions, make suggestions, and provide dictionaries, but refrain from making corrections.

Assessment

Use Generic Assessment Master 11 (Written Communication Rubric) to evaluate the final letters.

Assign Workbook p. 10 (Check Your Progress). Go over the self-assessment with learners. Be sure they understand how to complete it, especially the first part.

- Explain that the numbers represent a rating scale, with *1* being the lowest score and *5* being the highest.
- If learners have difficulty using the scale, explain that a *2* rating means "not very well, but improving" and that a *4* rating means "fairly well."

Use Unit Master 21 (Unit Checkup/Review) whenever you complete this unit.

Unit 2: Selling Your Skills

Materials for the Unit
- Magazine ads
- Product packaging
- Videotape of TV commercials
- Customizable Masters 2, 3, 5, 9
- Generic Assessment Masters 10 and 14
- Unit Masters 22–29

Selling Your Skills

Read the unit title; then review the unit goals listed below it.
- Tell learners in this unit they will focus on presenting their skills—something they need for school applications and job interviews.
- Bring in examples of magazine ads, product packaging, and TV commercials. Analyze with learners the various techniques used to sell products. Ask, "Can any of these techniques be used to sell your skills?" (Your packaging can be the way you dress for interviews. Your advertising can be business card, resume, and web site.)

Photo
- Read the question below the arrow. Then tell learners to look at the photo.
- Elicit as much information about the photo as you can. Ask questions like these:
  What is going on?
  Does the taxi look comfortable?
  Does it look safe?
- Ask learners what this picture has to do with selling your skills.

Caption

Read the caption with learners.
- Tell learners Hassam's selling strategy might work well in an urban environment. If learners are not from an urban center, ask them to suggest strategies appropriate to where they live.
- Ask learners where they have seen similar ads. What kinds of things do people advertise?

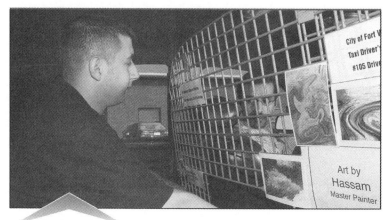

UNIT 2

Selling Your Skills

Presenting Your Skills

Home 1   Work/School 2   Community 3

- **Vocabulary** Interview words • Words for feelings
- **Language** Conditional contrary to fact • Indirect speech
- **Pronunciation** Sentence stress • Vowel sounds in *say, said,* and *says*
- **Culture** Expected behavior in the workplace

City of Fort W
Taxi Driver'
#105 Drive

Art by
Hassam
Master Painter

When have you found work by telling people about things you can do well?

Hassam Ahmad is from Egypt. He drives a taxi for ABC Taxi, but he wants to be an artist. He wants to meet customers. He also wants to meet someone who will help him sell his work. He puts photos of his artwork in the taxi for his passengers.

Think and Talk
1. What do you see in the picture? What is Hassam doing?
2. Does Hassam like his job? How do you know? What other work does he like?
3. How is Hassam telling people about his skills and his work? Is this a good idea? Explain your answer. What else could he do?
4. Do you like talking about and showing your skills? Why or why not?

What's Your Opinion? Is it right for Hassam to try to sell his work in the taxi when working for his employer? Explain your answer.

Extension

Talk about living in urban versus suburban or rural areas. Discuss the social and employment advantages and disadvantages of each.

Think and Talk
- Assign each group a question.
- Name a recorder and a reporter in each group. Tell recorders to write their group's responses. Then have reporters read the responses to the class.
- If a group finishes early, tell them to begin discussing (but not write about) the next question.

Possible Answers
1. The inside of a taxi, a driver, a passenger, some signs and photographs. Hassam is driving a taxi.
2. Answers will vary. He also likes making paintings.
3. He shows photos of his artwork in his cab. Answers will vary. Some learners may say this is an inexpensive and effective way to advertise; others may feel it is wrong to try to sell his artwork while doing his taxi job.
4. Answers will vary. Have learners explain their answers.

Vocabulary

Follow the suggestions on p. 6 for introducing and reinforcing the vocabulary words.

Network and *challenge* can be nouns or verbs. Give learners examples of each usage. Ask for other words used as both nouns and verbs.

Gather Your Thoughts

Use Customizable Master 5 (Idea Map). Follow the directions on p. 7 for customizing and duplicating the master and distributing the copies. Give one copy to each learner.

In this unit, learners will work toward achieving the goals set in Unit 1. Here, they take steps through *networking*—asking friends, family, co-workers, and others for information, advice, and support.

- Give learners examples of networking like these:

  A learner asks someone she knows from church if the place he works is hiring any new people.

  A new mother asks her own mother how to choose a good babysitter.

  You find a great sale on cereal and tell your neighbor about it.

- Have learners share their most recent networking experiences in their groups. Tell them to use the idea map in their books as a guide. The object is for learners to discover they have been using networking strategies all along.

- Emphasize that networking goes both ways—each person can contribute some information that will benefit the other.

What's the Problem?

Follow the suggestions on p. 5 for identifying and analyzing problems.

Some learners may say that they cannot network because they do not know anyone important or influential. Explain that networking is not

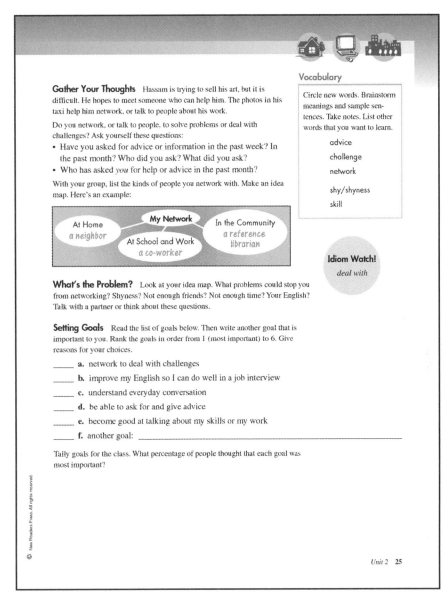

just a high-level activity or only for business.

Setting Goals

Follow the suggestions on p. 5 for setting goals.
- Have each learner write a personal goal in the space provided.
- Ask for a show of hands for each goal. Tally the results on the board or a transparency.
- Form small discussion groups of those who chose to work on the same goal. Have learners organize their discussions around questions like these:
  Why did you choose that goal?
  What do we all have in common?

Lesson 1: With a Little Help from My Friends ✳www✳

Read the title; then point out the lesson objectives listed below it.

Tell learners in this lesson they will talk about their skills and learn more about networking.

Question

Discussing this question may reveal a variety of attitudes towards asking for help. In some cultures, people do not believe in going outside the family for help. In others, asking for help is a sign of weakness.

Read the question aloud.

- Ask learners if their attitudes towards asking friends for help have changed since they came to the US.
- Ask learners if they know people who do a lot of networking. Is networking an effective way of getting things done?

Photo

Ask these questions:

- Is this a business or a social occasion? How do you know? Could it be a little of each?
- Can you tell anything about Hassam and Masa's place of birth and occupations? How?
- What time of day do you think it is? Why?

Listening Tip

Read the tip aloud. Tell learners that in this activity, they will need to listen for the *subscript* in a conversation.

Demonstrate the meaning of *subscript*.

- Say *I really need your help* in several different tones (e.g., desperate, playful, sarcastic).
- Ask learners which qualities in your voice changed the meaning of the words. Did you say some words louder? Softer? Did the rhythm change? Could they detect stress in your voice?

With a Little Help from My Friends

- Talk about your skills
- Use conditional contrary to fact

Who can give you advice about jobs, your plans, and your future?

- Listening Tip 🎧 If you know how the speaker feels, it's easier to understand the message. Through networking in his cab, Hassam has met someone who wants to interview him about his art. A friend gives him advice about how to prepare for his interview. Is Hassam worried? Tense? Excited? Does he feel some other way? Try to identify the tone of Hassam's voice in this conversation. The listening script is on page 136.

ingredients
label
professional

Idiom Watch!
go well
make a good impression
present yourself

Hassam and his wife, Masa, are talking with their friend Peter.

Talk or Write
1. How does Hassam feel about this meeting with Ms. Patterson? How do you know?
2. What does Peter mean when he says, "We never have enough time."
3. Hassam and Masa invited Peter to help Hassam prepare for an important interview. Was that a good idea? Why or why not?

26 Unit 2 Lesson 1

- Ask learners to think about talking on the phone. How do they know how the other person feels?
- Have a learner say a sentence in different ways. Ask the other learners which emotions he or she is trying to convey.

🎧 Play the audio or read the listening script on pp. 136–137. Follow the suggestions on p. 5 for listening comprehension.

Talk or Write

This exercise helps learners understand a conversation in English.

Have each group answer one question and report back to the class.

Possible Answers
1. He feels excited and nervous. He hopes she will sell his work, and he asks for advice about his meeting.
2. Hassam's friend means that there is never enough time to do things perfectly, but we should do the best we can with the time we have.
3. Answers will vary.

Vocabulary

Follow the suggestions on p. 6 for introducing and reinforcing the vocabulary words.

Class Chat

Use Customizable Master 3 (3-Column Chart). Follow the suggestions on p. 7 for customizing and duplicating the master. Make a copy for each learner.

- To keep the Class Chat short and lively, limit the time learners spend with each person.
- Tell learners to get answers from as many people as possible.
- Have learners greet one another before asking the questions and then thank each other before moving on.
- Tell learners to save the completed chart for Activity B.

Grammar Talk

Follow the suggestions on p. 7 for introducing the grammar point. Learners may recognize this point because they heard it used in the Class Chat and the listening section on the previous page.

Play the audio or read the listening script on pp. 136–137 again, this time in short segments. Ask learners to listen for sentences with *if* and *would.*

- After the selective listening, play or read some of the conditional sentences from the script. Ask for volunteers to repeat the statements.
- Ask learners to look at the printed script in the back of their student books (p. 136). Play or read the script again while learners underline the conditional sentences they hear.
- Ask learners to find a contraction of *I would* in one of the sentences.
- Tell learners to silently read the Grammar Talk information in their books. Ask them what they noticed about the sentences.

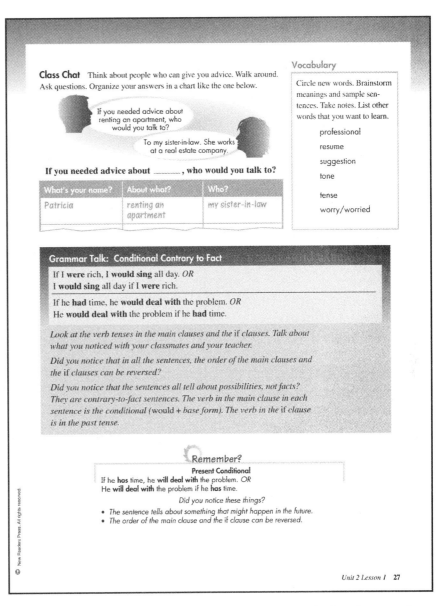

Unit 2 Lesson 1   27

Lead learners in writing rules for using the conditional with *would:*

- The sentences consist of two clauses.
- The verb of one clause is in the past.
- The other clause contains *would* and the base form of the verb.
- The clauses can be reversed without changing meaning.
- When the *if* clause comes first, it is followed by a comma. When the *would* clause comes first, there is no comma.

To practice using the conditional, use Unit Master 22 (Grammar: The Conditional) now or at any time during the rest of the unit.

Assign Workbook pp. 11–12.

Unit 2 *Lesson 1* **27**

Activity A

Answers

1. b	3. a	5. e
2. d	4. c	

The sentences containing *would* are contrary-to-fact sentences.

Activity B

- Model the *conditional contrary-to-fact pattern* by telling learners about people you would ask for advice.
- After they write their sentences, have learners exchange papers and help one another make any needed corrections.

Activity C

- Consider learners' needs as you start the activity. Make it a humorous retelling of social "bloopers" or a more serious discussion of roads not taken.
- Set a time limit for each interview.

Task 1

Guide learners in expanding and categorizing their lists of people.

- Write the categories on the board or an overhead transparency. Have learners copy them on a notebook page or four-column chart.
- Write a few sample questions for each category.
- Have partners ask each other their questions.

Ongoing Assessment

While learners practice their questions, walk around the room and listen. How well did they perform on the following features?
a. General quality of questions
   0 = incomprehensible questions
   1 = partially formed/partially understood
   2 = clear and appropriate
b. Use of vocabulary
   0 = limited/inappropriate
   1 = some problems using vocabulary
   2 = complete and appropriate

c. Features of language functions (conditional contrary-to-fact)
   0 = many problems/not understandable
   1 = some problem using language function
   2 = clear and accurate use of language function

With these categories in mind, take some notes. Which one or two categories were most difficult for the learners? In the follow-up period, select learners who scored 2 in any category and have them model appropriate communication.

Extension

Have learners ask family members and friends their questions. In a subsequent class, ask for reports on the interviews. Then ask questions like these:

- Why did you choose to ask that person that question?
- Were the answers helpful?
- How might you change the question to get a better answer?
- How did you feel asking the questions?
- How did the person you asked react?

Activity A With a partner, write the letter of the *if* clause that should follow each main clause. Then put a check mark in front of the contrary-to-fact sentences. Be careful! Only one *if* clause matches each main clause.

_____ 1. Hassam will make a better impression
_____ 2. Hassam wouldn't be so nervous
_____ 3. Peter would give suggestions
_____ 4. Ms. Patterson will try to sell Hassam's work
_____ 5. Hassam and Masa would take a vacation

a. if Hassam asked for help.
b. if Peter helps him.
c. if she likes his photos.
d. if he were ready for the interview.
e. if they had more money.

Activity B Class Chat Follow-Up Look at your Class Chat chart. Write about three group members. Who would they talk to if they needed advice?

1. _Patricia would talk to her sister-in-law, Tania._
2. _____
3. _____
4. _____

Activity C Think about a time when you wanted to make a good first impression and present yourself well. Was it a job interview? An open house at your child's school? A special party? Describe that experience to a partner. Your partner will ask you the questions in the chart below. Then switch roles.

Questions	Answers
When did you want to make a good impression?	When I talked to our teacher for the first time.
What happened?	I only said two words.
If you did it again, what would you do differently?	I would not act so shy.

One Step Up
Write your answers to the three questions in your notebook. Read your answers to the group. Then each group member says how he or she would deal with that same situation. Say, "If that happened to me, I would _____."

 TASK 1: Asking the Right Questions
Look at the kinds of people that your group listed in the idea map on page 25. Think about asking them questions. If you could ask questions to help deal with your challenges, what would you ask? Use these four categories: Work, Personal, Financial, Educational. Write the questions in your notebook.

Work: How can I ask for a pay raise?

Lesson 2: What Do I Do Now?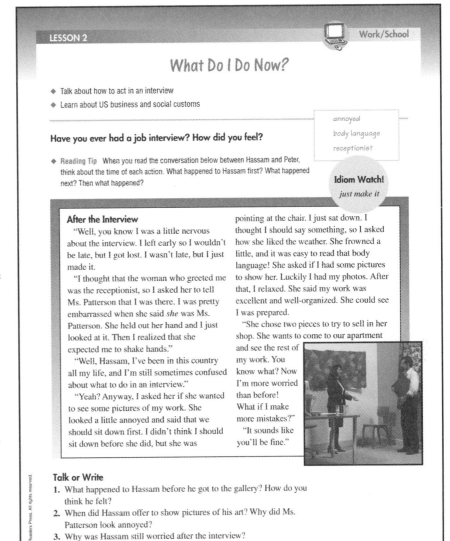

Read the lesson title and point out the objectives below it.

Tell learners that in this lesson they will prepare for an interview and learn about US business and social customs.

Questions

Read the questions aloud. If any learners have had interviews in the US, ask them questions like these:

- Was the interview in English or in your native language?
- Who interviewed you?
- What did you talk about?
- Do you remember what you were wearing on that day?

Attention Box

Read the words. Convey meaning by discussing and exemplifying, or by pointing and miming. This vocabulary should be understood, but learners should not be expected to produce the words at this point.

- Have learners identify the part of speech for each word.
- Tell learners to practice the words they do not know.

Idiom Watch

Have learners find the idiom in the story and tell its meaning from context.

Photo

Put learners in small groups to discuss the content of the photo.

Reading Tip

Read the tip aloud with learners.

- Guide learners in thinking about the sequence of events in the reading.
- Have learners read silently at first. Then read aloud to them. Have them make notes on the sequence of events as you read.

Finally, do the following:

- Have learners close their books.
- Read a sentence from the reading passage and ask learners to count

silently the number of words they hear.
- Repeat this activity with five sentences of various lengths.

Talk or Write

This exercise helps learners understand events in sequence.

- Put learners in small groups. Have each select a recorder to write members' answers on a large sheet of paper.
- Have groups display and compare their answers.

Possible Answers

1. He got lost. He probably felt anxious and upset. He was worried that he would be late.

2. He offered to show his pictures when he first met Ms. Patterson. She was annoyed because she wanted to sit down first.

3. He was worried that he would make more mistakes when Ms. Patterson came to his apartment.

To practice sequence, use Unit Master 23 (Comprehension: Hassam's Interview) now or at any time during the rest of the unit.

Inset page content

What Do I Do Now?

- Talk about how to act in an interview
- Learn about US business and social customs

Have you ever had a job interview? How did you feel?

annoyed
body language
receptionist

Idiom Watch!
just make it

◆ Reading Tip When you read the conversation below between Hassam and Peter, think about the time of each action. What happened to Hassam first? What happened next? Then what happened?

After the Interview

"Well, you know I was a little nervous about the interview. I left early so I wouldn't be late, but I got lost. I wasn't late, but I just made it.

"I thought that the woman who greeted me was the receptionist, so I asked her to tell Ms. Patterson that I was here. I was pretty embarrassed when she said *she* was Ms. Patterson. She held out her hand and I just looked at it. Then I realized that she expected me to shake hands."

"Well, Hassam, I've been in this country all my life, and I'm still sometimes confused about what to do in an interview."

"Yeah? Anyway, I asked her if she wanted to see some pictures of my work. She looked a little annoyed and said that we should sit down first. I didn't think I should sit down before she did, but she was

pointing at the chair. I just sat down. I thought I should say something, so I asked how she liked the weather. She frowned a little, and it was easy to read that body language! She asked if I had some pictures to show her. Luckily I had my photos. After that, I relaxed. She said my work was excellent and well-organized. She could see I was prepared.

"She chose two pieces to try to sell in her shop. She wants to come to our apartment and see the rest of my work. You know what? Now I'm more worried than before! What if I make more mistakes?"

"It sounds like you'll be fine."

Talk or Write

1. What happened to Hassam before he got to the gallery? How do you think he felt?
2. When did Hassam offer to show pictures of his art? Why did Ms. Patterson look annoyed?
3. Why was Hassam still worried after the interview?

Unit 2 Lesson 2 **29**

Vocabulary

Follow the suggestions on p. 6 for introducing and reinforcing the vocabulary words.

Extension

Play a word game:

- Write all the words from the vocabulary box on the board.
- Ask learners to close their eyes as you erase one word. Draw a horizontal line in place of the word. Ask learners to guess which word is missing.
- Repeat until all words have been erased and replaced by lines.
- Ask volunteers to come to the board and write the words on the correct lines.

Use Unit Master 24 (Game/ Vocabulary: What's Missing?) to play this game in small groups with word cards.

Technology Extra

Have learners find definitions of these words on the Internet or in the word-processing program of a computer.

In the US

Before reading, talk with learners about business and social customs. Ask these questions:

- Is making an appointment a business or a social custom?
- Is calling ahead before coming for a visit a business or a social custom?
- Can you think of more examples for business and social customs?

Then do the following:

- List learner responses on the board or a transparency.
- Have learners silently complete the reading.
- Ask learners which words or ideas they need to have pronounced or defined. Have other learners help pronounce and define.

Use Unit Master 25 (Life Skills: Business Customs in

In the US   Business Customs

In general, people in the US act quite formal in business situations. However, some businesses are more informal. For that reason, it's often difficult to know exactly how to act in business situations. Here are some things you can do.

If you are going to have an interview with a company, get all the information you can about that company from books, web sites, and people. Network with friends, classmates, and acquaintances, especially US-born people. Don't forget the library. Ask the librarian to help you find a book on business customs. In any business situation, watch what other people are doing. They can be models for the way you act.

Compare Cultures

Preparing a resume, researching a company, and interviewing for a job are common activities in the US, but not everywhere. Tell the class about experiences you or a family member had looking for a job in another country. What was similar? What was different? Which ways of finding jobs do you prefer?

Vocabulary

Circle new words. Brainstorm meanings and sample sentences. Take notes. List other words that you want to learn.

- body language
- custom
- situation
- annoyed
- confused
- embarrassed
- formal
- informal

Idiom Watch!
handle yourself

Pronunciation Target • Sentence Stress

Listen to your teacher or the audio. Listen for the stressed words in the sentences.

If I **needed** a **book**, I'd **go** to the **library**.
If I **wanted** a **job**, I'd **ask** my **brother** for **help**.

In English, you need to stress the right words to be understood. English speakers usually stress content words—the words that carry meaning. Those words sound a little longer and clearer than others. Did you hear the stress on the words in bold type? Say the sentences with a partner. Check each other's pronunciation.

Activity A Read the sentences below. Underline the stressed words. Practice with a partner. Listen carefully to your partner. Do you agree about which words should be stressed?

- If I had more time, I would work on my project.
- If I needed advice, I would ask my sister-in-law.
- If Peter hadn't helped Hassam, his interview wouldn't have gone so well.

Now write three sentences of your own with *if* clauses. Then do the same activity again with your partner.

---

the US) now or at any time during the rest of the unit.

Pronunciation Target

Play the audio or read the sentences in the student book aloud.

- Tell learners not to look at the text as they listen.
- Ask learners which words in each sentence sound longer and clearer.

Activity A

- After learners write their own sentences with *if* clauses, ask partners to exchange sentences.

- Tell learners to read their partners' sentences aloud. Circulate; listen to readers and help them stress the correct words.
- Ask some learners to read their sentences to you. Then ask their partner to tell you which words should be made longer and clearer.

 Assign Workbook pp. 13–14.

Activity B

Provide these examples for learners:

- If I am a man, should I get up for a woman on a crowded bus?
- Is it always appropriate for a man to let a woman walk into a room ahead of him?
- If I am annoyed by a cell phone conversation on a train, should I say something?
- Is it OK to call my boss by his first name? How friendly should I be with co-workers?

Have each group tally the number of learners confused by each situation.

- List on the board or an overhead transparency the 10 situations most learners find confusing. Discuss them with learners.
- Ask learners how they think they should behave in the various situations. Wait until as many as possible have answered before giving your opinion.

If possible, call in another "expert" on US culture (someone who works in the school, a friend, or another teacher) to give opinions.

Extension

- Before the discussion, have learners write in their notebooks the situation or custom they find most confusing.
- Then, after the discussion, have them write below it whichever solution they think is the best.

Activity C

Model completion of the Johari window using the example in the text or a class-generated example. Move from pair to pair to assist. Ask for volunteers to present their work.

Activity D

Encourage learners to use their own experiences in their stories.

One Step Up

Learners may make grammatical errors in this role-play. To encourage self-correction, follow these steps:

Activity B What social or business customs and situations in the US are confusing to you? In your group, list all the confusing situations you can. One person will write the group list on the board. When all groups have listed their situations, one student from each group will count how many students are confused in each situation. Make a class list of the 10 most confusing situations from all the lists.

Activity C With a partner, pick one of the confusing situations from Activity B. Think about how you and your partner would handle yourselves in that situation. Try to find something that you both would do. Then find something that neither of you would do. Complete a four-section square like the one below.

I	Both of Us
If I was worried about how to divide the check, I would ask the other person for help.	If we were worried about how to divide the check, both of us would ask the waiter for separate checks.
Neither of Us	**My Partner**
If we were worried about how to divide the check, neither of us would act nervous.	If Ricardo was worried about how to divide the check, he would pay for both of us.

 Eating in restaurants with people from the US is sometimes confusing. I am worried about how to divide the check.

Activity D With your group, sit in a circle. Tell a story about a person who went to a job interview and made a lot of mistakes. Each person in the circle can add a sentence with a new mistake to the story. You can make the story funny. One person in the group writes the story. Another person reads the story to the class.

One Step Up
With your group, role-play the story you write for your class. Remember to stress content words when you speak. Ask your classmates to suggest better ways to act in an interview.

TASK 2: Make a List of US Social and Business Customs
Make a list of suggestions that could be helpful to someone coming to the US. Include *do's* and *don'ts* about US business and social customs. Here are some examples:
Do: Stand when you are introduced to someone.
Don't: Don't be late for an interview. Give yourself extra time.

Technology Extra
Combine all the ideas from the lists into one brochure. Use a computer to write and design your brochure. Give a copy to other classes at your school.

Unit 2 Lesson 2   **31**

- Circulate during the activity. Make note of sentences with the most obvious errors. Write them exactly as they are spoken by learners.
- After the activity, bring learners back together.
- Referring to your notes, write up to six sentences on the board or an overhead transparency. Repeated mistakes should get preference.
- Ask learners to find the errors in the sentences and tell you how to correct them.

Task 2

Help learners generate ideas for their lists.

Technology Extra

The brochure can be simply a folded sheet of $8\frac{1}{2} \times 11$-inch paper.

- Help learners format the brochure as a horizontal document so that it reads correctly after it is folded.
- Have learners type a title and author on the cover and their *do's* and *don'ts* on the inside.
- Learners may want to include magazine pictures or drawings to illustrate the situations.

Lesson 3: Getting the Word Out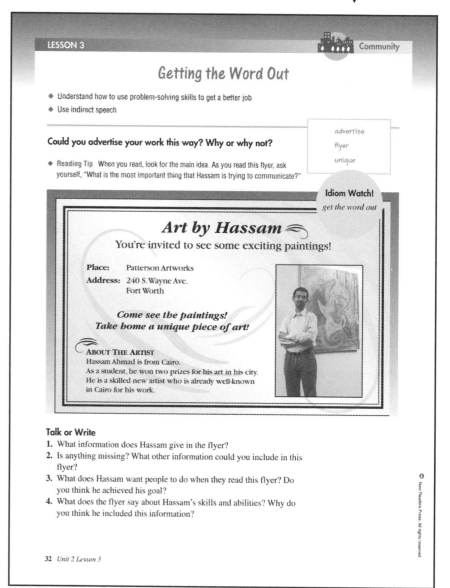

Read the title and point out the lesson objectives below it.

Tell learners in this lesson they will learn about ways to present their skills and achievements and get a better job.

Idiom Watch

- Ask learners what they think the idiom in the title might mean. If no one suggests the correct meaning, tell learners one meaning might be *to make information available to the public.*
- Have learners share similar expressions from their own languages. Ask them to translate the expressions into English if they can.

Questions

Read the questions aloud. Ask volunteers to answer the questions from their own work experience.

Reading Tip

Read the tip aloud. Then ask these questions:
- Why did Hassam include a painting in the photo?
- If you were to take a photo of yourself and your work, product, or any other object important to you, what would that object be?

Ask learners to bring such a photo or the object itself to school. Have them share the stories behind the photo or object.

Talk or Write

This exercise helps learners analyze an author's purpose.
- Have learners discuss the content of the flyer in small groups.
- Have a recorder in each group take notes and a reporter share the group's findings with the class.

Possible Answers
1. Hassam tells the name and address of the shop where his paintings are being sold. He tells something about himself.
2. Answers will vary. He could also include directions to get to the gallery, what school he went to, and prices for his art.
3. He wants people to come see his paintings and perhaps buy one. Answers will vary for the second part of this question. Ask learners to give reasons for their answers.
4. The flyer says that Hassam is a skilled artist, well known in Cairo, who has received prizes for his art. He included this information to show himself as a professional and to encourage people to come see his art.

Vocabulary

Follow the suggestions on p. 6 for introducing and reinforcing the vocabulary words.

Use Unit Master 26 (Vocabulary: Matching Game) now or at any time during the rest of the unit.

Group Chat

Use Customizable Master 3 (3-Column Chart). Follow the suggestions on p. 7 for customizing and duplicating the master. Make a copy for each learner.

Tell learners to save their completed charts for use in Activity A.

Extension

- Draw a two-column chart on a large sheet of paper.
- Have learners take turns writing on the chart the essential information from another learner's response (e.g., *Ana / fix cars; Mario / lay bricks*).

Ask questions like the ones below and have learners answer orally. Model the activity first.

- How many people said that they could do construction work? (____ *people said that they could do construction work.*)
- How many people said that they could do clerical work?
- How many people said that they could work with their hands?
- How many people said that they could operate a vehicle?
- How many people said that they could do artistic work?

Finally, create statistical data from learners' responses.

- Ask learners to convert the numbers into percentages [e.g., ____ (number of learners that can operate a vehicle) divided by ____ (total number of learners) = ____ percent (percentage of the class that can operate a vehicle)].

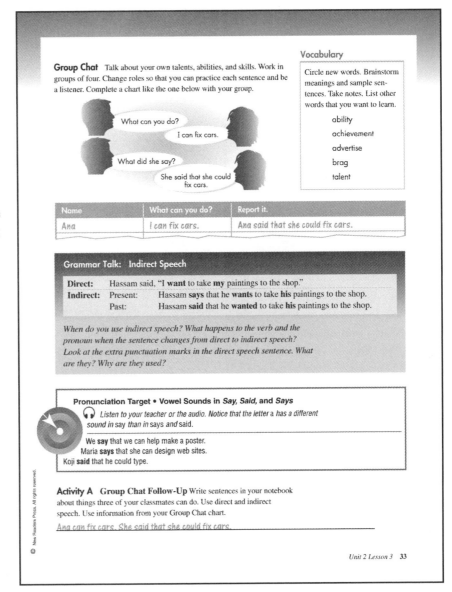

- Display the data on the board or an overhead transparency.
- Discuss the results.

Grammar Talk

Follow the suggestions on p. 7 for introducing the grammar point.

For further practice with indirect speech, use Unit Master 27 (Grammar: Indirect Speech) now or at any time during the rest of the unit.

Pronunciation Target

Play the audio or read the sentences in the student book.

- Ask if learners can hear the different sounds of *a*. Which two words have the same vowel sound? *(says and said)*
- The word *say* has a long *a*. Write on the board other words that have the same spelling *(hay, way, day, play, tray).*
- In the words *says* and *said,* the *ay* and *ai* have a *short e* sound, as in *let* or *again.* These are unusual spellings for *short e.*

Activity A

Guide learners by creating a few sample sentences before they write their own. Ask for volunteers to share their sentences.

 Assign Workbook pp. 15–16.

Activity B

Put learners in groups of four. Assign a reader, a repeater, a reporter, and a recorder in each group. Choose one group to model the procedure:

- The reader reads the sentence: *Hassam said, "I don't want to brag about myself."*
- The repeater repeats the sentence without looking at the book.
- The reporter restates the sentence as indirect speech: *Hassam said that he didn't want to brag about himself.*
- The recorder writes down the reporter's sentence.

After one round of reading, repeating, reporting, and writing, have learners change roles and repeat the exercise with the next sentence. Continue until all the sentences have been read.

Extension

Have learners copy the following sentences from the board and insert the correct punctuation marks:

1. *Mario said I can lay bricks.*
2. *Ms. Patterson said please sit down*
3. *The teacher said take out your notebooks.*
4. *Alice said show your best work.*
5. *Masa said have some cookies.*

Activity C

Keep the scripts in a class folder. Make them available to learners to review and practice whenever they choose.

For a multilevel group, ask some pairs to mime the interview and more advanced learners to write the dialogue for the mime.

Activity D

Encourage learners to practice correct sentence structure as they answer the questions.

Activity B In your group, one person reads the sentences. The others repeat. Then take turns using indirect speech to tell what someone said.

1. Masa said, "I think you should use a flyer."
2. They said, "We want to see your paintings."
3. Ms. Patterson said, "I like your work."
4. Peter said, "I'm still sometimes confused about what to do in an interview."
5. Hassam said, "I really want to sell my work."

Hassam said, "I don't want to brag about myself."

Hassam said that he didn't want to brag about himself.

Activity C On page 29, Hassam used reported speech to tell Peter about his interview with Ms. Patterson. With a partner, write and role-play the interview using direct speech. Be creative.

Activity D Ask your partner about an interview experience. It could be a job interview, a citizenship interview, a talk with a school official, and so on. You can also talk about an interview someone else had. Use the following questions. When you finish, your partner will interview you.

1. What was the purpose of the interview?
2. When was your interview?
3. What did you wear?
4. Where was the interview?
5. Who was the person you met? Do you remember the person's name or job title?
6. Do you remember any questions you had to answer? What were they?
7. How did it feel to talk about yourself?
8. What was the most difficult part of the interview?
9. If you could do or say anything differently, what would it be?
10. What did you learn from your interview?

One Step Up
Use your answers to Activity D to write about your interview or your partner's interview.

TASK 3: *Present a Collage of Your Skills and Achievements*
Plan a presentation for the class about your skills and achievements. Make a collage of pictures and words from magazines or newspapers as part of your presentation. Choose pictures and words that show your skills and achievements. Add small objects. Show the collage as you tell the class about your skills. These questions may help you:
- Which of these skills do I use in my current job or in daily life?
- Which skills would I like to use in my future jobs or in daily life?

One Step Up

Encourage learners to expand on each idea and provide details to make the story more interesting. Show learners how combining sentences makes the story more fluent:

It was in the winter. The weather was pleasant on that day.

Even though the interview was in the winter, the weather was pleasant.

Task 3

Assessment

Use Generic Assessment Master 10 (Oral Communication Rubric) to evaluate presentations.

Review Unit Skills

See pp. 8–9 for suggestions on games and activities you can use to review the unit vocabulary and grammar.

Unit 2 Challenge Reading 🌐

Reading Tip

Read the tip aloud with learners. Have them scan the reading before completing the reading activities below.

<u>Jigsaw Reading</u>

Divide the reading into three sections and assign each to a small group. If the class is very large, assign the same section to two groups.

- Have group members designate a recorder, a contributor, and a reporter for their group.
- Give each recorder a copy of Customizable Master 9 (Main Idea and Supporting Details).
- Tell recorders they will fill in the main idea and supporting details for their part of the reading. The contributor will lead the group discussion, and the recorder will take notes.
- Reconvene the whole group. Have reporters read from their master in the order of the assigned sections.
- Allow for a question-and-answer session between reporters and recorders so that recorders have time to complete the remaining sections of their master.

<u>Silent Reading</u>

- Have learners read the complete article silently. When they finish, tell them to add to their group's master by writing the main idea of the article.
- Ask group reporters to read their group's main idea to the class. Compare the responses.

<u>Extension</u>

Practice shaking hands by having learners stand in two lines facing each other. Tell learners to shake hands and greet each other as follows:

Student A: Hi, my name is ____.

Student B: Nice to meet you. My name is ____.

UNIT 2 Challenge Reading

◆ Reading Tip Reading an article quickly to find out what it is about or see how it is organized is a strategy many good readers use. Scanning, or doing a quick first reading, can help you get a general idea of what you will read. Later you can read the article again carefully for details. Read this article on business customs quickly. As you read, think about how the writer organized the ideas. Then read again more slowly and carefully before answering the questions on page 36.

Business Customs: How Should You Act?

How should you act at the workplace in the US? Customs for the workplace are always changing. For example, a few years ago, men and women were often treated differently at work. Today many men and women expect to be treated the same in the workplace, although in reality this does not always happen. Here are a few tips to help you avoid mistakes in the world of work.

Opening Doors Many men are confused about when to hold a door open for a woman. At work, a man should hold a door for a woman if he would hold it for a man in the same situation.

The following "rules" are true for both men and women:
- Hold the door open for a superior, male or female.
- Hold the door for anyone, male or female, who is carrying a lot of things.
- Hold the door for anyone, male or female, who is hurt or needs your help.

What about revolving doors? Since the person in front does all the pushing, you should enter the door ahead of a person in one of the categories above (a superior, a person carrying packages, or someone in need of help). And, of course, push the revolving door carefully so you don't hurt anyone.

Shaking Hands Both men and women shake hands in the same way in the workplace. Here's how it's done:
- Extend your right hand. It doesn't matter who extends a hand first.
- Look into the other person's eyes. This is called *making eye contact*.
- Present yourself as a serious but friendly person. You don't need to smile, but if you do, your smile should be sincere.
- Clasp the other person's hand. Apply some pressure, but not too much or too little. Practice makes perfect. Ask an American friend to check your handshake. Too much pressure? Too little? Keep practicing.
- Move your clasped hands up and down once or twice, and then let go. Easy? Now you know how to shake hands for business in the US.

Unit 2 Challenge Reading 35

As they finish, each learner moves on to the next person in the opposite line. Observe the handshakes, the eye contact, and the body posture. When there are problems, model for each pair.

Attention Box

Read the words, pointing or miming when possible to convey meaning. Brainstorm meanings and ask learners to identify parts of speech for each word.

This vocabulary should be understood, but learners should not be expected to produce the words at this point.

Talk or Write

Possible Answers

1. The main points are that in business, men and women are generally not treated differently, but sometimes superiors are treated differently.

2. Answers will vary. Hold the door open for a superior or for anyone who needs help. Shake hands firmly. Stand to greet a visitor to your office or a superior.

3. Answers will vary. In a social situation, a man must wait for a woman to extend her hand before shaking hands. In business, in doesn't matter who extends a hand first. But the Golden Rule is the same everywhere: Treat others the way you would want to be treated.

Writing Task

Tell learners to use the three subheads in the article as an outline for their paragraph. Encourage them to use their answers to the Talk or Write questions for ideas.

Learners can use Generic Assessment Master 14 (Writing Checklist and Error Correction Symbols) as they revise and edit their writing.

Is this any different from shaking hands socially? Well, a little. First of all, remember that at the workplace, it doesn't matter who extends a hand first. In social situations, this is still true when two women or two men shake hands. However, when a woman and a man shake hands socially, for example at a party or in a restaurant, the man should wait for the woman to extend a hand first. What if the woman doesn't extend a hand? That's easy. You don't shake hands. Just smile politely and keep the conversation going.

Standing and Sitting If you are in your own work area, you should stand to greet a visitor. You may also stand to meet a superior who you don't see every day—for example, the company president. This is done regardless of the gender of either person. In another person's office, wait to be invited to sit. If it's your space, don't forget to invite your visitor to sit.

This rule works another way. If you are very busy and don't have time for a long conversation, it's OK not to invite your visitor to sit. Your conversation will probably be shorter, and you will both be able to go back to work sooner.

The Golden Rule is the same everywhere: Treat other people the way you would like to be treated.

Talk or Write

1. What are the writer's main points about manners in a business situation?

2. Give one or more examples from the article of appropriate manners in a business situation.

3. What does the writer say about differences between business manners and social manners?

✏ **Writing Task** In your notebook, write a one-paragraph summary of the article. Summarize what the article says about business manners. Do this by listing the three areas that the article mentions. For each area, write about how to act in a business situation.

clasp
disability
extend
gender
regardless
revolving
superior
treat

Idiom Watch!
Practice makes perfect.

Unit 2 Project

Learners make a personal achievement record showing both documents and skills.

Get Ready

Have learners read the instructions in pairs. Tell them to make note of any questions or suggestions that might help them with the task.

Brainstorm with learners on how to complete the project. Ask questions like these:

• How long will the project take?
• What items and tools will you need?
• What things can you start working on immediately?

Do the Work

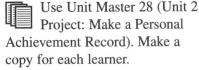 Use Unit Master 28 (Unit 2 Project: Make a Personal Achievement Record). Make a copy for each learner.

• Tell learners to use the master to keep track of their personal achievements as they continue through the course.
• Make sure learners have all the necessary materials, handouts, and time they need to finish the project.

Present

• Review the achievement records and make any suggestions for changes. Stress that the record is an excellent way to be prepared for an interview.
• Have learners practice their presentations with a partner. Then ask volunteers to present to the class.

Technology Extra

Help learners find clip art for their covers. Show them how to use the label-making feature of a word-processing program.

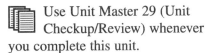 Assign Workbook p. 17 (Check Your Progress).

Use Unit Master 29 (Unit Checkup/Review) whenever you complete this unit.

UNIT 2 Project

Make a Personal Achievement Record

All people have to present their skills and achievements at one time or another. Be organized and prepare to brag about your achievements. Do this by keeping a record of your achievements and skills. Have it ready for times when you need to talk about yourself—an interview, a promotion review, a school application, or other important events.

| update |
| up-to-date |

Get Ready

1. Start with the list of skills and achievements you prepared for Task 3. Use the checklist your teacher gives you.
2. Buy a loose-leaf notebook or a folder to organize your achievement record. Buy plastic sheet covers to keep the pages in good condition.

Do the Work

1. In your achievement record, place copies of certificates, diplomas, letters of recommendation, your Social Security card, and immigration information.
2. Include photos of your achievements and talents. Do you paint houses? Care for children? Decorate cakes? Keep photos that show what you do.
3. You may also want to include an English paper that you are proud of.

As time passes, you will need to update your achievement record, or put new things into it to show new skills and achievements. Always keep your record up-to-date and ready to show.

Present

1. Before using your achievement record in an interview, show it to a teacher or someone else in your support network. Ask for comments and suggestions. Make changes.
2. Your achievement record is an excellent tool for helping you prepare for an interview. Practice talking about each item. Make sure the items are organized in a logical way. Begin and end with items that make a very good impression.
3. Remember that preparing for an interview means practicing your presentation many times until you can do it perfectly. You will have more confidence, and you'll feel less tense and shy.

Technology Extra

Use a computer to design a cover page for your achievement record. You can also use the computer to prepare labels for your photographs.

Unit 2 Project 37

Unit 3: Getting Help

- Protective plastic covers
- Sticky notes
- Phone directories
- Booklets listing domestic violence agencies
- Shoe boxes or large envelopes
- Index cards
- Customizable Master 6
- Generic Assessment Masters 10, 12–14
- Unit Masters 30–36

Getting Help

Read the title; then review the unit objectives listed below it.

- Follow the suggestions on p. 5 for talking about the title. Explore different cultural attitudes about seeking professional help with personal problems.
- This unit will focus on solutions to the problems of alcohol abuse, drug abuse, and domestic violence. Learners will also find out how to get support for themselves, friends, or family members.

Ask these questions to introduce the topic of getting help:

- Who do you ask for help with schoolwork?
- If a friend were sick or hurt, where would you take him or her for help?
- Where would you take a friend or relative for help with drug or alcohol abuse?

After learners answer, expand the topic with these questions:

- How else can you get help?
- What if your family and friends do not know how to help?

Photo

Follow the suggestions on pp. 4–5 for talking about the photo.

- Have learners cover the caption and look at the photo. Elicit as much information as possible.
- Ask what this picture has to do with getting help.

Caption

Have learners read the caption silently. Then ask these questions:
- What is Erin's dilemma?
- What reasons could she have for seeing Mark again after this?
- Why is she afraid to tell her mother what happened?

Question

Read the question below the arrow. Suggest the following possible actions:
- Never see Mark again.
- Get help for Mark quickly.
- Tell Mark he needs help. Refuse to see him until he gets it.

Take a poll of learners' opinions based on these three options.

Think and Talk

Follow the suggestions on p. 6 for comprehension questions.

<u>Possible Answers</u>
1. Answers will vary. They should include the punctured tire and Erin's shocked look.
2. Erin's boyfriend was drinking and was angry.
3. Answers will vary.
4. Answers will vary.

What's Your Opinion?

Have learners consider the issue and explain their opinions.

Vocabulary

Follow the suggestions on p. 6 for introducing and reinforcing the vocabulary words.

- Conduct a textbook word search. Tell learners to locate the vocabulary words in context on pp. 38 and 39. Give them the page numbers, activity titles, and line numbers below.
- Caution learners that some words are not in their simple form (e.g., *cope* appears as *coping*).

Locations and Answers

p. 39, Gather Your Thoughts, line 9 (*agency,* plural *agencies*)

p. 39, What's the Problem, line 2 (*barrier,* plural *barriers*)

p. 38, Unit Goals, line 2 (*issue,* plural *issues*)

p. 39, Setting Goals, item *e* (*resource,* plural *resources*)

p. 39, Gather Your Thoughts, line 9 (*strategy,* plural *strategies*)

p. 39, Setting Goals, item *d* (*communicate*)

p. 39, Gather Your Thoughts, line 9 (*cope,* participle *coping*)

p. 38, photo caption, line 6 (*abusive*)

p. 39, Setting Goals, items *a, b, c* (*abuse*)

p. 38, photo caption, line 6 (*violent*) [The noun *violence* is not used in the unit opener.]

Gather Your Thoughts

In Unit 2, learners moved toward achieving personal and professional goals through networking with friends and family. Unit 3 examines the idea of reaching out for more specialized help through community agencies and members of helping professions.

- Point out that together learners can be a *support group* for one another by offering support, referrals, and advice.
- Give learners a few minutes to read and think about the questions. Then ask volunteers to share their thoughts on each question.

These questions can generate discussion of differing cultural attitudes toward asking for help, whether from friends and family or from professionals.

What's the Problem?

Follow the suggestions on p. 5 for identifying and analyzing problems.

- If the barriers of embarrassment or of not wanting to appear weak or needy did not surface in the previous discussion, try to elicit them here.
- Other barriers may be the desire to fit in, fear of becoming an outsider, and not knowing whom to trust.
- Brainstorm strategies for overcoming these barriers.

Setting Goals

Follow the suggestions on p. 5 for setting goals.

Gather Your Thoughts Everyone needs help sometimes, but choosing how to get it depends on the person and the situation. Ask yourself these questions:
- Who have you asked for advice or help in the past week? In the past month? Is there anyone in your life with whom you can share your problems?
- Do you reach out for help easily, or do you try to solve problems alone?
- What resources—people, agencies, actions, coping strategies—do you use when you have a problem?

What's the Problem? Erin had reasons for not wanting to talk to her mother about what her boyfriend did. What are some barriers that may stop people from reaching out for help in situations that could be dangerous? Talk with a partner or think about these questions.

Setting Goals Read the list of goals below. Then write another goal that is important to you. Rank those goals in order from 1 (most important) to 6. Give reasons for your choices.

_____ **a.** identify community resources that deal with physical abuse and substance abuse

_____ **b.** protect myself from physical or mental abuse

_____ **c.** learn how to solve a problem related to substance abuse

_____ **d.** learn how to communicate with friends or family members who need help

_____ **e.** learn how to talk to agencies and other helping resources in English

_____ **f.** another goal: _____

Tally goals for the class. What percentage of people thought that each goal was most important?

Vocabulary

Circle new words. Brainstorm meanings and sample sentences. Take notes. List other words that you want to learn.

agency

barrier

issue

resource

strategy

communicate

cope

abusive/abuse

violent/violence

Remember?

situation

Unit 3 **39**

Lesson 1: Sharing Your Problems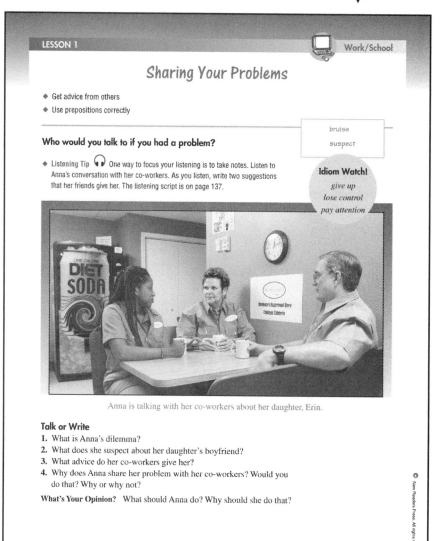

Read the title aloud.

- Explain that in this lesson learners will get advice from others. They will also start a personal resource guide.
- Tell learners the expression *sharing your problems* means "talking about your problems to someone else."
- Ask learners if they prefer to *share their problems* or *keep their problems to themselves* (not share them).

Question

Read the introductory question aloud. Then ask, "Why would someone discuss problems at work?"

Photo

Follow suggestions on pp. 4–5 for talking about photos. Have learners look at the photo as they listen to the audio.

Listening Tip

Read the listening tip with learners. Tell learners that taking notes helps us listen better and remember more of what we hear.

Play the audio or read the listening script on pp. 137–138. Follow the suggestions on p. 5 for listening comprehension.

- Ask, "What is Anna's problem?"
- Play the audio again. Ask, "Did you hear anything new the second time?"

Talk or Write

In this exercise, learners take notes during focused listening.

- Have learners answer in small groups. Tell each group to answer one question.
- Name a recorder and a reporter in each group. Tell recorders to write their group's responses. Then have reporters read the responses to the class.

LESSON 1   Work/School

Sharing Your Problems

◆ Get advice from others
◆ Use prepositions correctly

bruise
suspect

Idiom Watch!
give up
lose control
pay attention

Who would you talk to if you had a problem?

◆ Listening Tip One way to focus your listening is to take notes. Listen to Anna's conversation with her co-workers. As you listen, write two suggestions that her friends give her. The listening script is on page 137.

Anna is talking with her co-workers about her daughter, Erin.

Talk or Write
1. What is Anna's dilemma?
2. What does she suspect about her daughter's boyfriend?
3. What advice do her co-workers give her?
4. Why does Anna share her problem with her co-workers? Would you do that? Why or why not?

What's Your Opinion? What should Anna do? Why should she do that?

40 *Unit 3 Lesson 1*

- Have learners look up the word *dilemma* in a dictionary. Explain that one meaning of *dilemma* might be "a difficult choice between two actions."

Possible Answers

1. The dilemma is that Anna wants to ask Erin about her boyfriend but doesn't want Erin to stop talking to her. Anna wants to protect her daughter, but she also needs to keep communication open.
2. She suspects that he is abusive and has an alcohol problem.
3. Anna's co-workers tell her to stop Erin from seeing him, to be careful, to go to the police for protection, and to get out of the neighborhood.
4. Anna's co-workers are sympathetic and helpful. She sees them almost every day. Answers for the last two parts will vary.

What's Your Opinion?

Extension

Have learners write a paragraph on Anna's dilemma, including a topic sentence and supporting details.

Vocabulary

Follow the suggestions on p. 6 for introducing and reinforcing vocabulary words.

Partner Chat

Use Customizable Master 6 (Venn Diagram). Follow the suggestions on p. 7 for customizing and duplicating the master. Make a copy for each learner. Then follow these steps:

- Draw and label the diagram on the board or a transparency.
- Model the chat with a learner.
- Complete the diagram. Compare answers with the learner.
- Have pairs complete their diagrams.
- Ask pairs how their answers were both similar and different.

Have learners save the completed chart for use in Activity A.

Grammar Talk

Follow the suggestions on p. 7 for introducing the grammar point.

This section provides review, practice, and analysis of prepositional phrases.

- Prompt learners to identify the preposition, modifier(s), and object in each phrase.
- Ask for other modifiers. List them on the board or a transparency (e.g., *an, a, my, your, his*).
- Have partners make new sentences with prepositional phrases and read them aloud.

Pronunciation Target

Play the audio or read the phrases to the class, using a natural tone and pace. Follow the suggestions for pronunciation on p. 7.

- Have learners pronounce each phrase slowly after you, articulating each syllable.
- Repeat the phrase. Tell learners to focus on the placement and

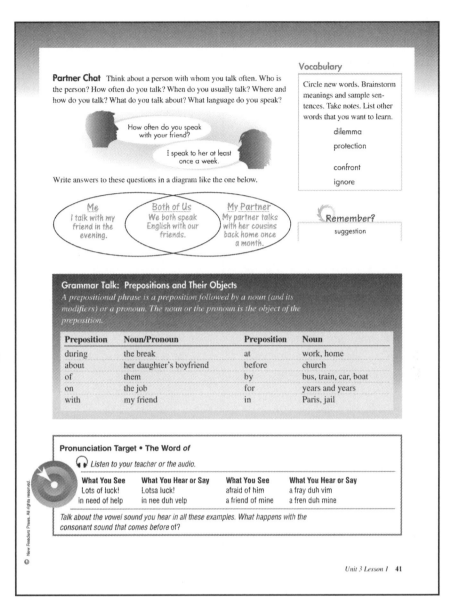

movement of their tongue, teeth, and lips. In the phrase *lots of luck,* for example, the tongue moves behind the teeth to pronounce the *l* sound, pulls back for *of,* and returns to the front of the mouth for *luck.*

- Have learners pronounce the reduced form *(lotsa luck)* several times, paying attention to the movement of their tongue.

Ask these questions:

- What is the difference in the way you move your tongue in the two pronunciations?
- Why do you think many people say this phrase the second way?

Learners may conclude that skipping the *v* sound in *of* makes the phrase easier to say.

Extension

Have learners take the lesson outside the classroom. Tell them to listen to people they think are good English speakers and observe which pronunciation they hear most. Point out that either is acceptable in spoken English.

 Assign Workbook pp. 18–19.

Activity A

Questions asking *who with, when, where, how,* and *what about* are usually answered with prepositional phrases.

Who with: Answers will vary, e.g., with (my) sister, with (my) mother, with (a) friend.

When: Answers will vary, e.g., on Saturdays, at lunchtime. When phrases usually do not take modifiers.

Where: Answers will vary, e.g., in (the) lunchroom, at (my) desk, in (the) park across (the) street.

How: Answers will vary, e.g., by long-distance telephone, in private. How phrases may or may not include modifiers.

What about: Answers will vary, e.g., about (our) problems, about (our) families, about (our) dreams.

Activity B

Possible Answers

2. to ___ (person)
3. to/with ___ (person)
4. in ___ (place)
5. to ___ (person/persons); for ___ (person, thing)
6. to/with ___ (person)
7. from ___ (person)

Activity C

This role-play should be done in small groups. Model the role-play with a learner. Then do the following:

- Assign roles within each group.
- Make *advisor* signs for those who will be giving advice. Have the "advisors" fold a sheet of paper in half vertically and write one of the advisor titles on it.
- Ask one member of each group to begin by telling the advisors about his or her problem.
- Group members give advice in turn. Then the person with the problem leaves the group to think

about the advice. Meanwhile, the group advisors reach a consensus on the best solution.

- The person with the problem makes a decision and returns to his or her group. Then the whole group compares their solutions.

After the first problem has been "solved," learners pass their signs to the right and repeat the role-play, with each group member taking a new role.

Task 1

Learners work in pairs to make an individual personal resource guide.

- First, have partners work individually to list the people they can

talk to. Then ask partners to share their lists with one another.

- Next, have partners ask each other these questions:
How do you contact the person?
When is the best time to contact him/her?
- Tell learners they may recommend other people to add to their partner's list.

Extension

Have learners rewrite their resource lists and put them in a protective plastic cover for future reference.

Activity A Partner Chat Follow-Up Look at the sentences in your Partner Chat diagrams. With your partner, copy the prepositional phrases from your sentences. Underline the noun or pronoun in the phrase. Circle the modifiers. With your class and your teacher, can you make general statements about phrases that have no modifiers?

with (my) friend _____

Activity B Read the first part of each sentence to your partner. Have your partner complete it with a prepositional phrase.

1. When I feel a lot of stress, I talk ___with my friends.___
2. When my boss yells at me, I complain _____
3. When I feel scared, I talk _____
4. When I need an emergency number, I find it _____
5. When I have a problem, I reach out _____
6. When I don't know what to do, I talk _____
7. When I need to find a doctor, I get a name _____

Activity C In a group of five, get and give advice. Each person chooses a role to play. Use the examples to the right or others that you create.

After the advisors give you their suggestions, leave the group to make a decision. Create your own solution, use a suggestion from one of your advisors, or combine two or more suggestions for a new solution. While you are gone, the rest of the group talks about the best solution to your problem. Return with your decision and compare it to your group's solution.

I would like to know what to do about my noisy neighbor. Her music is driving me crazy.

Friend: You should call the police.

Counselor: You should file a report at our town hall.

Boss: You should confront her first.

Co-worker: You should ask other neighbors for help.

TASK 1: Start a Resource Guide
Identify people that you can talk to about different kinds of problems. Write your ideas in a chart like this one.

Person	Problem	How to Contact	Notes
my boss	my schedule	go to his office	best time late afternoon
	where to find a good doctor		lives near me and knows the area

Lesson 2: Identifying Resources

Read the title and the objectives listed below it.

- Tell learners this lesson focuses on open, direct communication. In it they will gather and use informational literature from organizations that provide help.

Follow the suggestions on p. 5 for talking about the title.

- Ask learners what they think *resources* means in the title.
- Guide them to identify *resources* as people, places, or things they can turn to when they have problems.
- These *resources* might be other people (including friends and relatives), agencies, organizations, money, time, or personal qualities.

Question

Read the introductory question aloud.

- Share a personal anecdote about a time when you were misunderstood.
- Have learners reflect on the question in their notebooks. Ask volunteers to share their entries.

Reading Tip

This tip is to help learners focus on overall meaning as they read.

- Read the tip aloud.
- Tell learners that they can often skip over an unknown word and still understand what they are reading.
- Explain that readers who stop to look up or think about every new word are in danger of reading so slowly they lose the sense of the passage.
- After the first reading, ask volunteers to share what they understood. Defer discussion of underlined sentences until after learners have completed the Talk or Write exercise.

LESSON 2 Home

Identifying Resources

- Practice getting information about important issues
- Compare adverb and adjective phrases

alcoholic
rebellious
resentful

Have you ever had problems communicating with someone you love?

- **Reading Tip** You don't need to understand every word or sentence to understand a story. Read the story below twice. First, read without stopping. Focus on what the story is about. The second time, underline sentences that you don't understand. Then answer the questions below.

Confronting a Problem

As Anna prepared to talk with Erin, she was nervous. Some previous discussions had turned into upsetting arguments. Anna wanted to encourage her daughter to talk to her. She had read that she must not lose control or tell her daughter what to do. She knew that she had to ask Erin for her opinions. Anna planned to listen more and talk less. She wanted to reassure Erin that she loved her.

But on the day they finally spoke, Anna couldn't control her feelings. She shouted out her worst fears. She ordered Erin to stop seeing Mark immediately. She told her daughter that she was terrified for her. She said that Mark was an alcoholic and an abuser.

Erin had wanted to talk to her mother about the punctured tire, but she became resentful and rebellious. She had planned to tell Anna everything about her problems with Mark. She wanted to tell her that she sometimes felt afraid of him and that she needed help.

However, when her mother got upset, Erin got angry. She accused Anna of being too protective. She shouted at her mother, telling her that she could take care of herself and that she didn't need anybody telling her what to do.

"I *know* what to do!" she screamed as she slammed her bedroom door behind her.

It was then that Anna knew that she needed to find help and began to think about first steps to take.

Talk or Write
1. What was Anna's plan?
2. What happened to the plan when she tried talking to Erin?
3. Erin and Anna both wanted to talk. Why weren't they able to do so?

Unit 3 Lesson 2 43

Talk or Write

This activity helps learners find context clues in what they read.

- Tell learners to answer the questions in their groups.
- Have each group name a recorder and a reporter. The recorders will write their group's responses, and the reporters will read them to the class.
- Compare groups' answers.

Possible Answers
1. Anna had planned to listen more and talk less and to show her love for Erin. She planned to keep communication open by staying quiet and listening to Erin.

2. Anna could not stay calm. She shouted at her daughter. Erin got angry and shouted too. Anna's fear and Erin's pride prevented them from talking.

Vocabulary

Follow the suggestions on p. 6 for introducing and reinforcing the vocabulary words.

Ask learners to look back at the reading on p. 43. Tell them to add to this list any words they underlined.

Class Chat

- Have each learner write his or her name on three or four sticky notes.
- Poll learners about the issues listed in the graph in the student book. Eliminate any issues learners are not interested in.
- Have learners list the remaining issues vertically on the board; then ask them to call out other issues to add to the list. Write them on the board, or have a learner write them.
- If privacy is an issue, ask each learner to write one or more issues on a piece of paper and pass them up to you or the learner who is writing. (Other issues might include *money or time management, relocation,* and *employment.*)
- Redirect personalized accounts to more general categories (e.g., if a learner says, "I am always late," say that this might be a *time management* issue).

Have learners vote for the most important issues.

- Tell learners to line up their sticky notes end-to-end beside the issues they feel are most important. This will produce an instant bar graph illustrating learners' interests and concerns.
- Discuss the results. Then have learners answer the questions about the graph.

Grammar Talk

Follow the suggestions on p. 7 for introducing the grammar point.

- Ask learners how adjectives and adverbs function in a sentence. (Adjectives are words describing

nouns. Adverbs are words modifying verbs, adjectives, and other adverbs.) Give examples.

- Tell learners that prepositional phrases also can function as adjectives and adverbs.
- Have learners read and compare the sentences. The questions below each column should help them identify the differences.

 Use Unit Masters 30 (Grammar: Scrambled Sentences) and 31 (Grammar: Adverb Prepositional Phrases) now or at any time during the rest of the unit.

Pronunciation Target

Follow the suggestions on p. 7 for pronunciation.

 Play the audio or read the sentences.

- Have learners tell you if they hear breaks or stops between the words and which consonant sounds seem to last longer.
- Have partners read the words from their books and approximate the pronunciation.
- Ask them to write a rule about holding over final consonants (e.g., When a final consonant comes before a word that begins with a vowel, the consonant is transferred, duplicated, or added to that word.).

 Assign Workbook pp. 20–21.

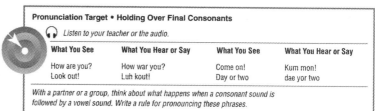

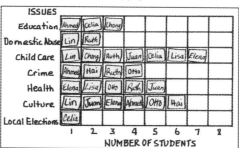

Class Chat Brainstorm some issues and create a bar graph like this one. Copy it onto the board. Write your name on some sticky notes. Place your name on the graph next to each issue that concerns you. Which issue is most important? Least important? How many people selected each issue?

Vocabulary
Circle new words. Brainstorm meanings and sample sentences. Take notes. List other words that you want to learn.

accuse
encourage
reassure

behavior

protective
rebellious
resentful
terrified

Grammar Talk: Adjective and Adverb Prepositional Phrases

Adjective Phrases	Adverb Phrases
Erin's boyfriend is the man **on the right.**	Erin hoped **for a peaceful discussion.**
She is the girl **in the bedroom.**	Anna needs to be patient **with her daughter.**
Erin's car is the one **with a punctured tire.**	They fought endlessly, **without any results.**

The phrases above modify nouns or pronouns. They answer these questions:
Which *man is Erin's boyfriend?*
Who *is she?*
Which *car has the punctured tire?*

The phrases above modify verbs, adjectives, or adverbs. They answer these questions:
What *did Erin hope for?*
Who *should Anna be patient with?*
How *did they fight?*

Pronunciation Target • Holding Over Final Consonants

Listen to your teacher or the audio.

What You See	What You Hear or Say	What You See	What You Hear or Say
How are you?	How war you?	Come on!	Kum mon!
Look out!	Luh kout!	Day or two	dae yor two

With a partner or a group, think about what happens when a consonant sound is followed by a vowel sound. Write a rule for pronouncing these phrases.

Activity A

Offer learners the option of writing about their own experience, about people they know, or about a conversation they heard that caused a misunderstanding or an argument.

- Get learners started with a few examples, e.g., this conversation between a worker and her boss:

   Boss: I've noticed that some supplies are missing from the storage room.

   Worker: I had nothing to do with that. What are you trying to say? That makes me angry.

   Boss: I'm not accusing you of anything. I only made a statement. But the way you've answered shows me that you may be a problem employee that gets angry before thinking.

- Have learners read or explain their conversations and talk about what went wrong.
- Ask for other statements that might have prevented the misunderstanding.

For more on conflict resolution and effective communication skills, use Unit Master 32 (Life Skill: Effective Communication) now or at any time during the rest of the unit.

Activity B

Have learners read the questions below the handbook before scanning for the specific information.

Possible Answers

1. State Child Abuse and Maltreatment Reporting Center and State Child Abuse Mandated Reporter's Line
2. State Domestic Violence Hotline, State Office for the Prevention of Domestic Violence
3. State Council on Alcoholism and Substance Abuse
4. Call the State Office for the Aging Senior Citizens Hotline.

Activity A Think about a time when you wanted to talk honestly and openly, but the other person got upset. Then do one of these things:

- Write a conversation showing what you both said.
- Draw pictures of your conversation. Use speech bubbles to show what you both said. Try to show emotion on the faces.

Try to use some of the words from the vocabulary box on page 44. If you want, share the drawings with your group members.

behavior
domestic
financial compensation
material
slap
victimization

Activity B Below are two pages from a handbook by a state Office for the Prevention of Domestic Violence. Scan the information. Then answer the questions below.

Resources

State Domestic Violence Hotline	
English	555-6906
Spanish	555-6908
State Child Abuse and Maltreatment Reporting Center	555-3720
State Child Abuse Mandated Reporter's Line	555-1522
Maternal and Child Health Hotline	555-5006

State Council on Alcoholism and Substance Abuse	555-5353
State Office for the Aging Senior Citizens Hotline	555-9871
State Office for the Prevention of Domestic Violence	555-6262
State Crime Victims Board	
Provides financial compensation to crime victims for certain expenses related to their victimization.	
Main Office	555-8727

1. Which two organizations would you call if you suspected a neighbor of abusing a child?
2. A friend tells you that her husband slapped her for complaining about his behavior. What organizations could she contact?
3. Which organization could you call for a relative who had a drug problem?
4. You volunteer at a home for older people. You notice that some workers treat the residents rudely. What can you do?

 TASK 2: *Gathering and Using Informational Publications*

Look for community, state, or national organizations that provide help with an issue that is important to you. Research their work and share your information with your classmates. Report to the class on one or two organizations that you would especially recommend. For example, you might say this:

"One organization that I have read about is the Child Abuse and Maltreatment Reporting Center. Their number is 800-555-3720. They also provide bilingual assistance. You can ask for someone who speaks your language. You should call them when you suspect that someone you know is abusing a child."

One Step Up

Practice calling a department in your state that deals with the issue that you think is most important. Request a handbook or a pamphlet. With a partner, role-play asking for help.

Unit 3 Lesson 2 45

Extension

Have learners find phone numbers and addresses of offices for prevention of domestic violence in their own community or state. Provide phone directories and booklets that list similar agencies.

Task 2

Tell learners to look at the bar graph and list of issues they made in the Class Chat. Use the most popular issues to complete this task.

- Tell learners that this task involves research that will require time outside of class.
- Help learners with computer research. If there is no computer

access at your site, offer to take learners to the nearest library so they can do their research there.

- For the oral report, have a few learners report in each class session for the duration of this unit. Allow 5 to 10 minutes per report.

One Step Up

Guide learners in selecting an issue to call about so that a wide range of information is collected.

Assessment

Use Generic Assessment Master 10 (Oral Communication Rubric) to evaluate presentations.

Lesson 3: Substance Abuse: Problems and Solutions

Read the lesson title and the objectives listed below it.

- In this lesson learners will use information to solve problems.
- They will also ask for information from an organization that can help them with a problem.

Question

Read the introductory question aloud. List learners' responses on the board or a transparency.

Discuss ways various pressures on young people might be reduced or eliminated. Ask these questions:

- What can an individual person do?
- What can an organization do?
- What can a community/society do?
- What can newspapers, television, and magazines do?
- What can businesses do?

Reading Tip

Read the tip aloud.

- Tell learners that by first reading the title and headings on a table or graph, they will be better able to predict its content.
- Point out that many good readers do this to see if the information in the table or graph will be useful to them.

Reading

Help learners interpret the tables by thinking aloud as you read them.

- Read across the first line of Table A. Model interpreting the data with sentences like these:

  In the year 2000, 2.4 percent of 12-year-olds had at least 1 drink each month. 1 percent of 12-year-olds engaged in binge drinking, and 0.1 percent drank heavily.

- Have learners take turns reading other lines in the tables in the same way.
- Point out the asterisks near some of the heads. Explain that these marks refer readers to notes in the tables.

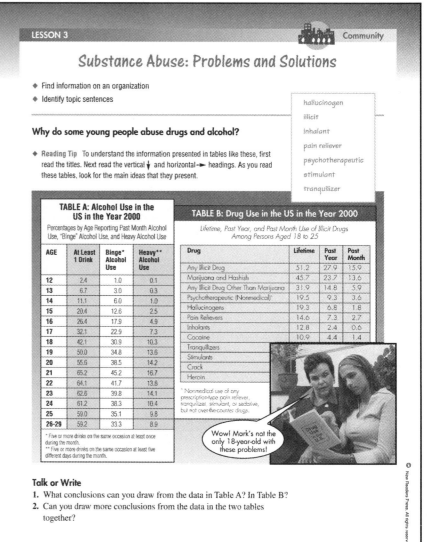

Talk or Write

This exercise helps learners become skilled at reading tables.

- Have learners work in small groups. Tell them to look at the highest and lowest percentages for each category in the tables.
- Make sure learners discuss the use of alcohol and compare it to that of other illicit drugs.

Possible Answers

1. Table A shows 21-year-olds drink the most. After that age, the use of alcohol declines. Table B shows half of those between ages 18 and 25 have used illicit drugs.

2. Together the two tables show that more young adults use alcohol than use illicit drugs.

Technology Extra

Point out that the statistical data may have changed since the year 2000. Ask volunteers to find more recent percentages on the Internet.

Vocabulary

Follow the suggestions on p. 6 for introducing and reinforcing vocabulary words.

To review all unit vocabulary, use Unit Master 33 (Vocabulary: Answering Questions) now or at any time during the rest of the unit.

In the US

Have learners read this paragraph and talk about it with a partner. Tell partners to clarify unknown words and phrases for each other.

One Step Up

Have a volunteer summarize the paragraph for the other learners. If this proves too challenging, provide an oral summary yourself.

Compare Cultures

- Prepare learners to share their thoughts in small groups. Allow them 10 to 15 minutes to reflect on these questions in their notebooks.
- If learners have difficulty drawing comparisons, suggest they compare a specific issue, such as drug use or domestic violence.

Activity A

Tell learners to look at the first underlined word in the reading.

- Explain that to be *concerned* is to be worried about something.
- Tell learners this is not a dictionary definition. Explain that the sentences following this word in the reading help define its meaning.
- Read a dictionary definition of the word *concerned* and compare it to the above meaning.

Have learners follow this model when defining other words in this story.

In the US   How to Get Help

In the US, people often get professional help for their problems. There are many low-cost or free programs. An alcoholic may go to a clinic for therapy. A victim of domestic violence may attend a group led by a counselor or psychologist. Sometimes workplace or community programs provide assistance. Schools and religious groups also have programs to help. These programs are usually private and confidential. Professionals can suggest strategies that relatives, friends, or neighbors may not be aware of. The programs can be long-term or short-term, and attendance may be mandatory or voluntary.

Compare Cultures

How do people in your home country deal with these issues? Do they rely on professional help? Do they depend on themselves and their families? What do most people think about these problems? What things are similar to the US? What things are different?

Activity A As you read the story below, try to understand the meaning of the underlined words by using the context of the story. When you finish, use the context clues to write a short definition for each word in your notebook. Then talk about your definitions with a partner and make changes. Finally, compare your definitions with a dictionary.

Vocabulary

Circle new words. Brainstorm meanings and sample sentences. Take notes. List other words that you want to learn.

clinic

counseling

counselor

psychologist

substance abuse

therapy

monitor

confidential

mandatory

voluntary

Remember?

long-term/short-term

At the Counselor's Office

When Erin's grades began going down, the high school counselor called her into the office. She told Erin that she was <u>concerned</u> about her grades. She asked if anything in her personal life was having a negative effect on her schoolwork. At first Erin was <u>reluctant</u> to talk about her problem. She <u>insisted</u> that everything was fine. However, she was <u>aware</u> that she needed help, so after a few talks, she decided to tell everything.

The counselor told her that their talks were completely confidential, but she <u>suggested</u> that Anna probably should also be <u>included</u> in the next meeting.

The next day Anna, Erin, and the counselor talked for an hour. The counselor offered a lot of <u>relevant</u> information, including <u>suggestions</u> on how to help Mark with his substance abuse problem. She gave them <u>pamphlets</u> to read and numbers to call. She said that the situation with Mark was <u>unpredictable</u> and could <u>escalate</u> and result in more <u>vandalism</u> or <u>violence</u>. She promised to speak to Mark and his parents immediately and to <u>monitor</u> the <u>situation</u>. She even <u>offered</u> to make some phone calls to legal organizations.

Unit 3 Lesson 3 **47**

- Make the activity move more quickly by telling partners to each find different words. Then have two pairs share their definitions.
- Read the story after all words have been defined. Talk about Erin and the help she received from the counselor.
- Make sure learners understand that this story demonstrates the kind of professional help described by In the US.

Use Unit Master 34 (Life Skill: Choosing a Helping Strategy) now or at any time during the rest of the unit.

 Assign Workbook pp. 22–23.

Activity B

Read the topic sentence from each paragraph aloud. Then do the following:

- Have learners read the paragraphs in pairs.
- Tell the pairs to discuss the sentences following each topic sentence and how they support or rephrase it.
- For the group brainstorming, provide each group with a shoe box or large envelope, index cards, and strips of paper.
- Tell learners to write topic sentences on the strips during the brainstorming process.
- After brainstorming, have individual group members each select a topic and write three or four sentences about it.
- Work with each group to create a paragraph from the sentences. Check for errors and for sentences that may not belong in the paragraph.
- Each group should have at least three topic-sentence strips and the same number of cards showing three or four supporting sentences. Tell learners to put all of their sentence strips and cards into the box or envelope.
- Have groups exchange boxes or envelopes and reconstruct the paragraphs written by other groups.
- Have learners read the assembled paragraphs to the class. Tell the other group members to listen for and confirm the matches.

One Step Up

Use topic sentences in a class debate.

- If you find that there are not enough members to debate the opposite point of view, join that team and model debate strategies.
- Assign a timekeeper who gives each side two to three minutes

---

Activity B Below are two paragraphs written by English students. Each has its own main idea, which is stated in the topic sentence at the beginning.

> Domestic violence is a taboo topic in my country. No one in my country talks about it. Everybody pretends that it doesn't exist. And so husbands continue to beat their wives. No one calls it abuse.

> I believe that psychotherapy is useless. People pay money to talk to a stranger who doesn't care about them. Instead, they should talk to caring people——their friends and families. That kind of counseling doesn't cost anything!

beat

caring

psychotherapy

taboo

In your group, brainstorm ideas for five more topic sentences related to the issues in this unit. You can state either an opinion or a fact. Write each idea on a separate strip of paper. Then individually, on a 3 × 5 note card, write three or four sentences supporting the idea of each topic sentence. *Do not copy your topic sentence onto this card.*

Next, as a group, put all your topic sentence strips and paragraph cards into an envelope or a small box. Mix them up and exchange envelopes with another group. Then match the other group's topic sentence strips with their paragraph cards. When you finish, read the topic sentences and paragraphs to the class.

 TASK 3: *Gather More Information on an Organization*

Look at the organizations that you researched in Task 2. List some of the things you would want the agency or organization to do for you. Choose a problem of your own or of someone you know, or a problem shown in one of the charts on page 46. Choose an organization that you think might be able to help you and your classmates solve the problem. Call that organization and ask them to send you more information.

✂✉💻 Technology Extra
See if the organization you chose has a web site. Log on to find more information and add it to the list you began in Task 2.

One Step Up
Debate an issue with your group members. In your group, choose sides, or *debate teams,* on the issue. Try to convince the other side that your debate team's ideas are right. Begin your statement by saying, "I strongly agree with . . ." or "I strongly disagree with . . ."

---

to make comments. Manage the debate by adhering to strict time frames.

Task 3

Remind learners that in Task 2 they researched an organization and talked about the help it offers. Task 3 asks them to focus on a specific, personal issue and to find an agency that can help them. Then it has them take action by making a phone call.

Review Unit Skills

See pp. 8–9 for suggestions on games and activities to review the unit vocabulary and grammar.

Reading Tip

Read the reading tip aloud with learners; then discuss the title of the brochure. Have learners predict the subject matter and possible advice.

- Write the title on the board or an overhead transparency.
- Ask learners, "Based on the title and the pictures, what type of information do you think you'll find in this brochure?"
- Write learners' responses on the board or transparency. Stress that their predictions do not have to be correct. (Some possible predictions include finding out about how to deal with an abusive husband, learning about substance abuse, and reading about things that can prevent abuse.)
- Divide the class into two groups. Assign one section of the brochure to each group. If the class is large, make four groups and have two groups use each section.
- Ask each group to look at the heading for their section and write questions about the topic. Then have them read to find answers to their questions.
- Talk to each group as they work. Ask if the brochure gave them the information they predicted and if they found the answers to their questions.
- Have each group prepare an oral presentation of the information in their section. Tell them to use their questions to help guide their presentation. Each person in the group should make one or two comments.
- If two groups have the same section, the two groups can present together so that information is not repeated.
- During the presentations, encourage further discussion and more questions from other learners.

UNIT 3 Challenge Reading

◆ **Reading Tip** Pamphlets and brochures are often easier to read than books or articles. The information often is separated into small sections, and there are photos and art that help make the meaning clear. Now look at this brochure from a community action agency. Read the headings and the introductory paragraphs. Look at the pictures. Then ask yourself what you think you will read about and what you will learn. As you read, underline unfamiliar words or write them in your notebook.

> approval
>
> tactful

Idiom Watch!
leave the door open

Action Plans:

How to Fight Domestic Abuse and Substance Abuse

There are several things that you need to do if you want to change an abusive situation. Stop being afraid to talk about your problem. Your conversation should be honest and direct, but always tactful. And no matter how the conversation goes, you need to leave the door open to talk again. Below are some specific and powerful things that you can do.

Fighting Physical or Psychological Abuse in Relationships

First, if you are abusive, get help. If you're not, share your strengths in the following ways:

▶ Accept that abuse affects a whole community. The community pays the price in juvenile crime, drug use, teen pregnancies, higher health care costs, and lost job time and job productivity.

▶ Teach your children that physical abuse and fear are never acceptable in relationships. Then set a good example and practice what you preach.

▶ Find out what services are available in your community. Be ready to refer a victim or an abuser to a place that can help.

▶ Take the problem personally. Your leadership and your involvement are important.

▶ Never say that a friend's or relative's abusive behavior is just due to stress, and never ignore it. Silence can be acceptance, and acceptance is a form of approval. If you don't speak up, the abuser can believe that the behavior is acceptable to you.

▶ Talk honestly with someone you think may be a victim of physical or psychological abuse. Remember that domestic violence could someday threaten the life of your friend or relative. Talking about the situation may not be easy for either of you. The victim may feel embarrassed or guilty. You must be honest but sensitive to her feelings, and you must never judge her. She may not want to talk the first time, but leave the door open by saying something like this:

"I'm worried about you. Are you OK? Do you want to talk about it? It's not your fault and you don't deserve it. I understand, and I won't talk about this to anyone else. I won't tell you what to do. I'll be your friend whatever you decide to do. Did you know there's a number to call to find out more about this? Do you want to call now, or shall I give you the number for later? If not, just remember that I have the number if you ever want to call."

▶ Don't plan a rescue or escape for your friend. And don't criticize her partner, even if you feel he deserves it. You need to try to break through her silence and isolation and be a resource she can use when she wants to.

Silent Reading

Have learners return to their books and read the brochure silently.

Talk or Write

Be sensitive to your learners' feelings about these personal issues. If you feel the topic or intensity is too much for some learners, wait a day before having them answer the Talk or Write questions.

Answers

Answers will vary.

Writing Task

- Allow at least 20 minutes for this task. Some learners may prefer to work in pairs to write the dialogue.
- Ask volunteers to read their letters or their dialogues.

Tell learners to use Generic Assessment Master 14 (Writing Checklist and Error Correction Symbols) as they revise and edit their writing.

Fighting Substance Abuse

Get early education on drugs so that you know what you are dealing with. Be able to recognize symptoms of substance abuse. Here are a few of the most common ones, although they can also be signs of other problems:

- **Physical signs:** repeated health complaints, red and glazed eyes, a lasting cough
- **Emotional signs:** personality and mood changes, irritability, irresponsible behavior, low self-esteem, poor judgment, depression, and a general lack of interest
- **Family:** arguing, breaking rules, withdrawing from the family
- **School:** low interest, negative attitude, lower grades, many absences, discipline problems
- **Social problems:** loss of interest in home and school activities, problems with the law

If these clues make you think someone you know and care about may have a problem, here's what to do. Find the right kind of intervention, or treatment. Try to match the place, the people, and the services to the person's problems and needs. Here are some guiding rules:

- ▶ Good treatment must consider the many needs of the individual, not just the drug or alcohol use. It must also deal with any possible medical, psychological, social, and learning problems. Substance abuse and mental problems often occur in the same person, so a substance abuse program should offer treatment for other types of problems as well.
- ▶ Medical detoxification is only the first step in substance abuse treatment. Used alone, it almost never gives long-term results for addicts.
- ▶ In good therapy, people learn to build skills to resist substance use and substitute positive actions for drug-using activities.
- ▶ Finally, don't give up! Remember that recovering from substance abuse can be a long-term process. Recovering abusers often need to return to treatment several times. Encourage the former abuser to participate in self-help programs during and after treatment.

Talk or Write

1. Can you think of another tip for helping an abusive person, a victim of abuse, or a substance abuser?
2. What do you think about the tips for helping a victim of abuse? Which of those tips was most surprising to you and why?
3. Many words in this reading were probably new to you. In your group, make a list of the words that any group member didn't understand. Help other group members with meanings that you know. Work together to guess the meanings of words that none of you know. First, look at the context—the rest of the sentence the word is in and the sentences before and after it. If you still can't guess the meaning, look at word parts, especially prefixes.

Writing Task Imagine that someone you care about is in an abusive relationship—either as a victim or as an abuser—or has a substance abuse problem. Do one of these things to help:

- Write a letter to the person.
- Write a conversation that you could have with that person.

Be as specific as possible with your comments, questions, and advice. Make sure that the advice fits the situation and the possible solutions in your community.

50 *Unit 3 Challenge Reading*

Learners make a community resource guide to help them find help with personal issues.

Get Ready

Post the questions below on a large sheet of paper. Add your own questions to the list.

- How long will you need to complete the project?
- What items and tools will you need to complete it successfully?
- What parts of it can you work on immediately?

Do the Work

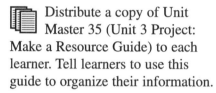 Distribute a copy of Unit Master 35 (Unit 3 Project: Make a Resource Guide) to each learner. Tell learners to use this guide to organize their information.

Have two or more group members work together on each of the group's chosen issues.

Present

Although learners are asked to present on only one problem, the Resource Guide itself should be an extensive booklet listing many issues and resources.

Learners can present these as resources for questions they wanted to answer for themselves, but remind them that the issues need not be their own.

Assessment

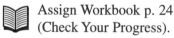 To do a formal assessment of this project, use Generic Assessment Master 10 (Oral Communication Rubric) to evaluate the presentations.

Assign Workbook p. 24 (Check Your Progress).

Use Unit Master 36 (Unit Checkup/Review) whenever you complete this unit.

Self-Assessment

Give each learner a copy of Generic Assessment Masters 12 (Speaking and Listening Self-Checks) and 13 (Writing and Reading Self-Checks). Go over the items together. These forms can be kept in the learners' portfolios.

UNIT 3 Project

Make a Resource Guide

As a class, create a Resource Guide that lists places to go for help on important issues. You can include government and community agencies and organizations that can help. Also try to find names and phone numbers.

Get Ready

Start by choosing several issues that you find most interesting and important. These can be the same issues you've already discussed in this unit, the issue that you chose for Task 3, or some new issues.

Do the Work

1. State each issue as a question at the top of a page of your guide. Use the form your teacher gives you—one page per issue. For example, you could include these questions:
   - How can I stop my neighbor from blasting her radio after midnight?
   - How can I protect my daughter from her violent boyfriend?
   - How can I get more information about alcohol treatment?
2. On the page, list names of organizations and people that might help with this issue. Also list all phone numbers, addresses, and e-mail addresses. Add notes and additional information.
3. Keep this reference and add to it in the future. Include new resources for new problems.

Present

Choose one issue and report to the class on it. One student reported on this question:

How can I get my landlord to fix the heat in my apartment?

Remember that you don't have to talk about your own issue. You can talk about any issue in this unit or about an issue that is important for a friend or relative.

One Step Up
If possible, publish your class guide on your school's web site.

Unit 3 Project **51**

Unit 4: On Your Own

Materials for the Unit

- Dictionaries
- Envelopes
- Pictures of home decorations, detergent, an electrical outlet, a fire extinguisher, a radiator, and a vacuum cleaner, or the objects themselves
- Customizable Masters 3–5, 7
- Generic Assessment Master 14
- Unit Masters 37–43

On Your Own

Read the title and the four groups of unit goals listed below it.

- Follow the suggestions on p. 5 for talking about titles.
- In this unit, learners will focus on making important decisions.

Find out how learners make decisions.

- Ask for examples of decisions learners have made recently (e.g., whether to go back to school; whether to rent or own a home; what car to buy).
- Ask how learners made the decision. Write their answers on a large sheet of paper.
- Tell learners in this unit they will share their decision-making techniques and learn new ones.
- Save the list of answers. Add to it at the end of the unit.

Question

Have learners silently read the question below the arrow. Ask a learner to read it aloud. Then ask these questions:

- What does it mean to be your own boss?
- Is anyone in the class his or her own boss?

Tally responses.

Photo

Follow the suggestions on pp. 4–5 for talking about the photo. Ask:

- What do the photo and the question in the thought bubble have to do with decision making?

- Who is making a decision?
- What is the decision about?

Ask for details and opinions about the photo with questions like these:

- Can you describe the two women?
- What time is it? Is it day or night? How do you know?
- What are they doing? Why do you think they are working so late?
- What items in the picture are used for business?
- What items tell you that there are children in the home?
- Is this a home or a business? Could it be both? How do you know?

Think and Talk

Follow the suggestions on p. 6 for comprehension questions.

Possible Answers

1. Answers will vary.
2. Answers will vary, but Donna and Sheba may be working on a budget. Donna is using a calculator. The other woman, Sheba, is working on a computer. They are working late because they have a lot to do.
3. Donna is worried about starting her own business. She is trying to make a decision.
4. Answers will vary.

Vocabulary

Follow the suggestions on p. 6 for introducing and reinforcing the vocabulary words.

- Ask learners to find as many of these vocabulary words as they can on the previous page.
- Have them guess the meaning of new words.

Gather Your Thoughts

Although the unit focuses on making career and business decisions, the techniques apply to making decisions in many contexts.

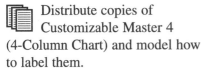 Distribute copies of Customizable Master 4 (4-Column Chart) and model how to label them.

- Point out that a good way to start decision making is by listing the good and bad points of each option in the decision.
- Depending on their language level, give pairs 5 to 10 minutes to complete the chart. Tell them to list everything they can think of. In brainstorming, *all* ideas should be included.
- Assign a recorder from one group to write the first list (Working for Someone Else/Good) on the board or a large sheet of paper. Have a group reporter read the list and ask if other groups have more to add. Repeat with the next three lists.
- Conclude the discussion by asking learners if they think making lists like these could help them make decisions. How?

What's the Problem?

Follow the suggestions on p. 5 for identifying and analyzing problems.

- Ask if anyone has ever put off or tried to avoid making an important life decision. Why do people sometimes avoid making even good changes?

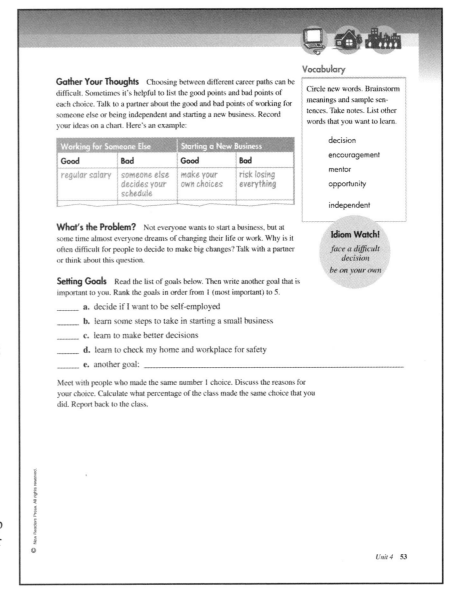

Gather Your Thoughts Choosing between different career paths can be difficult. Sometimes it's helpful to list the good points and bad points of each choice. Talk to a partner about the good and bad points of working for someone else or being independent and starting a new business. Record your ideas on a chart. Here's an example:

Working for Someone Else		Starting a New Business	
Good	Bad	Good	Bad
regular salary	someone else decides your schedule	make your own choices	risk losing everything

What's the Problem? Not everyone wants to start a business, but at some time almost everyone dreams of changing their life or work. Why is it often difficult for people to decide to make big changes? Talk with a partner or think about this question.

Setting Goals Read the list of goals below. Then write another goal that is important to you. Rank the goals in order from 1 (most important) to 5.

_____ **a.** decide if I want to be self-employed

_____ **b.** learn some steps to take in starting a small business

_____ **c.** learn to make better decisions

_____ **d.** learn to check my home and workplace for safety

_____ **e.** another goal: _____

Meet with people who made the same number 1 choice. Discuss the reasons for your choice. Calculate what percentage of the class made the same choice that you did. Report back to the class.

Vocabulary

Circle new words. Brainstorm meanings and sample sentences. Take notes. List other words that you want to learn.

decision

encouragement

mentor

opportunity

independent

Idiom Watch!

face a difficult decision

be on your own

Unit 4 **53**

- Have partners discuss the question for a few minutes and ask for volunteers to report their opinions.

Setting Goals

Follow the suggestions on p. 5 for setting goals.

- Ask for a show of hands to tally which goals learners think are most important.
- Find percentages for each goal, encouraging learners to compute the answers. Keep track of the numbers on the board or an overhead transparency.

Extension

Use this information to form small discussion groups of those who chose the same goal to work on. Have group members organize their discussion around topics like these:

- Why did we all choose that goal?
- What do we all have in common?

Lesson 1: Becoming Your Own Boss

Read the title and the lesson objectives below it.

- This lesson explores decision making in the context of starting a small business.
- Tell learners that in this lesson they will listen for details and practice debating an issue.

Question

Read the introductory question. Review the decision-making techniques from the unit opener.

Listening Tip

Read the tip aloud.

- Tell learners that making notes as we read helps us remember important numbers and details. The notes do not have to be grammatically perfect, but they do have to be clear and detailed enough to understand later.
- As learners listen to the audio or listening script, ask them to focus by listening for the most interesting number.

Play the audio or read the listening script on p. 138. Follow the suggestions on p. 5 for listening comprehension.

- After learners listen, ask, "How many people in the US were self-employed in 2001?"
- If necessary, review reading large numbers and placement of commas. Start with hundreds; move to thousands, then to ten thousands, hundred thousands, and millions.

Photo

Ask learners these questions:

- Where are they?
- Is it morning or evening?
- What are their jobs? How do you know?
- What is each one doing?
- What will happen next?

LESSON 1   Work/School

Becoming Your Own Boss

- ◆ Find information to support an opinion
- ◆ Use *who, which,* and *that* in adjective clauses

How do you make decisions that are good for you?

- ◆ Listening Tip   When you listen to something that contains numbers, it's a good strategy to write down the numbers. Listen to this conversation, and write down the number facts that you hear. Listen again if you don't catch everything the first time. Then check your notes with a partner. Tell your partner about the number fact that was most interesting to you. The listening script is on page 137.

businesswoman
fail
inspiring
retire
statistic
workforce

Waiting for the children to arrive, Donna and Sheba are watching a television program about starting a business.

Idiom Watch!
catch (something that is said)
Go for it!
write down

Talk or Write
1. What advice did Kim give? Do you agree with her? Why or why not?
2. What did you learn about small businesses? Are they important? Why?
3. Was Sheba correct when she said that 50 percent of businesses succeed? What did Kim say?
4. Look at the numbers that you wrote down. Did any of them surprise you?

What's Your Opinion? Why do you think so many small businesses fail?

54   *Unit 4 Lesson 1*

Talk or Write

This exercise helps learners listen for details.

Possible Answers

1. Answers will vary. Point out that Kim uses two expressions to give advice. To people wanting to start their own businesses, she says *go for it*. Review the meaning of the idiom. Her second piece of advice is *persistence pays*. Ask, "What does this mean to you? Do you know of similar sayings in other languages?"

2. Answers will vary. Small businesses are important to the US economy, as they employ 51 percent of the workforce. Most new jobs are in small businesses.

3. Kim said *over half* of small businesses *fail* in the first five years. That means *under half succeed.*

4. Answers will vary.

What's Your Opinion?

Discuss the question with the class. Provide a model for using modals (auxiliary verbs showing possibility) with the present perfect (e.g., They *may have run out* of money.)

Vocabulary

Follow the suggestions on p. 6 for introducing and reinforcing vocabulary words.

This vocabulary includes words used for work and job hunting. Create sentences showing different uses of *self-employment* (noun), *self-employed* (adj.), *persist* (verb), and *persistence* (noun).

Class Chat

 Give each learner a copy of Customizable Master 7 (Pie Chart).

Before doing the math part of the chat, check for prior knowledge.
- Many learners will find calculating percentages to be easy, while others may want a review.
- Point out that the *language* of mathematical processes is the focus here. Review the terms *divided by* and *equals*.

This chat also includes the skill of predicting outcomes.
- Have learners guess the number or percentage of classmates that would prefer a secure, salaried position with benefits. Then have them predict the number or percentage that would prefer starting their own business. Tell them to write the numbers in their notebooks.
- After the survey, ask how well they predicted. Ask what information they based their predictions on.

Grammar Talk

Follow the suggestions on p. 7 for introducing the grammar point. Introduce adjective clauses with people and objects in the classroom.

Extension
Play a modified Total Physical Response game.
- Put several yellow pencils or other similar objects around the room.

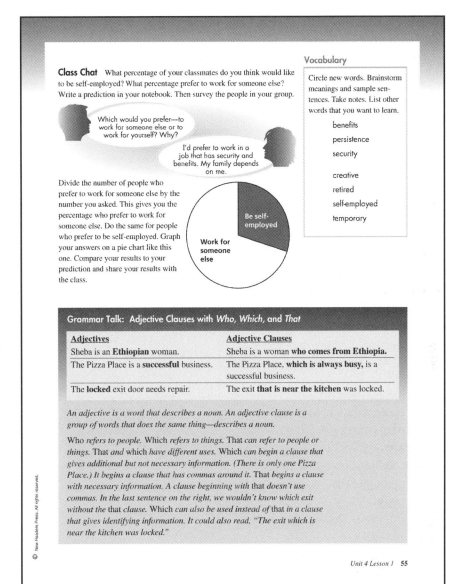

- Use polite commands that incorporate adjective clauses to help learners locate them (e.g., Please bring me the pencil that is on the table. Please bring me the pencil that is near the door.).
- Next have learners "hide" pencils and tell one another how to locate them using similar commands.

 Use Unit Masters 37 (Grammar: *Who, Which,* and *That* in Adjective Clauses) and 38 (Grammar: Information Gap) now or at any time during the rest of the unit.

Assign Workbook pp. 25–26.

Activity A

Divide the model sentence into *statement* (main clause) and *reason* (*because* clause). Have learners practice a few *because* sentences orally before writing.

Extension

- Collect the learners' sentences. Type them on a sheet of paper.
- Cut the sentences into strips. Then cut each strip before the word *because*.
- Divide the strips into envelopes. Give one envelope to each group. Have the groups put the strips together into new sentences.

One Step Up

Have learners write their group's new sentences in their notebooks.

Activity B

Possible Answers

1. I know a woman who/that started a successful daycare center.
2. Ms. Hellman is a teacher who also operates a small business in the summer.
3. Ethiopia is a country that is in East Africa.
4. Donna is a woman who is afraid to take chances.
5. Donna knows about a program that might help her.
6. The program, which is operated by the state, makes loans to small businesses.

Task 1

Assign learners to small groups according to whether they agree or disagree. Then follow the steps in the student book.

1. *Brainstorm.* Tell learners that supporting statements should use logic, facts, and experience.
2. *Find information.* Assign some group members to do research as suggested in the book and others to talk to small business owners.
3. *Debate.* Set a time limit of one or two minutes per speaker. The

captain states the first argument and supporting reasons. Then each debater does the same.

4. *Summarize.* Have team captains summarize the arguments.

Ongoing Assessment

During this activity, move from group to group. Listen to at least five interactions involving at least three different groups. How well did learners perform on these features?

a. General quality of stating opinions
   0 = no opinion stated
   1 = brief or halting statements/nonstandard sentence structures
   2 = opinions expressed clearly using standard structures
b. Features of language functions
   0 = many problems/not understandable
   1 = some problems with clarity
   2 = clear and appropriate, but not perfect
c. General quality of the debate
   0 = no debate or summary
   1 = debate unclear/not understandable
   2 = debate clear and appropriate, but not perfect

One Step Up

Alternatively, have learners write a group essay on their debate topic.

Lesson 2: Doing the Paperwork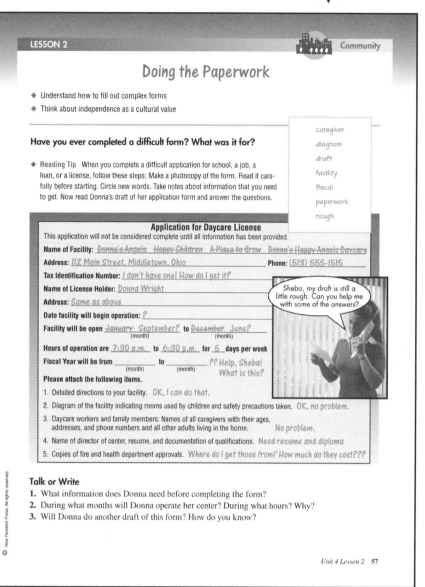

Read the title and point out the lesson objectives below it.

- In this lesson, learners learn how to fill out complex forms.
- They will also interview a guest speaker who is a small-business owner.

Questions

Read the introductory questions aloud. Brainstorm and list various complicated *forms* on the board (e.g., driver's license application, school registration, immigration forms).

Extension

Compare cultures by asking:

- Are forms in the US simpler or more complicated than forms in other countries you know? Why?
- In what other ways are forms in the US different? What might be the reasons for those differences?

Attention Box

Follow the suggestions on p. 6 for introducing and reinforcing vocabulary. Pronounce the words and ask learners to scan the graphic for these and other new words.

This vocabulary should be understood, but learners should not be expected to produce the words at this point.

Reading Tip

Read the tip aloud. Ask if anyone has other advice for completing forms. Write ideas from the book and from learners on the board.

Reading

Have learners read silently first. Then ask these questions:

- What is the application for?
- What do you see on the form?
- Why do you think the application looks the way it does?

Have learners work in pairs. Assign each pair a small section—one or two lines—of the form. Instruct pairs to study their sections.

- Write questions on the board or a transparency for pairs to answer (e.g., What information is asked for? Why do you think this information is needed? Does Donna have this information? If not, where can she get it?).
- Have pairs report back.

Talk or Write

This exercise helps learners become skilled at reading forms.

Most learners will be able to answer the questions by working together in groups or pairs.

Answers

1. Donna needs to choose a name for her business, get a Tax Identification Number, decide on an opening date, and find out what a *fiscal year* is.
2. September to June. 7:30 A.M. to 6:30 P.M., five days a week.
3. Yes. The form is messy. It has things crossed out and rewritten.

Vocabulary

Follow the suggestions on p. 6 for introducing and reinforcing vocabulary words.

- Study syllable stress by reading one of the longer vocabulary words (e.g., *independence*).
- Have learners look up the word in a dictionary, find the stress marks, and say the word. Then have them copy it with the stress marks into their notebooks.
- Repeat with the remaining words that have three or more syllables.
- Have learners read all the words from their notebooks again, following the marks they wrote.

Idiom Watch

Use the idiom *do paperwork* in a round-robin. Follow this example:
Teacher: Do you have to do a lot of paperwork?
Student 1: Yes, I do.
Student 1: Do you like to do paperwork?
Student 2: I usually like to do paperwork, except at tax time.

Repeat the round-robin with *run a business*.

<u>One Step Down</u>
Write one or two questions on the board for learners to ask each other.

Pronunciation Target

🎧 Play the audio or read the listening script on p. 138. If learners have done the dictionary exercise described above, have them write the *-tion* words with stress marks.

<u>One Step Up</u>
See how many *-tion* words learners can list in a given time, using dictionaries. Have learners practice their skills by marking, pronouncing, and defining each new word.

In the US

Learners may be skeptical that the behavior of at least some Americans

could stem from a strong belief in individual independence. After they read silently, give a few examples of Americans admired for their independence and strong will (e.g., Abraham Lincoln, Theodore Roosevelt, Franklin and Eleanor Roosevelt, Harriet Tubman, Rosa Parks, Geronimo). Ask for other examples from real life or fiction.

Ask learners if they agree that Americans value independence. Ask for supporting examples.

Compare Cultures

Form groups that include learners from different cultures.

 Distribute copies of Customizable Master 3 (3-Column Chart) to each group. Label the columns following the example in the student book. Have each group choose a recorder to write answers on the chart, or rotate the role for each question.

In the large group, tally the answers on the board or a transparency. See if everyone from the same country agrees. If not, have each person support his or her idea with an example.

 Assign Workbook pp. 27–28.

Pronunciation Target • *-tion* Ending

🎧 *Circle the vocabulary words that end in -tion. What part of speech are these words? Listen to your teacher or the audio. With a partner, mark the stressed syllable of each -tion word like this:*

op er **A** tion

Check a dictionary if you aren't sure. Then read the words to your partner. Together, brainstorm and write other words in the same word families, like this:

identification: identify, identity

⭐ In the US   The Value of Independence

Most people in the US believe in the value of *individual* freedom and independence. For example, many Americans value people who make their own decisions more than people who work as part of a group or for someone else. They admire people who overcome barriers and become independent and successful. Sometimes this belief in individual freedom can seem selfish to people from cultures that believe in group action and caring for all people.

☛ Compare Cultures

With your group, talk about what people in your home country and other countries think about the value of independence. Discuss this question: In your home country, do people value independence or cooperation more? Give an example to support your answer. Record your answers in a chart like this one. Report back to the class.

Country	Values Independence More	Values Cooperation More
Poland		✓

Vocabulary

Circle new words. Brainstorm meanings and sample sentences. Take notes. List other words that you want to learn.

cooperation
document
identification
independence
license
operation
precaution

indicate
value

detailed
selfish

Idiom Watch!
do paperwork
run a business

Poland is a country that values cooperation more.

Activity A

One Step Down

Have groups from the same country choose a hero from their country who demonstrates independence or cooperation. Tell the group to write their hero's name on a slip of paper and choose one person to be the storyteller. With a little help from the group, the storyteller will perform when the hero's name is chosen.

Activity B

Focus on the skill of organizing information into categories.

- Start with categories of everyday items in the classroom, such as *furniture* (desk, table, bookcase) and *supplies* (notebooks, chalk, pens).
- Explain that a *document* is an official paper; *information* is knowledge or facts needed to answer questions about something (e.g., a phone number). Brainstorm examples of *documents* and *information*.
- Go over the example and review reflexive pronouns (e.g., She will get it *herself*.).

Pronunciation Target

Although they may choose not to use them, learners need to be able to recognize these common reduced forms.

🎧 Read the examples or play the audio with books closed. Repeat.

- Ask learners to write this example:
  My plan *shoulduv been* more detailed.
- Write the correct form of the sentence on the board or an overhead transparency.
- Ask for a show of hands: Did anyone write *should of* when they heard *shoulduv?*
- Read the paragraph to find out why.

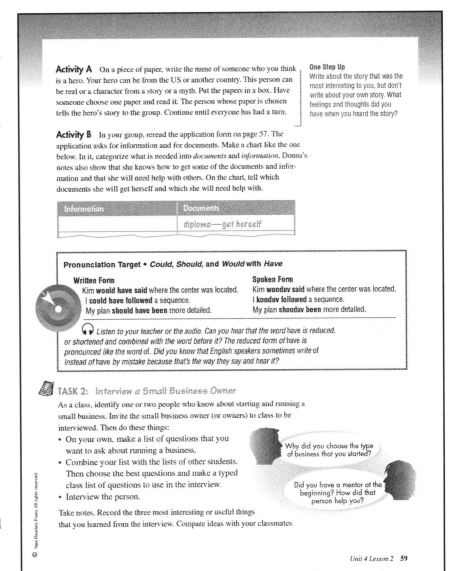

Activity A On a piece of paper, write the name of someone who you think is a hero. Your hero can be from the US or another country. This person can be real or a character from a story or a myth. Put the papers in a box. Have someone choose one paper and read it. The person whose paper is chosen tells the hero's story to the group. Continue until everyone has had a turn.

One Step Up
Write about the story that was the most interesting to you, but don't write about your own story. What feelings and thoughts did you have when you heard the story?

Activity B In your group, reread the application form on page 57. The application asks for information and for documents. Make a chart like the one below. In it, categorize what is needed into *documents* and *information*. Donna's notes also show that she knows how to get some of the documents and information and that she will need help with others. On the chart, tell which documents she will get herself and which she will need help with.

Information	Documents
	diploma—get herself

Pronunciation Target • *Could, Should,* and *Would* with *Have*

Written Form
Kim **would have said** where the center was located.
I **could have followed** a sequence.
My plan **should have been** more detailed.

Spoken Form
Kim **wooduv said** where the center was located.
I **kooduv followed** a sequence.
My plan **shooduv been** more detailed.

🎧 Listen to your teacher or the audio. Can you hear that the word have is reduced, or shortened and combined with the word before it? The reduced form of have is pronounced like the word of. Did you know that English speakers sometimes write of instead of have by mistake because that's the way they say and hear it?

📝 **TASK 2:** Interview a Small Business Owner
As a class, identify one or two people who know about starting and running a small business. Invite the small business owner (or owners) to class to be interviewed. Then do these things:

- On your own, make a list of questions that you want to ask about running a business.
- Combine your list with the lists of other students. Then choose the best questions and make a typed class list of questions to use in the interview.
- Interview the person.

Why did you choose the type of business that you started?

Did you have a mentor at the beginning? How did that person help you?

Take notes. Record the three most interesting or useful things that you learned from the interview. Compare ideas with your classmates.

Say the reduced models *shoulduv, woulduv,* and *coulduv,* but write them on the board using standard spelling.

- Ask, "Have you ever written *of* instead of *have* because that is what you heard?"
- If some learners think the reduced form is not proper English, ask them to listen carefully to good English speakers to hear if they use these reduced forms.

Task 2

Look for a person that owns a small business in your class or school. Someone who runs a shop nearby may agree to be interviewed.

- Assure the guest that the purpose of the interview is to practice English and learn about American business culture.
- Avoid questions about sensitive issues, e.g., sales, income, and other financial matters.

Technology Extra

Ask learners to find the Small Business Administration on the Internet. Have them report on how the US government supports small business owners.

Lesson 3: Safety First

Read the title and point out the lesson objectives below it.

Tell learners that in this lesson they will make a health and safety check of their home and workplace.

Question

Doing a home safety check may be new to some, but learners may be familiar with workplace safety rules. Ask, "Are there signs about safety where you work?"

Attention Box

• Practice stress on the multisyllabic words.

• Show the objects themselves or pictures to convey meaning.

This vocabulary should be understood, but learners should not be expected to produce the words at this point.

Photo

Give learners a few minutes to study the photo. Remind them of the title of this lesson.

• Ask learners how many things they see that are dangerous to small children. Tell them to list them in their notebooks.

• After they complete the reading, ask them to look at the picture again and add to their lists.

Reading Tip

• Write this sentence on the board or an overhead transparency: *The more you bring to your reading, the more you take away from it.*

• Ask learners what they think it means.

• Explain that if they read a story about a place they have been to, the story has more meaning.

• Have learners silently read the tip. Then ask them to do a mental safety check of their home or workplace and think about rules they already know.

Reading

After learners finish the reading, assign one or two safety rules to each pair. Ask these questions:

• Why is the rule important? What could happen if people did not follow it?

• Were there any rules in the reading that you had not thought of before?

• Why do you think the flyer asks for a diagram of the space?

Talk or Write

This exercise enhances reading with prior knowledge.

Follow the suggestions on p. 6 for comprehension questions.

Possible Answers

1. to prevent accidental burning (children could burn themselves.)
2. so children can get out if they close themselves in a closet
3. Germs could spread; children might get sick.

What's Your Opinion?

Ask learners to explain their opinions.

Vocabulary

Follow the suggestions on p. 6 for introducing and reinforcing vocabulary words.

Assign each pair a vocabulary word to find in the text. Have them copy the entire sentence and read the sentence to the class.

Group Chat

- Ask, "Why do we need safety rules?" (One idea might be that a government is responsible for the safety of its citizens.)
- Brainstorm some categories for which a government agency may make and enforce safety rules.
- Write learners' suggestions on the board or a transparency (e.g., safe housing and elevators, safe driving, public sanitation, doctors and hospitals, food in restaurants).
- Have volunteers model the question-and-answer pattern before breaking into groups.

Use Customizable Master 3 (3-Column Chart). Provide a copy for each group.

Extension

Practice questions and answers in a conversation circle.

- Arrange learners in two concentric circles facing each other. Student 1 in the inside circle asks the person he or she is facing in the outside circle a question, e.g., "What country are you from?" Student 2 responds.
- Student 1 then asks, "Are the rules in ___ stricter or less strict than they are in the US?" Student 2 responds. Finally Student 1 asks, "Can you give an example?" Student 2 responds.
- The inside circle then moves one person to the right. The outside circle stays in place. Repeat the process.
- When all learners have spoken to each other, change roles so

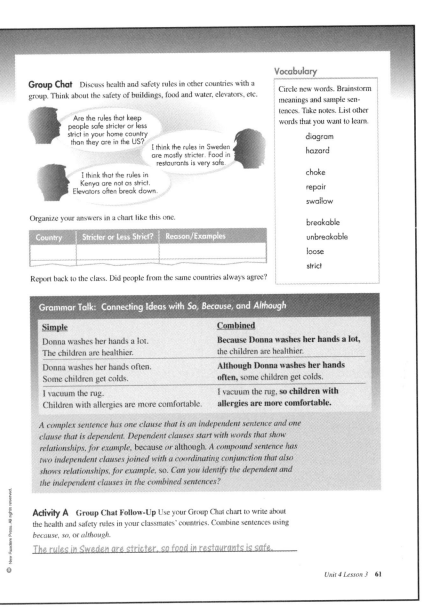

learners on the inside answer the questions those on the outside ask.
- The inside circle continues to move one person to the right after answering the questions. There may be some false starts, but most will get the idea after a few times.

Grammar Talk

Follow the suggestions on p. 7 for introducing the grammar point.

If students seem confused by the sentence using *so*, point out that *so* can also be used to make a complex sentence. In such cases, *so* is a subordinating conjunction and

means "for the purpose of ensuring that" (e.g., I vacuumed the rug *so the children with allergies would be more comfortable.*).

Use Unit Master 39 (Grammar: Cause and Effect) now or at any time during the rest of the unit.

Activity A

If you used the conversation circle instead of the three-column chart, review some safety rules and have learners work from notes.

Assign Workbook pp. 29–30.

Activity B

Tell learners that *although* shows that in spite of effort, the outcome is the *opposite* of the expected one. *Because* indicates that the outcome is the expected one.

Answers

3. Because we forgot to put the detergent away, someone almost swallowed some.
4. Because Donna provided a detailed diagram, the city gave her a license.
5. Although we bought a new fire extinguisher, we failed inspection.
6. Because Sheba washes her hands often, the children are healthy.

Extension

Remind learners that the order of the clauses may be reversed and the comma omitted (e.g., Someone almost swallowed some detergent because we forgot to put it away.). Have them write sentences 4 through 6 in reverse order.

Activity C

Use Customizable Master 5 (Idea Map). Make a copy for each group.

- After groups have completed their idea maps, have a learner from each group list on the board or a large sheet of paper safety tips for one room (e.g., the kitchen).
- To encourage more participation, have one learner dictate and another write.
- When the group's entire list has been written, ask if anyone can add more safety tips. Add learner contributions to the list.

Repeat the process for each of the rooms. Keep adding to the lists until everyone is satisfied.

Task 3

Use Unit Master 40 (Life Skill: A Safety Checklist) to help learners complete Task 3.

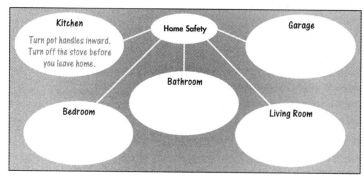

Activity B In your notebook, combine the pairs of sentences below with *because* or *although*. Use *because* to show cause and effect. Use *although* to show contrast. Then exchange papers with a partner to check your answers.

1. We locked up the cleaning products. Everyone felt safe.
   Everyone felt safe because we locked up the cleaning products.
2. We removed breakable objects. Someone broke a drinking glass.
   Although we removed breakable objects, someone broke a drinking glass.
3. We forgot to put the detergent away. Someone almost swallowed some.
4. Donna provided a detailed diagram. The city gave her a license.
5. We bought a new fire extinguisher. We failed inspection.
6. Sheba washes her hands often. The children are healthy.

Activity C Make your own safety suggestion list. Brainstorm with your group. Use an idea map like the one below. Think of safety tips that are *not* on the list on page 60. Think about safety tips for each room of a house.

Kitchen — Turn pot handles inward. Turn off the stove before you leave home.
Home Safety
Garage
Bathroom
Bedroom
Living Room

TASK 3: Safety Check

1. Check your living or work space for hazards. Use the list on page 60 and the health and safety tips that you wrote in Activity C.
2. Answer these questions: Did you find any hazards? What were they? Which was the most serious? Report back to your group.
3. Think about how to fix the hazards. Which ones could you repair yourself? Which ones need professional repair?

One Step Up
List ways to fix the hazards. Try to find out the costs for fixing the problems. Are the more serious hazards the most expensive to fix? Can some simple, inexpensive changes make a big difference?

62 *Unit 4 Lesson 3*

Have learners add their ideas to the checklist or create their own checklist.

- If possible, tell learners to make this a family project by involving children in looking for hazards in the home.
- Have learners report the results of their home safety check to the class, using the questions in the student book as a guide.
- Ask each learner to identify one hazard and describe a plan to correct it.

One Step Up

Have learners work together to list other ideas for fixing or eliminating hazards.

Extension

Use One Step Up as a writing assignment. Have learners write about how to fix their safety hazards. Alternatively, choose one hazard and ask learners to write about why it is dangerous and how they could correct it.

Use Unit Master 41 (Thinking Skill: Working with a Circle Graph) now or at any time during the rest of this unit.

Review Unit Skills

See pp. 8–9 for suggestions on games and activities to review the unit vocabulary and grammar.

Reading Tip

📑 Use Customizable Master 3 (3-Column Chart) to create the KWL chart. Label the three columns *Know, Want to Know,* and *Learned.* Make a copy for each learner. Then do the following:

- Read the reading tip with learners and point out the three columns on the chart.
- Tell learners to look at the article and read the title and the subheads; this will give them an idea of the subject. Brainstorm a few *Know* items by asking learners what they know about small businesses in the US.
- List learners' responses on the board or a transparency. Then give learners a few minutes to complete the *Know* column on their own charts.
- Brainstorm again with the *Want to Know* column. Have learners record things they would like to know about small businesses.
- Have learners read the passage silently. Tell them to write brief notes in the *Learned* column as they learn new things.
- When learners finish reading, ask them to review what they had wanted to learn. Were their questions answered? Ask if they still have questions about small businesses in the US. Discuss where they can find the answers.

Extension

Illustrate the power of prior knowledge with a "Visiting Expert" activity. Divide learners into three groups. Assign each group one section of the reading as follows:

- from the title through the section titled "Jobs Created"
- the "Getting Started" section
- "Running a Home Business" to the end

Have groups read their part of the article silently, discuss it briefly, take notes, and choose a spokesperson. This person will be the "expert" on that part of the article.

- At your signal, each expert moves to another group and, using his or her home group's notes, tells the new group as much as possible about that part of the reading.
- After a few minutes, the experts move on to the next group and tell them about that part of the article.
- Continue until all parts of the article have been heard by all groups.

Finally, have all learners read the entire article silently. Ask these questions:

- Did you remember more from the reading when you knew something about it in advance?
- How can this help you be a better reader?

UNIT 4 Challenge Reading

◆ **Reading Tip** Before you read, take a few minutes to think about the topic. Write down a few things that you already **know** about small businesses, including things you learned in this unit. Then write down things that you **want** to know about small businesses and the people who run them. After you read, think about the topic again and write down new things that you **learned** from reading the article. You can use a chart like the one on page 64 to record your ideas. This is called a **KWL** chart.

audit

blueprint

Idiom Watch!
Business is slow.
get started

SMALL BUSINESS REPORT

Source: US Small Business Administration

Small businesses are important in keeping the US economy strong, according to a recent *Small Business Profile,* which is a report from the US Small Business Administration. The report shows that small businesses create jobs and new opportunities for many people in or near their homes. Some small businesses are not really small. The definition of a small business is a business that employs fewer than 500 people.

Number of Businesses In the year 2000 the US had 5,812,100 businesses that employed one person or more. Nearly 99.7 percent of those were small businesses.

Success Rate About half of all new businesses stay open for four years. The Small Business Administration reports that 66 percent of businesses remain open at least 2 years, 49.6 percent at least 4 years, and 39.5 percent at least 6 years.

Not all businesses close because they are failures. In fact, 57 percent of owners of businesses that closed said that their business was successful at the time it closed. Sometimes, however, business people move, retire, or close one business and open a different one.

Jobs Created Small businesses create jobs. Almost all companies begin small. They need to grow to stay in business. Small businesses create about two-thirds to three-quarters of new jobs each year. Just over half (50.9 percent) of the nation's employees work in small businesses.

Getting Started Thousands of people across the US are learning that starting their own business is a good way to take care of family and other responsibilities, have a good income, and get great satisfaction from work. But it's important to remember that starting a small business requires a lot of careful planning and preparation if you want to succeed.

Begin by looking at your reasons for starting your own business and for choosing a particular type of business. Ask yourself hard questions, for example: Do you really want to be independent, or do you want the security of working for someone else? What kind of work are you interested in doing? Do you have the skills you will need for that work?

When you decide what kind of business you want, think about the opportunities and the competition. Will there be customers for that kind of business? Can you do better than your competition?

Finally, create a clear business plan. You will need information on legal and financial requirements. You will also need to give details of what you plan to do and how you expect to keep the business running. The business plan is a kind of map for starting and running your new business.

Running a Home Business For many people who want to be their own boss, a home business is a good way to start. Careful preparation and a good business plan are still important. Even though you are "at home" every day, you still need to think like a businessperson. Here's some advice on making sure your home business succeeds.

Unit 4 Challenge Reading **63**

Talk or Write

<u>Possible Answers</u>

1. The article says about half of all new businesses stay open at least four years and about 40 percent stay open at least six years. It does not state a specific number for five years.

2. If learners answered the question in What's Your Opinion in Lesson 1 (p. 54), briefly review their list of reasons small businesses fail. Positive reasons for closing a business include making enough money to retire or wanting to open a different kind of business. Negative reasons might include financial difficulties or family problems. Some people find they do not enjoy running their own business and decide to take a job as an employee.

3. Small businesses create jobs. They create new opportunities. People can work near their homes. They can get more satisfaction from their work. They can take care of family and other responsibilities and still work.

4. Answers will vary.

<u>Extension</u>

Ask these discussion questions:

• What is the definition of a small business in the US?

• Do you agree with this definition?

• Do you think other countries define small businesses the same way?

Writing Task

Encourage learners to use their completed KWL charts as they write their paragraphs. Ask if anyone still has questions. Brainstorm places where they can find answers.

Have learners use Generic Assessment Master 14 (Writing Checklist and Error Correction Symbols) as they revise and edit their writing.

• Act like a businessperson during business hours. Separate your home life and your business life. Rent a post office box and use that address on mail and stationery for your business. Have a phone line in your home just for your business, or use an answering machine for incoming business calls.

• Discipline yourself. Follow a schedule as if you were working for someone else. Unless it's an emergency, do not baby-sit or visit with neighbors during work time.

• Organize your workspace carefully.

• Find a mentor, someone who will answer questions, make suggestions, and help you evaluate ideas. You should also join professional associations.

• Ask your regular customers to suggest new customers.

• Keep accurate records of your expenses. The Internal Revenue Service (IRS) audits home-based businesses more frequently than it audits individuals.

• This is most important: Put some of your earnings into a savings account for times when business may be slow.

Talk or Write

1. In Lesson 1 of this unit you learned that more than 50 percent of small businesses close in the first five years. Do you think that the numbers in this report agree with that success rate? Why or why not?

2. Why might a successful small business close? With a partner, list as many reasons (both negative and positive) as you can for a small business closing.

3. List three or more reasons why small businesses are important to the US economy.

4. Think about a small business that you know. In your opinion, is it successful? Why or why not? Report to the class.

Writing Task Look at the KWL chart you made before starting to read. Think about what you learned from the article. Complete the third column of the chart.

What I **Know** about Small Business	What I **Want to Know** about Small Business	What I **Learned** about Small Business

Use the list in the third column to write a paragraph in your notebook. Give your paragraph this title: "What I Have Learned about Small Businesses."

Look at the second column again. Did you find out what you wanted to know? If you want to learn more, share your questions with your teacher and the class.

Unit 4 Project

Learners explore opening their own small businesses.

Get Ready

For background on small businesses in the US, call the US Small Business Administration or visit the U.S. Small Business Administration web site. Learners can also call their local office of the Small Business Administration or the Chamber of Commerce, or talk to someone in a similar business.

Creating a virtual business can provide a rich context for meaningful conversation, reading, and writing.

- Join learners in writing for two minutes on this topic: *If money were no object and you could start any kind of business anywhere in the world, what would it be? Where would it be?*
- Remind learners that the writing is for them alone. They should write without correcting, editing, or self-censoring.
- Ask for a few volunteers to read what they wrote to the class.
- Do the group brainstorming activity from the student book.

Alternatively, use the text questions for a guided fantasy as in Unit 1.

- Have learners imagine their own businesses as you read the questions aloud.
- Ask learners to review the questions and take notes on their answers.
- Break into small groups. Have learners take turns describing a business they would like to open.
- Have group members suggest names for one another's businesses.

Each learner will now have an idea and a name in mind and be ready to make a business plan.

Do the Work

- Have learners write answers to the questions under Get Ready.

- Tell them to develop their answers by adding details and examples.
- Have them review their freewriting exercise for ideas and then organize them under the three categories suggested in the student book.
- Have each learner write a rough draft about his or her small business. Then have writing partners help one another edit and polish their work.

Present

Choose one way of presenting for all learners, or tell learners to choose the form of their own presentations.

UNIT 4 Project

Create a Business

Many of us will never run our own small business, but many of us think about it sometimes. What kind of small business would you like to run?

Get Ready

In a group, brainstorm types of businesses that you think might be successful in your area. Ask group members what businesses they think you would be good at. Use those ideas to choose one business that you personally want to run. Then answer these questions about it:

- What business did you choose? What product or service will you provide?
- What skills and experience do you have that are needed for this business?
- Who would be the boss? How many employees would be needed?
- What would be a good location for this business?
- Are there many other businesses of this kind in the area?
- What kinds of people would use this business? Do many of them live close to the business location?
- How can you get more information and help?

Do the Work

Use your answers to the questions above to write about your idea for a small business. Organize the information into three categories:

- description of the business (including why it is a good business for you)
- location and competition
- customers and need for the business

Put the information into three paragraphs. Give your work the title "My Dream Business." Illustrate your work. For example, illustrate the description with pictures of similar businesses.

Present

Present your dream business to your classmates in *one* of these ways:

- Read the description to your classmates.
- Make notes and tell about your business in a one-minute speech.
- Make a poster or bulletin board display.
- Create another kind of presentation. (Suggestions: Make a video, have someone interview you, write a song about your new business, create a computer presentation, etc.)

Unit 4 Project **65**

Assessment

 Use Unit Master 42 (Project Assessment Form) to assess each learner's writing and presentation. The completed form can become a part of each learner's portfolio.

Assign Workbook p. 31 (Check Your Progress).

Use Unit Master 43 (Unit Checkup/Review) whenever you complete this unit.

Unit 5: Think before You Buy!

Materials for the Unit

- News articles about ethical and unethical business practices
- Food or drink for taste-testing, plastic spoons/cups
- Consumer magazines containing product ratings
- Customizable Masters 2, 4–6
- Generic Assessment Masters 11 and 14
- Unit Masters 44–50

Think before You Buy!

Read the title; then review the unit objectives listed below it.

- Follow the suggestions on p. 5 for talking about titles.
- Tell learners that this unit will focus on becoming educated consumers. Together they will create a consumer guide using the commercial products examined in the three lesson tasks.
- Have learners list some of the things they think about before they go shopping.
- Ask learners to bring in some examples of product ads. Create a display of these ads.

Photo

Follow the suggestions on pp. 4–5 for talking about the photo. Then read the question below the arrow.

- Talk about products that learners have purchased.
- Ask those who answer *yes* to the question why they think they bought the wrong product. Was it their fault or the fault of someone or something else?

Have learners look at the photo and read the caption. Elicit both details and opinions by asking questions like these:

- Do you think Bill has a headache? What makes you think that?
- Do you think he should try to fix the camera or buy a new one?
- What should Bill have done before he bought the camera?

- What should he have done before he decided to fix it?

Think and Talk

Follow the suggestions on p. 6 for comprehension questions.

<u>Possible Answers</u>

1. There are camera pieces, lenses, an assembly manual, and a warranty.
2. He probably has a headache and feels upset because he can't understand the instructions.
3. Answers will vary. Have learners explain and support their answers.
4. Answers will vary. Have learners explain and support their answers.

Vocabulary

Follow the suggestions on p. 6 for introducing and reinforcing vocabulary words.

Gather Your Thoughts

Use Customizable Master 6 (Venn Diagram). Follow the suggestions on p. 7 for customizing and duplicating the master. Make a copy for each learner.

Model the activity by drawing a large Venn diagram on the board or an overhead transparency.

Include several examples in each circle. For example, inside the circle for *My Shopping Habits,* write habits like these:
• I buy only what I need.
• I buy at the last minute.
• I buy only on sale.
• I buy recommended products.

Inside the circle for *Smart Shopping Habits,* write habits like these:
• Buy after comparing prices.
• Buy from a reputable dealer.
• Buy only what you need.
• Buy recommended products.

Now copy the sentences that describe your smart shopping habits (those that are in both circles, that is, the last two if you are using the *Smart Shopping Habits* above) into the middle overlapping section of the Venn diagram.

What's the Problem?

Follow the suggestions on p. 5 for thinking about the problem.
• Help learners focus their conversations by providing a sentence starter for learners to complete (e.g., People make mistakes when purchasing because ____.).
• Have pairs of learners compete to see which can generate the most sentence endings.
• Remind them that each sentence ending must be logical and clearly different from the others.

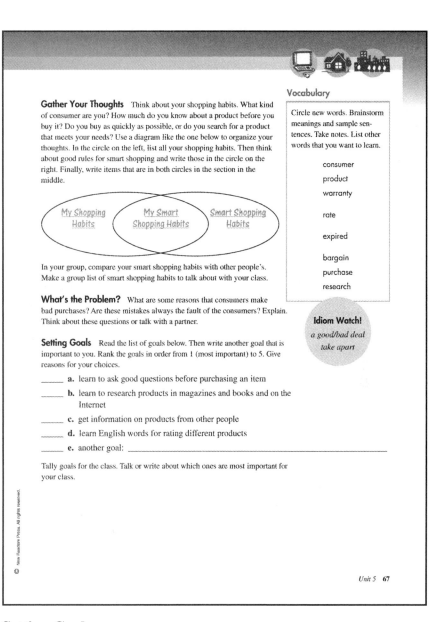

Gather Your Thoughts Think about your shopping habits. What kind of consumer are you? How much do you know about a product before you buy it? Do you buy as quickly as possible, or do you search for a product that meets your needs? Use a diagram like the one below to organize your thoughts. In the circle on the left, list all your shopping habits. Then think about good rules for smart shopping and write those in the circle on the right. Finally, write items that are in both circles in the section in the middle.

My Shopping Habits — My Smart Shopping Habits — Smart Shopping Habits

In your group, compare your smart shopping habits with other people's. Make a group list of smart shopping habits to talk about with your class.

What's the Problem? What are some reasons that consumers make bad purchases? Are these mistakes always the fault of the consumers? Explain. Think about these questions or talk with a partner.

Setting Goals Read the list of goals below. Then write another goal that is important to you. Rank the goals in order from 1 (most important) to 5. Give reasons for your choices.

_____ **a.** learn to ask good questions before purchasing an item

_____ **b.** learn to research products in magazines and books and on the Internet

_____ **c.** get information on products from other people

_____ **d.** learn English words for rating different products

_____ **e.** another goal: _____

Tally goals for the class. Talk or write about which ones are most important for your class.

Vocabulary

Circle new words. Brainstorm meanings and sample sentences. Take notes. List other words that you want to learn.

consumer
product
warranty
rate
expired
bargain
purchase
research

Idiom Watch!
a good/bad deal
take apart

Unit 5 **67**

Setting Goals

Follow the suggestions on p. 5 for setting goals. To clarify each goal, provide the following examples:

a. Ask questions like, "What are its special features? Do you provide a written guarantee?"

b. Locate web sites that compare products and prices.

c. Ask your friends, "Are you satisfied with this product? How did you find out about the best place to buy it?"

d. Learn words such as *strengths, weaknesses, quality, pros and cons,* and *ratings.*

Lesson 1: Shopping Smart 🔆

Read the title and point out the lesson objectives below it.

- Tell learners that in this lesson they will do an informal product analysis.
- Explain that the *-ing* form of many verbs is used with the word *smart* (e.g., shopping smart, working smart, playing smart). Tell them this expression is an informal idiom and not for formal speaking or writing.

Question

Read the question aloud.

- Tell learners about a time you asked someone for advice when deciding which car, camera, computer, or other item to buy.
- Have learners share their experiences.

Photo

Follow the suggestions on pp. 4–5 for talking about photos. After learners study the photo, ask them what they think is happening (e.g., Bill is on some steps talking with two men and a woman. Their body language suggests an important discussion.).

Listening Tip

Read the tip aloud.

- The target skill in this activity is listening for idioms. Before learners listen, read some idioms from the script (e.g., *figure out, on a tight budget, come up with*) and ask learners to guess the meaning.
- As learners respond, point out how difficult it is to understand the meaning of these expressions without their context.

🎧 Play the audio or read the listening script on p. 139. Ask learners to listen for the idioms as they are used in context. Follow the suggestions on p. 5 for listening comprehension.

LESSON 1   Work/School

Shopping Smart

- Analyze a product you want to buy
- Use present and past participles as adjectives

Who do you talk to when making decisions about a purchase?

- Listening Tip 🎧 If you are listening to a conversation in English and hear an idiom or expression that you don't know, try to think about the meaning of the whole sentence. Sometimes there are clues in the sentence to help you decide what the idiom means. Try this as you listen to a conversation between Bill and his friends at school. The listening script starts on page 137.

> genius

Idiom Watch!
come up with (an idea)
figure out
be on a tight budget

Bill is talking with three classmates about the problem with his camera.

Talk or Write
1. What are three things that Bill's classmates tell him to do?
2. What do they think is the best way to learn about new products?
3. What does Bill know about the differences between digital and traditional cameras? Do you know about other differences?

68   *Unit 5 Lesson 1*

Talk or Write

In this exercise, learners use context to understand idioms.

Play the audio or read the listening script again. If learners are ready, have each group answer one question. One learner can take notes and another can report back to the class.

Possible Answers
1. Bill's classmates tell him to research cameras on the web; read special product magazines; look for ads for buying cameras through an 800 number or the web.

2. They think he should visit a library and read the latest issues of consumer magazines.
3. He knows that the traditional camera uses film and the digital doesn't. He also knows that he can send pictures over the web using the digital camera. Remainder of answer will vary. As learners suggest other differences between the two types of cameras, write them on the board or an overhead transparency.

Vocabulary

Follow the suggestions on p. 6 for introducing and reinforcing vocabulary words.

Use the listening activity on p. 68 so learners can hear the words in context.

Play the audio or read the listening script for the conversation again, this time in small segments. Ask learners to listen for the vocabulary words.

- Have learners turn to the script on p. 137 in their books. Ask learners to underline the words as they listen to the conversation once more.

Group Chat

Use Customizable Master 4 (4-Column Chart). Follow the suggestions on p. 7 for customizing and duplicating the master. Make a copy for each learner.

- Keep the Group Chat short and lively by giving learners limited time to come up with names of equipment or materials.
- Each learner should generate at least five answers but no more than eight. Class size will determine the exact time limit, but 10 minutes is a good target time.
- Tell learners to save the completed chart for use in Activity B.

Grammar Talk

Follow the suggestions on p. 7 for introducing the grammar point. Learners will have passive recognition of this point because they heard it used in the Group Chat and in the conversation on the previous page.

- Have learners silently read the Grammar Talk information.
- Have volunteers report the information back to the class.

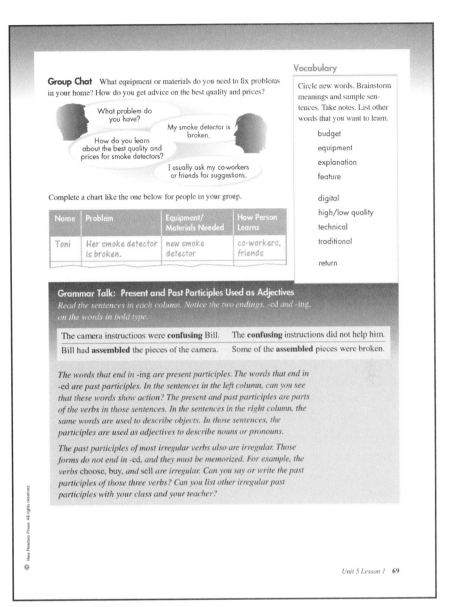

- Help learners make a list of the characteristics of present and past participles as adjectives:
  1. They look like verbs but act like adjectives.
  2. They can be regular or irregular.
  3. Like adjectives, they come before a noun in a sentence.
  4. Some participles have both *-ed* and *-ing* forms as adjectives.

Use Unit Master 44 (Grammar: Participial Adjectives) now or any time during the rest of the unit.

 Assign Workbook pp. 32–33.

Activity A

Model the activity by giving learners these examples:

1. We heard *breaking* news on the radio.
2. The amount is *budgeted* for your lunch.
3. The *chosen* learners participated in a presentation.

Point out that in examples 1 and 3, a present participle and a past irregular participle are used to describe objects. Example 2 uses a regular past participle as part of the verb, not as an adjective.

Activity B

- To begin, have partners decide which verb can be converted to either a past or present participle and used as an adjective.
- Then have learners write sentences using information from their Group Chat charts.

Activity C

Use Customizable Master 2 (2-Column Chart). Follow the suggestions on p. 7 for customizing the master. Make a copy for each learner.

Extension

After individual learners finish working on their charts, involve them in this guessing game activity:

- Tell learners they will play a game called *What's My Task?*
- Student A reads a sentence from column B (e.g., I use my *ironing* board.) and asks the large group, "What's my task?"
- Other learners respond, "You *iron* your clothes." OR "You *are ironing* your clothes."

Task 1

Copy and distribute Customizable Master 2 (2-Column Chart). Have learners write the heads *Weaknesses* (in the left column) and *Strengths* (in the right column). Do the following to prepare learners for the task:

- Read Bill's chart with learners.
- Review the concept of *pros and cons* so they can brainstorm.
- To help them choose a product to research, suggest that they make a list of various products and select the one they need the most.

Have learners begin gathering information by asking other learners. Tell them to make a list of questions like these to ask about their product:

- How would you rate the quality of ___ (the product)?
- What is the best price for ___?
- How soon will ___ break down?
- Is there another brand that is better?

Activity A In your notebook, write sentences using the present or past participles of six of these verbs as adjectives:

break	buy	purchase	return	speak
budget	choose	research	sell	write

When you finish, check your sentences with a partner. Have you used the participles correctly?

Activity B Group Chat Follow-Up In your notebook, write sentences about at least two problems you discussed in your Group Chat. In the second sentence about each problem, use a participle as an adjective.

Toni needs to buy a smoke detector. Her old one is broken.

I can't always answer my phone. I need an answering machine.

Activity C Write about the tasks for which you use machines or equipment at home. Write your tasks in Column A of a chart like the one below. Then use participles as adjectives to tell more about each task in Column B.

A	B
I iron my clothes.	I use my <u>ironing</u> board. I hang the <u>ironed</u> clothes in the closet.

 TASK 1: Do an Informal Product Analysis

Think about one product that you want to buy. Gather information about the product from classmates, co-workers, friends, and a local store. Record the weaknesses *(cons)* and strengths *(pros)* in a chart like the one below. Bill created this chart after gathering information about digital cameras.

Product: Digital Camera

Weaknesses	Strengths
printed photos may be poor quality	some cameras record sound and make videos
too much time spent uploading to Internet	can share photos easily with others on e-mail
difficult to get printed photos	can review photos instantly and delete poor ones

Lesson 2: Doing the Research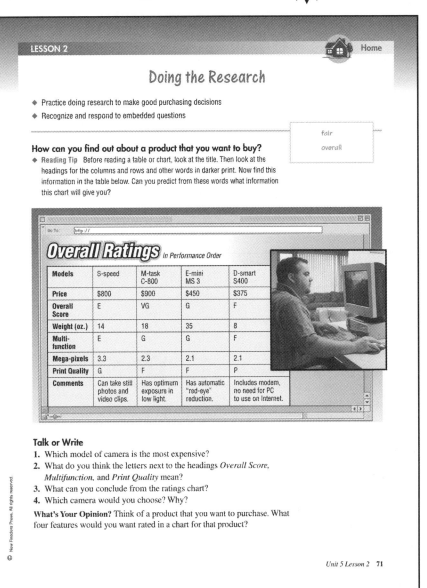

Read the title and point out the lesson objectives below it.

- Tell learners in this lesson they will learn to do consumer research to make good purchasing decisions.
- They will also research and rate a product.

Question

Read the question aloud with learners.

- Allow learners about five minutes to discuss the question with their groups before having them give their answers.
- Some ways to find out about a product include television and radio commercials, magazine and newspaper ads, friends, and consumer magazines.
- Point out that sometimes you can become familiar with a product by trying it before purchasing it.

Reading Tip

Read the tip aloud to the class.

From reading the headings and other words in darker print, learners should be able to predict what information the chart will give them:

- Prices of various digital cameras
- Different types of cameras
- Various capabilities of the product
- Print quality for each camera
- Weight of each camera

Discuss the layout and organization of the chart.

Reading

Have groups of learners find specific information. Ask questions like these:

- Which product costs $800?
- Which camera includes a modem?
- Which got the best overall score?
- Which is least expensive?
- Which has the poorest ratings?

Doing the Research

- ◆ Practice doing research to make good purchasing decisions
- ◆ Recognize and respond to embedded questions

fair

overall

How can you find out about a product that you want to buy?

◆ **Reading Tip** Before reading a table or chart, look at the title. Then look at the headings for the columns and rows and other words in darker print. Now find this information in the table below. Can you predict from these words what information this chart will give you?

Go To: http://

Overall Ratings In Performance Order

Models	S-speed	M-task C-800	E-mini MS 3	D-smart S400
Price	$800	$900	$450	$375
Overall Score	E	VG	G	F
Weight (oz.)	14	18	35	8
Multi-function	E	G	G	F
Mega-pixels	3.3	2.3	2.1	2.1
Print Quality	G	F	F	P
Comments	Can take still photos and video clips.	Has optimum exposure in low light.	Has automatic "red-eye" reduction.	Includes modem, no need for PC to use on Internet.

Talk or Write
1. Which model of camera is the most expensive?
2. What do you think the letters next to the headings *Overall Score, Multifunction,* and *Print Quality* mean?
3. What can you conclude from the ratings chart?
4. Which camera would you choose? Why?

What's Your Opinion? Think of a product that you want to purchase. What four features would you want rated in a chart for that product?

Talk or Write

This exercise gives learners practice in reading a table.

Follow the suggestions on p. 6 for comprehension questions.

Answers
1. The M-task C-800 is the most expensive model.
2. The letters stand for quality. (P = poor, F = fair, G = good, VG = very good, and E = excellent.)
3. Answers will vary. One possible answer is that the best camera to buy may be the E-mini MS 3.

It is not the most expensive camera, and two of its features are rated as good.
4. Answers will vary.

What's Your Opinion?

Have learners reflect a few minutes and make notes before giving their opinions to the class.

Vocabulary

Follow the suggestions on p. 6 for introducing and reinforcing vocabulary words.

- Ask learners to list other words they would like to learn. Suggest they look through the unit and add unfamiliar words.
- Remind them that the list can include words from activities as well as words from directions for any activity.

Class Chat

 Use Customizable Master 2 (2-Column Chart). Copy and distribute the chart to learners.

- To begin the activity, review question formation.
- Elicit the questions learners will use for each item and list them on the board or a transparency. Then have learners write the questions on their charts.

Tell learners to save their charts for use in Activity B.

Questions

1. Have you learned how to shop on the Internet?
2. Do you know where to find bargains on appliances or technology?
3. Do you find out/Have you ever found out how much a product should cost before buying?
4. Do you know which stores offer the best prices on technology?
5. Do you know where to find information comparing different products?
6. Do you read product ratings?
7. Do you know how to find consumer information sites on the Internet?

Grammar Talk

Follow the suggestions on p. 7 for introducing the grammar point. Learners will have passive recognition of this point because embedded questions were included in the Class Chat.

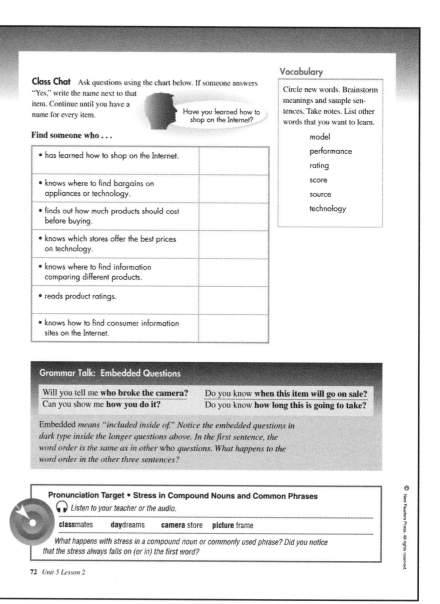

Class Chat Ask questions using the chart below. If someone answers "Yes," write the name next to that item. Continue until you have a name for every item.

Have you learned how to shop on the Internet?

Find someone who . . .

• has learned how to shop on the Internet.	
• knows where to find bargains on appliances or technology.	
• finds out how much products should cost before buying.	
• knows which stores offer the best prices on technology.	
• knows where to find information comparing different products.	
• reads product ratings.	
• knows how to find consumer information sites on the Internet.	

Vocabulary

Circle new words. Brainstorm meanings and sample sentences. Take notes. List other words that you want to learn.

model
performance
rating
score
source
technology

Grammar Talk: Embedded Questions

Will you tell me **who broke the camera?**
Can you show me **how you do it?**
Do you know **when this item will go on sale?**
Do you know **how long this is going to take?**

Embedded *means "included inside of." Notice the embedded questions in dark type inside the longer questions above. In the first sentence, the word order is the same as in other* who *questions. What happens to the word order in the other three sentences?*

Pronunciation Target • Stress in Compound Nouns and Common Phrases
Listen to your teacher or the audio.

classmates   **day**dreams   **camera** store   **picture** frame

What happens with stress in a compound noun or commonly used phrase? Did you notice that the stress always falls on (or in) the first word?

- Read the question about word order inside the embedded question.
- Have learners rephrase the embedded questions as normal questions to see what happens to the verb.

Answer

In the other sentences, the verb in the embedded question follows the subject instead of the question word.

 Use Unit Master 45 (Grammar: Embedded Questions) now or at any time during the rest of the unit.

Pronunciation Target

 Play the audio or read the words in the student book.

Learners should not look at their books as they listen.

- Explain that the first word in the compound is stressed, that is, pronounced longer and louder.
- Model both correct and incorrect stress and ask learners to listen to identify the correct pronunciation.

 Assign Workbook pp. 34–35.

Activity A

Have learners work in pairs. One reads the original question, and the other creates the embedded question. Provide more examples:

1. Did you say how much this camera costs?
2. Can you tell me which one is better?
3. Do you know where the expiration date is?
4. Can you tell us where you found it?
5. Did you explain to her why it is so expensive?
6. Would you mind telling me where I can find it?

Activity B

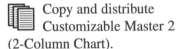 Copy and distribute Customizable Master 2 (2-Column Chart).

- Have learners write the heads *Sentence* (in the left column) and *Question for Class* (in the right column).
- This writing activity further reviews embedded questions. Learners may work in pairs or individually to change a sentence into an information question.

Review embedded questions in a later class by asking the questions from this activity and having learners answer in complete sentences. Ask questions like these:

- Can you tell me who knows how to shop on the Internet?
- Can you tell me who knows where to find bargains on household appliances?

Task 2

Talk with learners about products they would like to research.

- Suggest that their first source of information is other learners. Have them look for people who already have some information about their product.

- Tell them to request information using embedded questions. Write these sample questions on the board or a transparency:
  Do you know how much ____ costs?
  Do you know how ____ performs over time?
- Provide learners with consumer and specialized magazines that rate products. (You could create a permanent class library that includes many of these magazines.)
- Allow learners time to browse the materials. Encourage them to use the guide questions to limit their research to specific information.

Technology Extra

Assist learners in using the table-making feature in a word processing program.

Activity A In your notebook, embed these questions in other questions. Check the word order in your sentences carefully. Then read your sentences to a partner.

1. How much does this camera cost? *Do you know how much this camera costs?*
2. Which one is better? *Can you figure out* ____?
3. Where is the expiration date?
4. Where did you find it?
5. Why is it so expensive?
6. Where can I find it?

Activity B **Class Chat Follow-Up** Write sentences using the information from your Class Chat chart. Then write a question about each sentence using words and phrases like these: *Can you tell me . . . ? Do you know . . . ? Did you figure out . . . ?* When you finish, ask the class one or more of your questions. Remember that more than one answer may be possible.

Mohamed has learned to shop on the Internet.

Can you tell me who has learned to shop on the Internet?

TASK 2: Research and Rate a Product
Alone or with a partner, rate a product that you need or want to purchase—food, over-the-counter medicine, a technology product, and so on. First, look for information about the product. If there are similar brands of the same product (such as a refrigerator or a frozen pizza) or companies that offer the same service (such as two airline companies), choose two or three and compare their features, price, and quality. Use the information and questions below as a guide for your research. After doing the research, would you still buy the product? Why or why not?

Sources of Information
- consumer product magazines (in library)
- specialized magazines for products, such as car magazines (in library)
- advertisements and product information sheets
- recommendations from friends
- conversations with sales clerks
- web sites

Questions to Answer
- What is the name of your product?
- Where can you purchase it?
- What is the price range for your product?
- What kind of warranty does it provide, if any?
- What did you learn that surprised you?

Technology Extra
Using the information from your research, make a table on the computer similar to those in consumer guides.

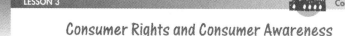

Read the title and point out the lesson objectives below it.

- In this lesson learners will read and analyze a passage from a textbook. They will also create an original product ad.
- Introduce the task of creating a product ad (p. 76). Tell learners to begin thinking of a product to advertise and to start collecting materials (e.g., pictures) to use in the ad.

Question

Read the question aloud to learners.

- Have learners work in pairs to create a list of consumer rights. Provide these examples:

We have the right to return defective products.

We have the right to complain to the manager.

- Create a class list on a large sheet of paper. As each pair reads their list, add only new ideas to the class list.
- Post the list.

Photo

Ask these questions:
- What is Bill reading?
- What kind of information do you think he is looking for?
- How can he use the information?

Reading Tip

Read the tip aloud with learners.

Warn learners that some English words look like words in other languages but have different meanings.

Reading

Ask learners if they know how and when the consumer-protection movement began in the US.

- Tell learners to read the passage silently. Have them use a highlighter to mark important names and dates, or have them write these in their notebooks.

- Read the article aloud to model pronunciation and stress.
- Learners can now make the list of words that look like words in another language. Likely choices include *organization, protection, product, informed, commission, bureau, violated, company,* and *especially.*

Talk or Write

This exercise helps learners read for supporting details.

Possible Answers
1. Two important events are the beginning of the consumer-protection movement in 1962 and the forming of the Consumer Product Safety Commission in 1973.
2. *Movement* here means "actions by groups of people that cause changes."
3. Answers will vary.

Extension

Share newspaper and magazine articles about ethical and unethical business practices.

Vocabulary

Follow the suggestions on p. 6 for introducing and reinforcing vocabulary words.

- After the brainstorming, identify the sentences that use the words correctly, write them on a sheet of large paper, and post them for learners to refer to during the rest of this unit.
- Review other strategies for learning new words (e.g., guessing meaning from context; using a dictionary).

To review all unit vocabulary, use Unit Master 46 (Game: Vocabulary Review) and 47 (Vocabulary: Learner-to-Learner Dictation) now or at any time during the rest of the unit.

Idiom Watch

Ask learners if anyone knows the meaning of *keep up with the times*. Write one or two correct responses on the board or a transparency. Tell learners to watch for this idiom as they read In the US.

In the US

Read the passage to learners. Then ask them to read it silently.

Extension

Have learners discuss the reading in pairs. Use these questions to guide their conversations:

- Do you agree or disagree with each sentence about Americans? (Have each partner respond for each sentence.)
- Can you think of an example of technology, besides the car, that is used by some people in the US when they do not need it?
- Why do *you* think people use technology that is not necessary in their lives?

Conclude the activity by having several pairs respond to each question.

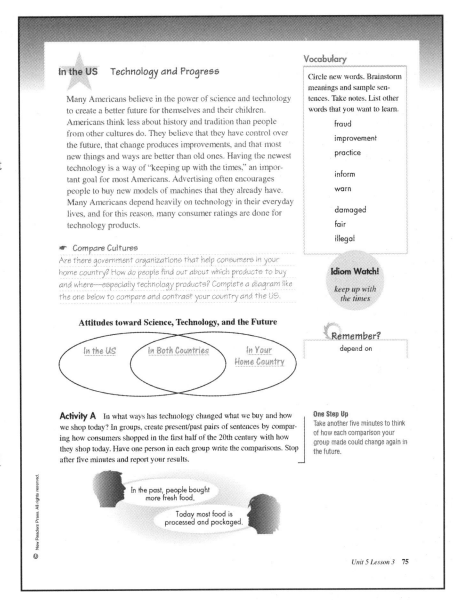

In the US   Technology and Progress

Many Americans believe in the power of science and technology to create a better future for themselves and their children. Americans think less about history and tradition than people from other cultures do. They believe that they have control over the future, that change produces improvements, and that most new things and ways are better than old ones. Having the newest technology is a way of "keeping up with the times," an important goal for most Americans. Advertising often encourages people to buy new models of machines that they already have. Many Americans depend heavily on technology in their everyday lives, and for this reason, many consumer ratings are done for technology products.

Compare Cultures

Are there government organizations that help consumers in your home country? How do people find out about which products to buy and where—especially technology products? Complete a diagram like the one below to compare and contrast your country and the US.

Attitudes toward Science, Technology, and the Future

In the US   In Both Countries   In Your Home Country

Activity A In what ways has technology changed what we buy and how we shop today? In groups, create present/past pairs of sentences by comparing how consumers shopped in the first half of the 20th century with how they shop today. Have one person in each group write the comparisons. Stop after five minutes and report your results.

In the past, people bought more fresh food.

Today most food is processed and packaged.

Vocabulary

Circle new words. Brainstorm meanings and sample sentences. Take notes. List other words that you want to learn.

fraud

improvement

practice

inform

warn

damaged

fair

illegal

Idiom Watch!

keep up with the times

Remember?

depend on

One Step Up

Take another five minutes to think of how each comparison your group made could change again in the future.

Unit 5 Lesson 3 75

Compare Cultures

Use Customizable Master 6 (Venn Diagram). Follow the suggestions on p. 7 for customizing and duplicating the master. Make a copy for each learner.

Extension

Form groups of learners from the same country. Ask them to discuss attitudes toward technology and progress held by people from different groups or regions in their home country. Then have them compare those attitudes with attitudes toward technology and progress in the US.

Activity A

Guide groups away from reporting sentences or ideas already read by another group. Ask group recorders to cross out any repeated sentences or ideas before reporters give their account.

One Step Up

As learners think of how their comparisons might change again in the future, remind them that technology is not the only reason for change.

 Assign Workbook pp. 36–37.

Activity B

Instruct the groups to anticipate what points the other group will make. Tell them to prepare their arguments with the purpose of convincing members of the opposing group to join theirs.

Activity C

Many products have multiple brands that can be used for the taste test, including beverages, bread, jam, condiments, desserts, ice cream, and milk products. Encourage group members to suggest additional products for their taste test.

Write the class list of test results on a large sheet of paper and post it. The list should include the following:
- General product category (e.g., mustard, cola, coffee)
- Name of each brand
- Taste words next to each brand (e.g., smooth, crunchy, sweet)
- Number of learners who would buy each brand

Task 3

Allow plenty of preparation time for this task of creating a product ad. If you introduced the task at the beginning of this lesson, learners should have gathered ideas and pictures for their ads by now.

Follow these steps, which correspond to the numbered steps in the student book:

1. Ask learners to bring in either the actual product or a picture of it.
2. Have learners keep notes about the product in a folder.
3. Have learners use the slogans from the list or create their own.

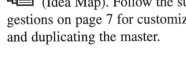 Use Customizable Master 5 (Idea Map). Follow the suggestions on page 7 for customizing and duplicating the master.

4. Give each learner a copy of the idea map.
5. Encourage creativity by making your own ad poster. If possible, work with a learner on the task. You and the learner can model the presentation, using humor or drama if possible. Make your presentation fairly simple and direct.

One Step Up

As an additional step, encourage some learners to do an ad for an idea or concept (e.g., good health, world peace, an exercise routine, universal health coverage), rather than for a commercial product ad.

Assessment

 Use Generic Assessment Master 11 (Written Communication Rubric) to evaluate product ads.

Review Unit Skills

See pp. 8–9 for suggestions on games and activities to review the unit vocabulary and grammar.

Activity B   Your teacher will divide the class into two equal groups, Group A and Group B. Each group will support one of these opinions:

A. Technology makes it easier to be an informed consumer.
B. Technology makes it more difficult for consumers to choose well.

In your group, prepare to support your opinions with good examples from the US and other countries that you know. Your teacher will tell you how much time you have. At the end of that time, each group will present its opinions to the other group. After both groups present, discuss the ideas as a class, vote, and take a class survey on the issue.

Activity C   In a group, do a taste test of three different brands of a food product. Each group has three samples—for example, three brands of peanut butter. Each person uses a clean plastic spoon to taste each brand. Describe differences you taste. Which sample tastes the best? Create a class list or chart with the result. Tally how many students would buy each brand.

 TASK 3: Create an Original Product Ad
With a partner, follow these steps to create an ad for a product:

1. Choose something that you would like to sell to your classmates.
2. Gather as much information about it as you can.
3. Brainstorm slogans often used in ads. This list can help you:
   - last chance to buy
   - the best deal
   - the greatest offer
   - while supplies last
   - a great opportunity
   - our lowest prices ever
   - only in our store
   - new and improved
4. Complete an idea map with the most important or interesting information and the best slogans that you gathered. Use these phrases and sentences in your product ad.
5. Make an advertising poster using your phrases and slogans with pictures of the product.
6. Convince your classmates to buy your product by presenting your poster. Read your ad or role-play it. Make the presentation funny, serious, or dramatic, but make it as convincing as possible. Students can rate the ads by telling which products they would or wouldn't buy and why.

> convincing
> dramatic
> slogan
> supplies

Unit 5 Challenge Reading ☀www☀

Reading Tip

Read the tip aloud with learners.

- Demonstrate how reading phrases rather than isolated words improves comprehension.
- Ask learners to look at the attention boxes on this page and the next and identify any word they do not know. Then provide a sentence that illustrates its meaning accurately.
- Brainstorm the meaning of the title with learners. Tell them that the word *beware* means "be careful," "be aware," or "be cautious."

Extensions

1. Substitute a jigsaw activity for a third reading. Follow the suggestions for jigsaws on p. 8.
2. Divide the second part of the reading ("To make a complaint about a business . . .") among three groups.

Provide each group with three questions like the ones below. These will guide group members as they prepare a report for the class:

- If you want to make a complaint, is it best to contact the store or the headquarters of the company?
- How should you report the problem?
- Why should you keep records of how you tried to resolve the problem?
- What should you write to the company?
- How can you protect your original proof of purchase and other documents when you send these to the company?
- What are some additional solutions if your problem is not resolved by anyone from the company?
- What kind of agencies can help you with your problems as a consumer?
- What legal action can you take?
- Do you always need a lawyer?

UNIT 5 Challenge Reading

◆ **Reading Tip** One way to better understand what you read is to first skim it quickly. Then read again slowly, reading word groups—phrases and clauses, or even whole sentences. It's easier to understand when you read this way. Try it with this reading.

Let the Buyer Beware

This advice is provided by the Federal Citizen Information Center. The FCIC can help you find information about federal government agencies, services, and programs. It tells you which office can help with problems. The FCIC does not handle consumer complaints, but it helps consumers send complaints directly to companies and agencies through its web site.

If you take these steps before making a large purchase, you have a good chance of avoiding problems and being happy with what you bought:

- Decide exactly what you want, need, and can afford.
- Research the product or service using information from the Federal Citizen Information Center in Pueblo, Colorado. The FCIC's toll-free number is 1-888-878-3256, and its web site is www.pueblo.gsa.gov.
- Ask family and friends to share experiences and give recommendations.
- Compare prices. Get several price estimates.
- Learn about and compare warranties. Some warranties are required by law. Call a state or local consumer protection office to find out more.
- Research a company's complaint record with your local consumer affairs office and the Better Business Bureau. Find out how many and what kinds of complaints have been filed. For a large purchase, look at the complaint files to see what the company did about the complaints.
- Read and understand any contract that anyone asks you to sign. Are all the blanks filled in? Are any promises included in writing?
- Extended warranties or service contracts help businesses make extra money. Someone may talk to you about these as you are paying. Think in advance if not having to worry about problems is worth the price.
- Check out a seller's return policy and get it in writing.
- Consider paying by credit card. If you later have a legitimate complaint against the seller, you may not have to pay a charge on your credit card.

To make a complaint about a business, use these tips:

- It's usually best to contact the business that sold you the product or performed the service. Most companies want to keep you as a customer.
- Many stores also have a toll-free number. If you can't find it, dial toll-free directory assistance at 1-800-555-1212. Contact the headquarters of the company or manufacturer by phone or the Internet. Ask for the consumer affairs office. Describe the problem calmly. Tell in as few

complaint
extended
headquarters
legitimate
policy
toll-free

Unit 5 Challenge Reading **77**

Challenge Reading

This reading is intended to make learners "stretch" slightly beyond their comfort level. If you find learners struggling, tell them that the reading is meant to challenge them and that they do not have to understand everything to answer the questions successfully.

Go over the reading several times and discuss it until learners feel comfortable with the content.

Talk or Write

<u>Answers</u>

1. Answers will vary. Ask learners how reading the article a few times has helped them understand these words. If learners are still struggling with the text, ask if the oral reports by other learners helped them. Why or why not?
2. Answers will vary. After learners write their responses, volunteers can report on what additional clues helped them understand the article.
3. extended, certified

Writing Task

Use Customizable Master 5 (Idea Map). Make a copy for each learner.

After brainstorming, learners should use the five questions to structure their responses in their notebooks.

Learners can use Generic Assessment Master 14 (Writing Checklist and Error Correction Symbols) as they revise and edit their writing.

---

words as possible the action you would like the company to take. Ask for the name of the person that you talk to. Take notes on the date, what the person said, what you said, and the next steps you agree on.

- If this doesn't work, write a letter stating what happened. Describe the problem, what you have done to resolve it, and the solution you want (for example, your money returned or the product repaired or exchanged). Include a copy of the receipt, the date of purchase, the name and address of the store where you purchased, and information about the warranty. Do not send original documents, only copies. Send your complaint by first-class certified mail to be sure it reaches the person.
- After you call or write, give the person time to resolve your problem. Save copies of *all* letters to and from the company.
- If the company won't help, contact a local, state, or federal agency to tell you your rights and investigate or resolve an issue. Try the Better Business Bureau or the Consumers' Union for help.
- If your case still is not resolved, you can take legal action. Small Claims Court will usually resolve cases quickly and inexpensively, and you won't have to hire or pay a lawyer. Small Claims Court deals with cases in which the amount of money is limited. The maximum amount varies from state to state. It may be between $2,000 and $5,000.

certified mail

investigate

receipt

resolve

Talk or Write

1. Which new words could you understand when you read in word groups?
2. What was still difficult to understand? What other clues do you need?
3. With a partner, list all participles used as adjectives in this reading and write their meanings.

Writing Task

In an idea map, brainstorm answers to these questions about a time when you purchased a product that you were not happy with in either the US or your home country. Then write a one-paragraph story about your experience.

- What did you buy?
- What was wrong with it?
- What did you do or say to complain?
- What happened as a result?
- What would you do differently now that you have read the article above?

78 *Unit 5 Challenge Reading*

Unit 5 Project 🌐

Learners create a consumer guide for products examined in the unit.

Get Ready

- Tell learners to read the project instructions in pairs, listing any questions or suggestions that might help them.
- Next, have learners brainstorm ideas for completing the consumer guide. Remind them that the guide must have a contents page, a resource page, and individual product pages, and that each product page must have the four elements listed in the student book.

Guide the brainstorm session with questions like these:

- How long will it take to complete the guide?
- What items and tools will you need to successfully complete the project?
- What things can you begin working on immediately?
- What information do you already have that you can use in the guide?

Do the Work

Distribute copies of Unit Master 48 (Unit 5 Project: Checklist for Class Consumer Guide) to each learner to help learners organize their work on this project.

Present

Assessment

During the presentation, complete a copy of Unit Master 49 (Project Assessment Form) for each learner. The completed form can become part of each learner's portfolio. Notice that some items are collective scores for all learners' efforts on the product, while others are scores on the product pages created by individual learners.

UNIT 5 Project

Create a Class Consumer Guide

With your class, create a consumer guide for some or all of the products that you looked at in the following tasks in this unit:

- Task 1, Do an Informal Product Analysis, page 70
- Task 2, Research and Rate a Product, page 73
- Task 3, Create an Original Product Ad, page 76

Get Ready

Choose the products that you will review. Use the checklist that your teacher gives you. Each student should present at least one product review. Plan a page with these features for each product:

- name of product at the top of the page
- general information about the product
- rating charts for each product from the Internet or consumer magazines
- short summary of information at the bottom of each page

Do the Work

1. For each product that you include, gather or create the information that you need.
2. Divide the guide into sections like these: Food Products, Technology, Services, Home Appliances. Decide where each product should go.
3. Number your pages. At the beginning of the guide, add a contents page. List the page numbers of the sections and the products in each section.
4. Add a resource page at the end of your guide. List all your research resources there—names of web sites, magazines, books, and so on.
5. Ask for comments and suggestions from your teacher. Make changes if necessary.
6. Design a cover for your class consumer guide. You can include photos, drawings, or symbols of products. You may want to make a collage cover using pictures and words cut from magazines.

Present

As a class, present your guide to another class in your school or program. Put your guide in a school or program library so that other students can look at it closely.

Technology Extra
If some students know how to work with computer graphics and type, let them suggest how to make a cover design on the computer.

Technology Extra

If some learners can use a computer but are unsure of assembling graphics and type, assist them in making the cover design.

 Assign Workbook p. 38 (Check Your Progress).

 Use Unit Master 50 (Unit Checkup/Review) whenever you complete this unit.

Unit 6: Protecting Your Rights

Materials for the Unit

- Magazine and newspaper ads and brochures with pictures of automobiles
- Examples of fine print in contracts, other legal documents, or product information sheets
- Local telephone books
- Customizable Masters 2, 3, and 8
- Generic Assessment Masters 10, 12–15
- Unit Masters 51–54

Protecting Your Rights

Read the title aloud to learners.

- Review the four groups of unit goals listed below it.
- Tell learners that the goal of this unit is to raise awareness of their rights as consumers.

Elicit learners' experiences with consumer fraud by asking these questions:

- Has anyone ever been cheated by a salesperson who made false promises?
- What did you do?
- Did your actions produce results?

Photo

Follow the suggestions on pp. 4–5 for talking about the photo; then read the question below the arrow.

Caption

Read the caption with learners. Then ask these questions:

- What else could they have done?
- What would you have done in the same situation?
- Should the Wus have taken the car *as is?* Explain.

Extension

Balance the discussion by looking at the salesman's point of view:

- Why did he try to pressure them to take the car?
- Could he also be under pressure? Explain.
- Is it his fault that the car was not satisfactory?

UNIT 6

Protecting Your Rights

Understanding Your Rights
- ◆ Vocabulary Legal terms
- ◆ Language Adverbs of time with the past perfect • Special problems with prepositions, articles, gerunds, and infinitives
- ◆ Pronunciation Consonant blends
- ◆ Culture Written and verbal contracts

Home 1   Work/School 2   Community 3

> But we said that we wanted a sunroof and four-wheel drive.

Has a salesperson ever tried to cheat you?

Last week Mr. and Mrs. Wu put a $500 deposit on a contract to buy their dream car. Today, when they go to pick up the car, they discover that it doesn't have the features that they wanted. They ask for their $500 deposit, but the dealer refuses. He tries to pressure them into taking the car anyway. The Wus refuse. They leave disappointed and angry, without their deposit or the car.

Think and Talk
1. What do you see in the picture? What's the problem?
2. Has anything like this ever happened to you or to someone you know?
3. What should the Wus do next? What advice would you give them?
4. How important do you think it is to get a contract in writing?

What's Your Opinion? The car dealer said that he was keeping the deposit because he had to pay for delivery. Was it right for him to keep the deposit? Explain.

dealer
dream car
four-wheel drive
sunroof

80 *Unit 6*

Attention Box

Bring in pictures of cars from magazines, papers, and dealers' brochures. Briefly discuss the specific features the Wus ordered.

This vocabulary should be understood, but learners should not be expected to produce the words at this point.

Think and Talk

Assign one question to each group.

The recorder in each group records group members' responses on a large sheet of paper. The group reporter reads the responses back to the class.

Possible Answers
1. They are outside at an automobile showroom. The couple looks angry. The man has a paper in his hand. The salesman is turning up his hands. The problem is that the couple did not get everything they ordered on their new car. The salesman isn't helpful.
2. Answers will vary. Ask learners who answer *yes* to explain the problem and its solution.
3. Answers will vary. Add your own relevant experiences to the discussion.
4. Answers will vary.

What's Your Opinion?

Give learners a few moments to formulate their opinions.

Vocabulary

Follow the suggestions on p. 6 for introducing and reinforcing vocabulary words. Ask learners to classify the words in each of the three clusters (*nouns, verbs, adjectives*).

Gather Your Thoughts

- Have each group draw an idea map on a large sheet of paper and complete the map together.
- As you move from group to group, help learners progress by asking where people get more information. Where can *they* get information about where to get more information?

Responses may include ideas like these:

- Ask friends and family for advice.
- Ask the salesman for the name and phone number of a satisfied customer.
- Read consumer reports. Look up information on the dealership or the car on the Internet.
- Shop around and compare features and prices before you buy. Do not be in a hurry.

Have a reporter from each group report by posting the group map and talking about it.

Extension

Draw a large idea map for all learners on the board or another large sheet of paper, adding new suggestions as each group reports. Have learners copy the large map into their notebooks.

What's the Problem?

Follow the suggestions on p. 5 for identifying and analyzing problems.

- Allow five minutes for learners to discuss the question with a partner. Then have one partner from each pair report briefly on their discussion.
- Elicit examples. Everyone can be cheated, but very young people,

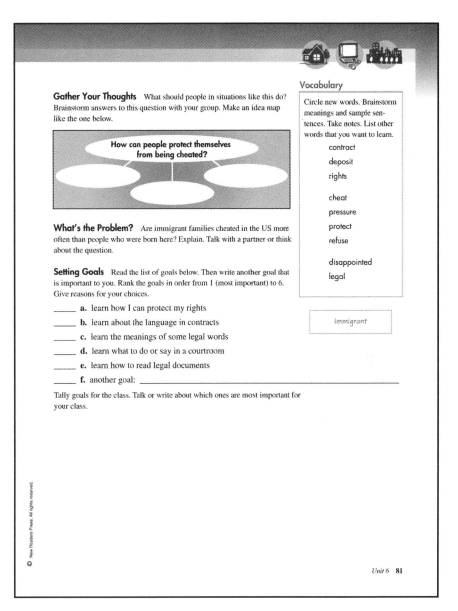

the elderly, and new immigrants may be cheated more often.
- Ask learners if they know of anyone that has been cheated who is not in one of these categories.

Setting Goals

Follow the suggestions on p. 5 for setting goals.

Lesson 1: Read the Fine Print!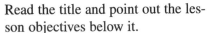

Read the title and point out the lesson objectives below it.

- Tell learners that this lesson will show them how a contract can protect their rights. They will also make a class list of legal terms.

Tell learners that *fine* means *small*. Show examples of *fine print* in a contract, other legal document, or product information sheet. Then ask these questions:

- Why do you think some things are written in *fine print?*
- Is it always important to read the *fine print* in an ad or contract? Why or why not?

Question

Read the question aloud. Ask learners if they have ever signed a contract in English without reading it.

- Is it sometimes OK to sign a contract without reading carefully? If yes, when and why?
- When should you read every word?
- When should you talk to a lawyer before signing?

Attention Box

This vocabulary should be understood, but learners should not be expected to produce the words at this point.

Photo

Follow the suggestions on pp. 4–5 for talking about the photo.

- Have learners read the question in the speech bubble aloud. Ask who can answer the question.
- Encourage learners to tell more about Mr. and Mrs. Wu from what they see in the photo.

Reading Tip

Have learners read the tip silently. Point out the bold type in the contract and have learners scan the bold print. Then ask these questions:

- What did you learn?

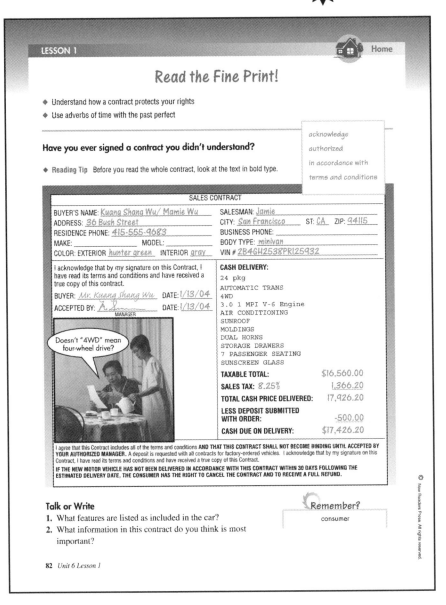

- Why was some information in bold print?

Learners may now contrast *fine print* with *bold print*. Ask these questions:

- What kind of information is usually printed in *fine print?*
- What kind of information is usually in *bold print?*

Have learners read the contract again more carefully.

Talk or Write

This exercise builds skill in reading contracts.

- After groups answer the questions, ask one group to answer each for the class.

- Ask if other groups agree or can add anything to the answer.

Answers

1. 24 pkg.; automatic transmission; four-wheel drive; 3.01 MPI V-6 engine; air conditioning; sunroof; moldings; dual horns; storage drawers; 7 passenger seating; sunscreen glass.

2. Answers will vary, but may include the cost of the car; the condition that the car must be delivered within 30 days or the consumer can cancel the contract and receive a full refund; and the list of features.

Vocabulary

Follow the suggestions on p. 6 for introducing and reinforcing vocabulary words.

- Have learners look again at the contract.
- Ask if they found any other unfamiliar words that are not in the vocabulary list.
- Have learners write the unfamiliar words in their notebooks. Then have them look the words up in a dictionary or ask another learner for the meaning.

Group Chat

Use Customizable Master 3 (3-Column Chart). Make a copy for each learner.

- Tell partners to choose one of the questions in the book and change it from present perfect to past perfect.
- Have them write the questions they chose as headings at the top of their charts.
- Tell the pairs to ask five classmates both questions.
- Do a quick whole-group survey to assure that all five questions are being asked.
- Allow a set time (e.g., between 5 and 10 minutes) for the interviews.
- Ask one learner from each pair to report the answers to their questions while the other learner tallies the responses on the board.

Grammar Talk

Follow the suggestions on p. 7 for introducing the grammar point. Learners will have passive recognition of this point because they heard it used in the Group Chat.

- Review the difference between main and dependent clauses. (Main clauses can stand alone; dependent clauses cannot.)
- After a volunteer reads a main clause and its dependent clause,

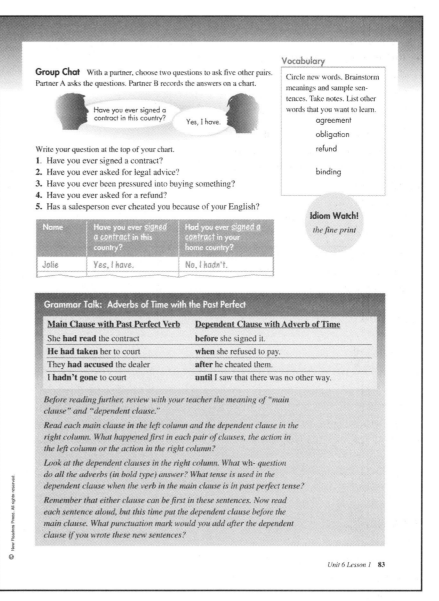

ask which happened first, the action on the left or the action on the right.

- Learners may be confused by the negative with *until* in the last sentence. Provide these examples:

I hadn't studied English until I came to the US. *(First I came to the US, and then I studied English.)*

I hadn't met my friend until I came to this school. *(First I came to this school, and then I met my friend.)*

- Ask for volunteers to answer the questions at the bottom of the box.

Answers

In the first sentence, the action in the *left* column happened first. In the other sentences, the action in the *right* column happened first.

The adverbs in bold type answer the question *when*. The simple past is used in the dependent clause.

A comma follows the dependent clause when it comes before the main clause.

 Assign Workbook pp. 39–40.

Activity A

Tell learners to look at their Group Chat charts from the previous page.

- Read the example in the student book aloud. Then create a similar model sentence using information from a learner's chart.
- Have partners trade notebooks and read one another's sentences.

Activity B

Make the eight cards according to the instructions in the book. Mix up the cards and lay them facedown on a table or desk.

- Have two learners begin playing Concentration, following the directions in the student book. Have remaining learners gather around as observers.
- When all the cards have been matched, mix them up, lay them facedown again, and start another game with two different learners.
- Expand the game. Have groups of four or more make their own sets of cards based on their Group Chat charts. Have them play Concentration in their groups.

Use Unit Master 51 (Grammar: Concentration) to provide additional cards for Activity B.

- After groups have played the game a few times, have all groups pass their cards to another group and play again.
- At the end of the activity, collect the cards, band them in sets, and save them for future reviews or individual enrichment.

Activity C

Put learners in groups to brainstorm answers to the three questions.

- Write these three headings on a large sheet of paper: *Teacher, Student, School*.
- As each group reports its answers, ask the class, "Do you agree? Should it be part of the class contract?"

Activity A   Group Chat Follow-Up Work with your partner. In your notebook, write sentences with the answers from the Class Chat chart.

Jolie has signed a contract in this country, but she hadn't signed a
contract in her home country before coming here.

Activity B   Play Concentration with your group. On a set of 3 × 5 cards, write these clauses, each clause on a separate card:

- I had decided to take an English class . . .
- I had planned to write you a note . . .
- I hadn't thought about our agreement . . .
- He took her to court . . .

- . . . before I came to the US.
- . . . when I had the time.
- . . . until you asked me to pay.
- . . . after she refused to pay the bill.

Using these cards as models, each person should make another set of eight cards with his or her own clauses. The first clause in each sentence should have a past perfect verb. The second clause should begin with an adverb of time and have a past tense verb.

Put all the cards together, mix them up, and put them on a table with the words down. The first player turns over any two cards. If they make a logical, realistic sentence, the player keeps them and turns over two more. If they do not make a logical sentence, the next player takes a turn. The game ends when all cards are matched. The person with the most cards win.

If someone doesn't think that a sentence is logical, that person explains why. The player who made the match explains why it is logical. The group can discuss and vote to decide whether the player should keep the cards.

Activity C   Do you have a class contract? Think about these questions, and brainstorm answers in your group.

- What does your teacher expect from you as a student?
- What do you expect from your teacher?
- What obligations do you and your teacher have to the school?

TASK 1:   *Make a Class List of Legal Terms*

Follow these steps to make a class list of legal terms (words or expressions that have a legal meaning). You can use the list as a reference during the rest of this unit. Be sure to leave room for more terms.

1. Reread the contract on page 82. Pay special attention to the small print.
2. Make a list of the *legal terms*, or words and expressions that have a legal meaning. Talk about their meanings in your group. If no one in your group knows a word, find it in a dictionary.
3. Work together with your teacher to make the class list of legal terms.
4. Make a wall chart of the terms and their meanings.

84 *Unit 6 Lesson 1*

- As learners accept conditions for the class contract, enter them under the appropriate heading.
- Review the contract periodically, adding or deleting items.

Task 1

Use the vocabulary lists learners generated earlier in this lesson (p. 83).

- Tell groups to write a brief definition for each term, using prior knowledge or a dictionary.
- Combine lists to make a class list. Assign several learners to work on a reference wall chart of legal terms. Be sure to leave room to add new terms.

- Post the chart for learner reference for the remainder of the course.

Lesson 2: Taking Legal Action

Read the title and point out the lesson objectives below it.

- Tell learners that in this lesson they will learn how to take legal action.
- They will also learn to listen to recorded messages in English.

Question

Read the introductory question aloud.

Photo

Follow the suggestions on pp. 4–5 for talking about the photo. Ask if anyone has ever received help from co-workers in the way Mrs. Wu does in the photo. If not, ask learners who usually gives them advice about legal matters.

Listening Tip

Read the tip aloud. Ask learners about strategies they use to understand recorded messages. Do they use any of the five listed here?

Play the audio or read the listening script on pp. 139–140. Follow the suggestions on p. 5 for listening comprehension.

- Ask learners to take notes as they listen.
- Play the tape or read the script as many times as learners request it. Tell learners that there is no limit to the number of replays.
- Allow time for pairs to talk about the message. Tell learners, "Your partner may have understood some parts that you've missed. Share these with each other."

Talk or Write

This exercise helps learners understand a recorded message.

Possible Answers

1. She must first try to resolve the problem out of court. She must notify the car dealer she plans to sue. She must get the forms at the Municipal Building and pay the $20 fee. She must collect

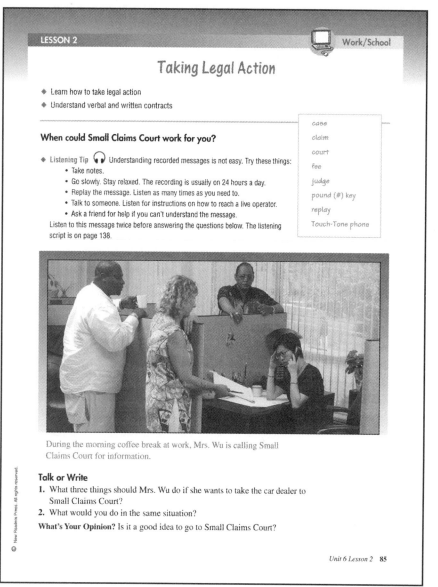

LESSON 2 — Work/School

Taking Legal Action

- Learn how to take legal action
- Understand verbal and written contracts

case
claim
court
fee
judge
pound (#) key
replay
Touch-Tone phone

When could Small Claims Court work for you?

- Listening Tip 🎧 Understanding recorded messages is not easy. Try these things:
  - Take notes.
  - Go slowly. Stay relaxed. The recording is usually on 24 hours a day.
  - Replay the message. Listen as many times as you need to.
  - Talk to someone. Listen for instructions on how to reach a live operator.
  - Ask a friend for help if you can't understand the message.

Listen to this message twice before answering the questions below. The listening script is on page 138.

During the morning coffee break at work, Mrs. Wu is calling Small Claims Court for information.

Talk or Write

1. What three things should Mrs. Wu do if she wants to take the car dealer to Small Claims Court?
2. What would you do in the same situation?

What's Your Opinion? Is it a good idea to go to Small Claims Court?

Unit 6 Lesson 2 **85**

any papers or contracts that support her case and present the case in court.
2. Answers will vary.

What's Your Opinion?

Extension

Set up a debate activity.

- Divide the group into two camps—those who support going to Small Claims Court and those who do not.
- Ask each group to present its point of view. Tell learners to convince the opposition to change sides, literally, so that members of the other side cross the room to their camp.

- Have group members alternate speaking in two-minute turns. Set a rule that no one is to interrupt a speaker during the allotted two minutes.

Vocabulary

Follow the suggestions on p. 6 for introducing and reinforcing vocabulary words. Then do the following:

- Review the list of legal terms learners made for Task 1 (p. 84).
- As learners add new words to their lists, remind them of this learning strategy: *Select and practice only words you do not know.*

Pronunciation Target

Before learners listen to the words, make sure they understand them. If some do not, ask those who speak the same first language and *do* understand to explain the words or translate them. Allow no more than five minutes for this activity.

Play the audio or read the words. Follow the suggestions for pronunciation on p. 7.

Activity A

Read your own or these additional examples to learners:

- The **pl**aintiff did not **pl**an to **sp**end a lot of time on his **cl**aim form.
- The **sm**all company takes **pr**ide in its **pr**oducts.
- The **st**udents felt **pr**essured to **sp**eak in **cl**ass.

For additional pronunciation practice, use Unit Master 52 (Vocabulary: Syllable Stress) now or at any time during the rest of the unit.

Technology Extra

This is a good activity for individual learner practice.

 Assign Workbook pp. 41–42.

Activity B

Direct learners' attention again to the listening tip on p. 85.

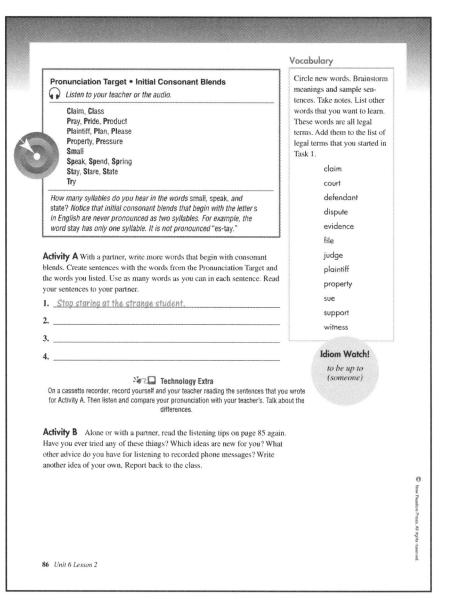

Pronunciation Target • Initial Consonant Blends

Listen to your teacher or the audio.

Claim, Class
Pray, Pride, Product
Plaintiff, Plan, Please
Property, Pressure
Small
Speak, Spend, Spring
Stay, Stare, State
Try

How many syllables do you hear in the words small, speak, *and* state? *Notice that initial consonant blends that begin with the letter* s *in English are never pronounced as two syllables. For example, the word* stay *has only one syllable. It is not pronounced "es-tay."*

Activity A With a partner, write more words that begin with consonant blends. Create sentences with the words from the Pronunciation Target and the words you listed. Use as many words as you can in each sentence. Read your sentences to your partner.

1. *Stop staring at the strange student.*
2. _____
3. _____
4. _____

Technology Extra
On a cassette recorder, record yourself and your teacher reading the sentences that you wrote for Activity A. Then listen and compare your pronunciation with your teacher's. Talk about the differences.

Activity B Alone or with a partner, read the listening tips on page 85 again. Have you ever tried any of these things? Which ideas are new for you? What other advice do you have for listening to recorded phone messages? Write another idea of your own. Report back to the class.

Vocabulary

Circle new words. Brainstorm meanings and sample sentences. Take notes. List other words that you want to learn. These words are all legal terms. Add them to the list of legal terms that you started in Task 1.

claim
court
defendant
dispute
evidence
file
judge
plaintiff
property
sue
support
witness

Idiom Watch!
to be up to (someone)

- On a large sheet of paper, write the head *Listening Tips for Recorded Messages.*
- Write only the first part of each tip under the head.
- Have learners suggest additional tips. Add them to the list.

If learners are unable to generate more tips, provide these:

- Listen for words that tell you to go back to the menu if you want to hear the message again.
- Write the message and have someone read it for you.
- Listen to the message again while looking at the words you wrote.
- Listen to the message again without looking at what you wrote.

In the US

Before learners read the passage, ask these questions to elicit examples of written and verbal contracts:

- Do you have a verbal or a written agreement with your landlord? If it is written, what do you call that agreement?
- Do we have a verbal or a written agreement that gives student/teacher obligations?
- Have you ever loaned money to someone? Did you write down the conditions for the return of the loan or did you agree verbally?

Write learner responses on the board. After learners read the paragraph silently, read it to them.

Compare Cultures

Put learners in groups by nationality. If there are more than a few learners for any country, create another group for that nationality.

To help learners compare countries, provide the following example:

In some countries, when people lend each other money (even large amounts), the verbal agreement is honored. In the US, most people think that verbal agreements are too risky. They want written contracts.

Activity C

If no one has seen or knows about a Small Claims Court case, ask learners to provide the same information about the Wus' case.

One Step Up

After learners practice the role-plays in their groups, they can perform them for the class.

- Assign a role for each learner.
- Before the role-play, provide some preparation time for learners to write the script.
- The defendant and the plaintiff should prepare a statement and a rebuttal for the presentation.

In the US   Written and Verbal Contracts

Mr. and Mrs. Wu had a written contract with the car dealer. Informal verbal agreements between friends are common when small amounts of money are involved. However, in the US a formal written contract is expected if the amount of money is large or if people don't know each other well. People in the US use contracts often and expect them in many situations.

Compare Cultures

In your home country, do people often make agreements without written contracts? When do people use written contracts? Work with a group of learners from your home country or culture. Talk with your teacher and your class about differences between the way people use contracts in the US and the way they use them in your home countries.

Activity C   Ask group members to tell about any court cases that they have seen or participated in. Choose one case and answer these questions:
- Who was the plaintiff?
- What was the dispute about?
- What evidence did the plaintiff present to support the case?
- What evidence did the defendant present?
- What was the decision? Did you agree with it?

In a group, present the case to the class. Explain clearly what happened.

One Step Up
In a group, take the roles of judge, plaintiff, defendant, and witnesses. Role-play the Wus' Small Claims Court case or the case that your group presented in Activity C.

Technology Extra
Students who have a VCR or a DVD recorder can record a TV show with a court scene. Watch the show in class. As you watch, stop the recording frequently to review legal terms used by the characters. Add any new terms to the list that you started in Task 1.

TASK 2: Listen to a Recorded Message
Listen to a recorded phone message. You and a partner call the same number and listen to the message. You could call the Small Claims Court number, another government service number, the 800 number of an airline, a movie theater for its schedule, etc. Take notes and compare. Report back to the class. Use the questions below as a guide for your report.
- Did both of you get the same message?
- Did you understand most of the message?
- How many times did you have to replay it?
- What parts were difficult to understand?

Unit 6 Lesson 2 87

- The judge and the witness should have at least two statements ready.

Technology Extra

If no learner has a VCR or a DVD recorder, record the program yourself.

Task 2

Bring in phone books so learners can find phone numbers for this task.

- Have partners decide on a business or agency to call and find the number in the phone book.

- If there is no telephone access for learners at your school or learning center, assign the phone calls as homework. Since partners are calling the same number, they can finish the task in class.
- Allow time in class for pairs to compare notes before they report back.

Lesson 3: Speaking Up for Your Rights 🔆www

Read the title and point out the lesson objectives below it.

- Tell learners that in this lesson they will learn more about their rights and court procedures. They will also learn to present an argument in Small Claims Court.
- Ask learners to define the idiomatic expression *speak up for.* If they cannot, tell them it means *to express an opinion freely and directly.* It can also mean *to demand or insist on.*

Question

Read the question aloud to learners. Assign the question as a one-paragraph essay. Have some volunteers read their essays to the class.

Photo

Tell learners to look at the photo of Mr. and Mrs. Wu in court. Ask a learner to read Mr. Wu's speech bubble.

Reading Tip

Read the tip aloud; then do the following:

- Ask learners how they imagine the courtroom. How does their image compare with the one in the photo? Is their courtroom filled with people, or is it only the Wus and the judge?
- Have learners share their experiences and describe the physical environment of a courtroom they have been to in the past, whether in the US or their home countries. Discuss how such images help them understand the story.
- Tell learners that they will read the story silently twice. As they read the story the second time, have them pay close attention to the images in their mind.
- Help learners visualize the story. Ask them to try to see Mr. Wu's facial expression as he speaks; Mr. and Mrs. Wu reading the cue cards; the judge's reaction, facial

---

---

expressions, and actions as she tells them the verdict; and the reaction of Mr. and Mrs. Wu when they receive their check.

Conclude the reading activity by reading the story to learners.

- Point out the pronunciation of initial consonant blends and word stress.
- Ask them to circle words with initial consonant blends and underline words that are stressed in each sentence.

Talk or Write

This exercise helps learners visualize what they read.

Possible Answers

1. They felt nervous because this was the first time they had to defend their rights in court. They controlled their feelings by preparing well. They prepared their speech and wrote notes on cards.
2. They feel proud and confident.

Vocabulary

Follow the suggestions on p. 6 for introducing and reinforcing vocabulary words.

 To review all unit vocabulary, use Unit Master 53 (Game: Vocabulary Race) now or at any time during the rest of the unit.

Class Chat

 Use Customizable Master 2 (2-Column Chart). Follow the suggestions on p. 7 for customizing and duplicating the master. Make a copy for each learner.

If there are more than 10 learners, assign one question to a pair. One person asks the questions; the other writes the responses.

Grammar Talk

Follow the suggestions on p. 7 for introducing the grammar points.

Box 1: Provide more examples for each of the three prepositions:
- Americans celebrate Independence Day <u>on</u> July 4.
- Our lunch break is <u>at</u> noon.
- Some places get snow <u>in</u> January.

<u>One Step Up</u>

Ask learners to write sentences using the prepositions correctly. Ask them if there are any sentences with these prepositions that confuse them. Discuss the examples and the rules.

Box 2: Ask learners for more examples using each article. Write learners' sentences on the board. Monitor errors by asking whether the statement is nonspecific, general, or specific.

Box 3: Write some sentences showing incorrect use of gerunds and infinitives on the board or an overhead transparency. Use sentences like the ones below. Ask learners why they are wrong:

Mr. Wu wants winning the case.

He will have suing the dealer.

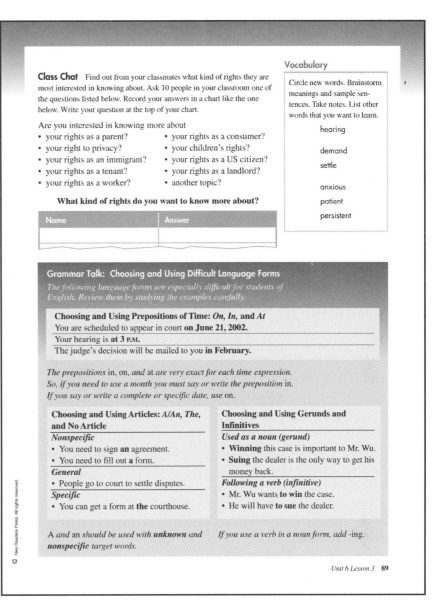

Class Chat Find out from your classmates what kind of rights they are most interested in knowing about. Ask 10 people in your classroom one of the questions listed below. Record your answers in a chart like the one below. Write your question at the top of your chart.

Are you interested in knowing more about
- your rights as a parent?
- your right to privacy?
- your rights as an immigrant?
- your rights as a tenant?
- your rights as a worker?
- your rights as a consumer?
- your children's rights?
- your rights as a US citizen?
- your rights as a landlord?
- another topic?

What kind of rights do you want to know more about?

Name	Answer

Vocabulary

Circle new words. Brainstorm meanings and sample sentences. Take notes. List other words that you want to learn.

hearing

demand

settle

anxious

patient

persistent

Grammar Talk: Choosing and Using Difficult Language Forms

The following language forms are especially difficult for students of English. Review them by studying the examples carefully.

Choosing and Using Prepositions of Time: *On, In,* and *At*
You are scheduled to appear in court **on June 21, 2002.**
Your hearing is **at 3 P.M.**
The judge's decision will be mailed to you **in February.**

The prepositions in, on, and at are very exact for each time expression.
So, if you need to use a month you must say or write the preposition in.
If you say or write a complete or specific date, use on.

Choosing and Using Articles: *A/An, The,* and No Article
Nonspecific
- You need to sign **an** agreement.
- You need to fill out **a** form.

General
- People go to court to settle disputes.

Specific
- You can get a form at **the** courthouse.

A *and* an *should be used with* **unknown** *and* **nonspecific** *target words.*

Choosing and Using Gerunds and Infinitives
Used as a noun (gerund)
- **Winning** this case is important to Mr. Wu.
- **Suing** the dealer is the only way to get his money back.

Following a verb (infinitive)
- Mr. Wu wants **to win** the case.
- He will have **to sue** the dealer.

If you use a verb in a noun form, add -ing.

Unit 6 Lesson 3 **89**

Learners' reason should be the rule in the book: *You cannot use a gerund if it follows a verb.*

 Assign Workbook pp. 43–44.

Activity A

Learners take turns dictating complete sentences and filling in the blanks. Model the first two sentences with a learner.

Activity B

Have learners look at their charts from the Class Chat. Assign learners in groups according to the question they expressed interest in.

- Limit groups to four learners. If more learners are interested in the same topic, form a new group.
- Point out some strategies for effective communication. Tell learners to prepare a few short sentences that argue their point clearly.
- Model statements like these:

  We believe that a parent has a right to discipline her child.

  Interference from government agencies results in a parent's loss of authority at home.

- Be sure each learner has an opportunity to speak. Each should make at least two statements, one giving the point of view, the other stating the rationale.
- If two groups are making the same argument, have all learners analyze and compare their quality. Then have a vote for the most effective one.

Task 3

Have the class form a circle to talk about the problems.

- Provide an example of a good case for Small Claims Court, such as this one:

  The parking garage attendant scratched my car when he parked another car too close to mine. It will cost $200 to repaint my car.

- Ask learners if anyone would like to share their experiences. How did they defend themselves? What did they say?

Activity A   You are Partner A or Partner B. Cover your partner's side of the exercise. Dictate, or read, the sentences printed in red to your partner. Then listen to your partner's dictation. Fill in the blanks.

Partner A

1. Mr. Wu's case was heard on January 4.
2. He arrived _____ 3 P.M., exactly on time.
3. In February he'll get his money back.
4. _____ the day he gets his money back, he'll be very happy.
5. Winning his case in court made him very proud.
6. He wanted _____ the dealer from cheating other people.

Partner B

1. His case was heard _____ January 4.
2. He arrived at 3 P.M., exactly on time.
3. _____ February he'll get his money back.
4. On the day he gets his money back, he'll be very happy.
5. _____ his case in court made him very proud.
6. He wanted to stop the dealer from cheating other people.

Activity B   Look at your Class Chat responses. Form a group with three people. Discuss your rights. Use the idea map below as a model. Present your map to your class. Your classmates have the right to disagree with you. As a group, defend your point of view.

Rights as a Parent

- I have the right to
- teach my child how to behave
- protect my child from physical danger
- speak to my child's teacher
- educate my child in my culture
- have my child tested for learning disabilities

 TASK 3:   *Present Your Argument*

Think of a problem in your own life or the life of someone you know that could be settled in Small Claims Court. Describe the problem and the arguments that would be made during the court hearing:

- arguments used by you
- arguments used by the defendant
- the defendant's response to your arguments
- your response to the defendant's arguments

Use Customizable Master 8 (Johari Window). Make a copy for each learner.

- After the general discussion, have learners work with Johari Window organizers.
- Learners may work alone or in pairs. Those who work alone should present their ideas to a partner. Those who work in pairs should present to the class.

Peer Assessment

Give a copy of Generic Assessment Master 15 (Peer Assessment Form for Projects and Tasks) to each learner.

Follow the suggestions for peer assessment on p. 4.

Have partners practice their presentation to another pair before presenting to the class.

Tell learners to complete and exchange the forms before doing their final presentations.

Assessment

Use Generic Assessment Master 10 (Oral Communication Rubric) to evaluate presentations.

Review Unit Skills

See pp. 8–9 for suggestions on games and activities to review the unit vocabulary and grammar.

Unit 6 Challenge Reading ⟨www⟩

Reading Tip

Read the tip aloud with learners. Then have learners skim the questions.

Ask learners to predict what might be included in this article. Predictions might include these:

- The article is about different types of service contracts.
- It is about the advantages and disadvantages of buying a service contract.
- The article describes the difference between service contracts and warranties.

List learner predictions on the board or a large sheet of paper. Compare these with the actual information after the final reading of the article.

Challenge Reading

- Tell learners to look first at the questions following the article. Then have learners read the article silently, looking for the answers.
- Instruct pairs of learners to read the article as if it were an interview. First one learner asks the question, and the other answers it. Then learners switch roles.
- Circulate to monitor individual pronunciation of consonant blends and take notes on errors.
- Listen for the pronunciation of these words: con**tr**act, **pr**oduct, **tr**ansportation, la**st**s, co**st**s, again**st**, comp**l**ete.

After the reading, create a minilesson on pronunciation.

- List the above words on the board or an overhead transparency.
- Have learners identify all the consonant blends they have practiced in this unit.

◆ **Reading Tip** Before you read, look over the entire guide. Skim over some of the questions to get an idea of what the guide covers. Then read the guide carefully, looking for the main ideas.

Have you ever bought a technology product that needed repair after its warranty expired? Did you know that many manufacturers and stores offer to fix your product if you purchase a service contract when you purchase the product? Here is some information to remember the next time you need to decide whether to buy a service contract. As you read this guide, think about whether a service contract could have been useful to you in the past.

Service Contracts and Extended Warranties

To Purchase or Not to Purchase?

Q. *What is a service contract?*

A. A service contract is a kind of repair insurance, sometimes called an "extended warranty" or a "service agreement," that you buy separately from the product.

Q. *How is a service contract different from a warranty?*

A. Essentially, a warranty is not bought separately. It comes with the product you purchase.

Q. *Are there different kinds of service contracts?*

A. Yes, there can be many different kinds of service contracts. For example, a service contract may require you to pay a certain amount for repair service. Or it may require you to pay labor or transportation charges.

Q. *Are you saying that a service contract may not pay for repair service when I need it?*

A. It may not pay for everything. For example:
- It may pay for labor only or parts only.
- It may not pay for every part.
- It may limit the number of repairs.
- You may have to pay a certain amount for each service call.
- It may not pay for in-home service.

Q. *What are some pros and cons of service contracts?*

A. Service contracts may help you pay for expensive repairs and routine maintenance. On the other hand, be sure the service you receive is given by technicians who are trained to work on your product brand and who will use appropriate replacement parts.

Unit 6 Challenge Reading **91**

Talk or Write

<u>Possible Answers</u>

1. One main point of this article is that it is very important to read the terms of any service contract offered at an extra cost.
2. Answers to the first part of the question will vary. Some of the most important terms and expressions to remember are *service contract, warranty, weigh the cost, routine maintenance,* and *compare.*
3. An important question relates to different types of coverage and whether the services they provide are worth the money.
4. Answers will vary.

Writing Task

Tell learners to write their first draft quickly, without worrying much about grammar or spelling. After finishing a first draft, they should go back to look at organization and move ideas around until they have a well-organized essay.

Have learners trade papers with a partner for a peer edit. They should tell their partners one thing they liked about the paper and one thing that was not clear. Then they can help each other correct any grammar or spelling mistakes.

Learners can use Generic Assessment Master 14 (Writing Checklist and Error Correction Symbols) as they revise and edit their writing.

Q. How can I make sure that the service contract I buy with a new product does not duplicate the warranty or overlap it?

A. Read the warranty to find out how long the warranty lasts and what it covers. Your new electronic product warranty may cover most repair costs, sometimes for 90 days, sometimes for a year or more.

Q. My VCR needs maintenance service to keep the heads clean. Can a service contract help pay the cost?

A. Yes, some service contracts do cover routine maintenance.

Q. How can I decide whether to buy a service contract?

A. Read the warranty, read the service contract, and compare. Weigh the cost of the service contract against maintenance and repair bills you may have later. If you cannot first read the service contract, do not buy it! Make sure all the blank lines are completed.

Q. Who sells service contracts?

A. The retailer who offers you a service contract may be selling it for the dealer, the manufacturer, or a separate service company. Ask the salesperson for time to study the contract. Also ask if the retailer sells more than one kind of service contract. If so, compare them.

Q. What happens if my service contract company goes out of business?

A. Unfortunately, there is little you can do if this happens. The best way to protect yourself is to make sure before purchase that the company is reputable and has insurance so you can get a refund.

Talk or Write

1. What are some of the main points of this guide?
2. Did you learn any new words? What are the most important terms to remember?
3. Which questions do you feel are most important?
4. Which information surprised you?

Writing Task Use an idea map to list the five most important points you want to remember from the article. Then write a short paragraph that describes the most important parts of a service contract. Include a title and a topic sentence.

<u>92</u> *Unit 6 Challenge Reading*

Unit 6 Project

Learners create a personal glossary of legal terms.

Get Ready

- Tell learners that this is a project that requires time and group effort to complete.
- Ask learners the meaning of the word *glossary.* If they have difficulty responding, tell them it is "a list of specialized or technical words with their definitions."
- You may want to have learners use bilingual dictionaries to find legal terms, since they may know the terms in their first language but not in English.

Do the Work

Assign different pairs of volunteers for each task:

- One to alphabetize the words
- One to type them on a computer or write them
- Two or three to do research and write rules of conduct for local courts
- Two or three to report on court procedures

Present

Each group can choose any of the three ways to do the presentation.

Use Unit Master 53 (Game: Vocabulary Race). Learners can use this list of words to create their glossary.

Learners who chose to create and distribute the glossary should talk about their effort to the class. Have them use these questions below as a presentation guide:

- Who received the copies?
- How did you decide who would receive them?
- How did people react to the glossary? What did they say?
- How did you distribute the glossary? (e.g., in person? by mail or e-mail?)

UNIT 6 Project

Create a Personal Legal Glossary

A glossary is a mini-dictionary of words used for a specific purpose. Develop a glossary of legal terms.

Get Ready

Look at the list of legal terms you started in Task 1 and any new legal words from Lessons 2 and 3. Brainstorm other words that would be useful to people in legal situations.

Do the Work

1. Create a legal glossary by alphabetizing your word list and adding definitions. Check the dictionary for exact meanings.
2. Type your list on a computer, or have a group member who has good handwriting write it.
3. Add other useful information. For example, what are the rules for court conduct in your area? Check the Small Claims Court or the Internet. Call Small Claims Court in your area for a brochure, or ask someone in the group who knows someone who has been to court.
4. Have group members watch a court TV program and report back to the group their observations on courtroom procedures and vocabulary.

Present

Present your project in a way that you enjoy.

- Give your glossary a title and simple cover. Publish it for students in another class.

OR

- Make copies of your list for people from other countries who need to know more about the US legal system.

OR

- Dramatize your courtroom knowledge:
  - Brainstorm to choose an issue.
  - Assign roles: plaintiff, defendant, judge, witnesses, and other roles.
  - Plan a simple court scene and practice it in your group.
  - Present the case to classmates.
    Note: The judge can decide who wins the case, or you can ask classmates to vote on the winner.

Unit 6 Project **93**

Learners who chose to dramatize their courtroom knowledge will need time to rehearse. Provide classroom time for different groups to prepare their presentations.

Assessment

To do a formal assessment of this project, use Generic Assessment Master 10 (Oral Communication Rubric) to evaluate the presentations.

Assign Workbook p. 45 (Check Your Progress).

Use Unit Master 54 (Unit Checkup/Review) whenever you complete this unit.

Self Assessment

Give each learner copies of Generic Assessment Masters 12 (Speaking and Listening Self-Checks) and 13 (Writing and Reading Self-Checks). Go over the items together. The completed forms will become part of each learner's portfolio.

Unit 7: Participating in Your Community

Materials for the Unit

- Voter registration form for each learner
- Letters to the editor from newspapers and/or magazines
- Card stock or colored paper
- Clips or rings to hold papers
- Customizable Masters 3–5, 8, 9
- Generic Assessment Masters 14, 15
- Unit Masters 55–59

Participating in Your Community

Read the title; then review the four groups of unit goals listed below it.

Ask learners what it means to participate in your country and community. Then ask these questions:

- Do you think it is important to participate actively in your country and community?
- Do you participate actively? Why or why not?

Photo

Follow the suggestions on pp. 4–5 for talking about the photo. Talk about the thought bubble. Ask what Galina is referring to when she thinks, "Why didn't I know about this?"

Question

Read the question below the arrow.

- Ask learners to tell about their first voting experience in the US or another country.
- Have learners who have never voted describe attitudes in their home country toward voting.

Caption

Have learners read the caption silently.

- Ask if there are words you need to explain. For example, learners may know the word *proposal* only as a *proposal* of marriage. Ask what kind of a *proposal* would be on a voting ballot.

Participating in Your Community

Becoming an Active Community Participant

Work/School 1   Home 2   Community 3

- ◆ **Vocabulary** Language for participating in a democracy
- ◆ **Language** Present and past participles used as adjectives • Past participles of irregular verbs
- ◆ **Pronunciation** Disappearing /h/ of function words
- ◆ **Culture** Tradition of self-reliance and community involvement

> Why didn't I know about this?

What do you like and not like about voting in your home country or in the US?

Galina, a new citizen, is voting for the first time. She becomes anxious when she sees proposals on the ballot. She selects her candidates, but she doesn't know how to react to the proposals. People are waiting, so she makes a quick choice and leaves, feeling that she has wasted her vote.

Think and Talk
1. Where is Galina? What do you see in the picture?
2. What happened? Why do you think Galina felt she wasted her vote?
3. Has anything like this happened to you or to anyone you know? Explain.
4. How should people prepare to vote?

What's Your Opinion? If you are not sure about a candidate or an issue, should you vote anyway? Why or why not?

candidate

waste

94 *Unit 7*

- After explaining any new words, have learners check the dictionary definitions.
- Ask volunteers to close their books and paraphrase the caption orally or in writing.

<u>One Step Up</u>

Have partners write their own photo caption, using some new words from this unit.

Think and Talk

Follow the suggestions on p. 6 for comprehension questions.

<u>Answers</u>
1. Galina is in a voting booth.
2. Galina became anxious when she saw proposals that she hadn't

expected on the ballot. She voted without fully understanding them. She was prepared to vote for candidates but not for proposals.
3. Answers will vary.
4. Answers will vary. They should prepare by reading, attending meetings, asking for opinions, and studying the issues.

What's Your Opinion?

Learners may not know that people do not have to vote on every issue and candidate on the ballot. Galina could have voted for the candidates but not for the proposals.

Vocabulary

Follow the suggestions on p. 6 for introducing and reinforcing vocabulary words.

- First brainstorm meanings. Then have groups of learners use all of the vocabulary words to write sentences about governments, citizens, and elections in the US or other countries.
- Circulate among the groups to give advice and assistance.

Gather Your Thoughts

Distribute a copy of Customizable Master 5 (Idea Map) to each group, or tell each group to create an idea map using the map in the book as a model.

- Brainstorm what a responsible citizen needs to know and do.
- Have groups use their idea maps to organize the ideas generated during the brainstorming activity.
- Circulate among groups. Offer suggestions for categorizing their ideas. Ask why they included a particular item in a category. If their ideas do not fit the categories given in the text, tell them to make new headings.
- Draw an idea map on a large sheet of paper. Incorporate learners' ideas and post it in the room.

What's the Problem?

Follow the suggestions on p. 5 for identifying and analyzing problems.

Learners may say that limited English language skills prevent them from being well informed on issues. Respond with this research project:

- Ask if anyone knows how to get information on national and community issues in languages other than English.
- Appoint learners to research national and community issues and report back to the class.
- List sources on the board (e.g., foreign language newspapers,

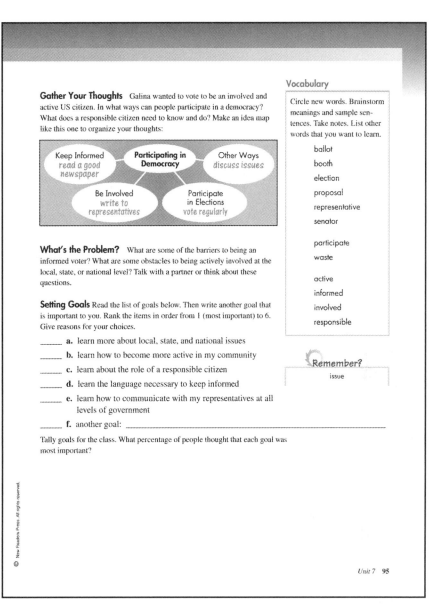

Gather Your Thoughts Galina wanted to vote to be an involved and active US citizen. In what ways can people participate in a democracy? What does a responsible citizen need to know and do? Make an idea map like this one to organize your thoughts:

Keep Informed
read a good newspaper

Participating in Democracy

Other Ways
discuss issues

Be Involved
write to representatives

Participate in Elections
vote regularly

What's the Problem? What are some of the barriers to being an informed voter? What are some obstacles to being actively involved at the local, state, or national level? Talk with a partner or think about these questions.

Setting Goals Read the list of goals below. Then write another goal that is important to you. Rank the items in order from 1 (most important) to 6. Give reasons for your choices.

_____ a. learn more about local, state, and national issues

_____ b. learn how to become more active in my community

_____ c. learn about the role of a responsible citizen

_____ d. learn the language necessary to keep informed

_____ e. learn how to communicate with my representatives at all levels of government

_____ f. another goal: _____

Tally goals for the class. What percentage of people thought that each goal was most important?

Vocabulary

Circle new words. Brainstorm meanings and sample sentences. Take notes. List other words that you want to learn.

ballot

booth

election

proposal

representative

senator

participate

waste

active

informed

involved

responsible

Remember?

issue

Unit 7 **95**

web sites, organizations that provide services for immigrants from specific parts of the world, service organizations).

- Assign specific learners to research organizations and publications and report back. They can ask friends and neighbors, call organizations to ask what services they provide, check phone books, and use a search engine to find web pages.

Some learners may feel that their vote or effort will not make enough difference. Others may feel that since they are not enthusiastic about any specific candidate, it will not matter for whom they vote.

- As learners present such barriers, ask the class to suggest ways to overcome them.
- List the suggestions next to each barrier on a large sheet of paper and post the list in class.

Setting Goals

Follow the suggestions on p. 5 for setting goals.

Lesson 1: Participating in Elections

Read the title and point out the lesson objectives below it.
- Tell learners that in this lesson they will learn about voting and fill out a voter registration form.

Question

Have pairs of learners discuss the question and share their responses with the whole class.

Attention Box/Idiom Watch

Model pronunciation and discuss the meanings of the words and idiomatic expressions. Tell learners that this unit will help them understand these words and expressions in context.

Photo

Follow the suggestions on pp. 4–5 for talking about the photo. Then ask these questions:
- Where is Galina standing?
- Where did the voting take place? Where does it usually take place in your neighborhood?
- Do you think Galina is proud? Explain.

Reading Tip

Read the tip aloud. Then follow the suggestions on pp. 5–6 for in-class reading.
- Have partners read the interview twice, taking turns being the reporter and Galina.
- As pairs read, circulate to take notes on pronunciation. Practice pronunciation at the end.

Talk or Write

This exercise develops skill in reading an interview.

Follow the suggestions on p. 6 for comprehension questions. Where possible, use the questions to stimulate further discussion.

Possible Answers
1. Answers will vary. Discuss the meaning of the word *conscientious*. Have learners support their opinions with evidence from the reading.
2. The best answer would be *both*. She felt proud and happy to vote but a little frustrated because she was not completely informed.
3. Voting is also a little intimidating; I hope my vote was correctly recorded; I was too embarrassed; part of the ballot was confusing; I wish that I had learned more.
4. She had talked about the candidates. She could have read the ballot before voting.

Extension

In her response to the question, "Do you believe that one person's vote can make a difference?" Galina shows that she thinks this is a unique quality of the US. Discuss this point. Ask, "Can one person really make a difference in the US? Can one person make a difference in other countries too?"

One Step Up
Have pairs of learners role-play the interview using the reporter's questions but creating their own responses.

Vocabulary

Follow the suggestions on p. 6 for introducing and reinforcing vocabulary words.

Class Chat

 Use Customizable Master 4 (4-Column Chart). Follow the suggestions on p. 7 for customizing and duplicating the master. Make a copy for each learner.

- Have learners walk around and ask the questions of at least five other learners.
- Using verbs of emotion, write a short list of past participles on a large sheet of paper. Post the list for learners to use in answering the questions. Include these participles:

  confused   fascinated
  intimidated bored
  embarrassed amazed

- Ask learners to add to this list if they use other verbs of emotion in their responses. Refer back to the list when you discuss the grammar point in this lesson.

Ongoing Assessment

While the learners are completing this activity, circulate and listen to their conversations. Monitor at least five different interactions, involving at least three pairs of learners. Take notes on how well the learners performed on these features:

a. General quality of responses
   0 = no response/wrong response
   1 = incomplete response
   2 = fluent response
b. General quality of interaction
   0 = confusion and breakdown in communication
   1 = inappropriate requests for repetition
   2 = smooth interaction
c. General quality of pronunciation
   0 = incomprehensible response
   1 = wrong word stress interrupting comprehension
   2 = comprehensible response

Class Chat Talk about your voting experience in the US or in your home country. How did you feel? What surprised you about the process? Record your answers in a chart like the one below.

Name	When did you vote?	How did you feel?	What was surprising?
Andrew	a year before I came to the US	excited	the large number of voters
Anna	a few months after I became a US citizen	intimidated	other parties on the ballot

Vocabulary

Circle new words. Brainstorm meanings and sample sentences. Take notes. List other words that you want to learn.

candidate

district

affordable

conscientious

democratic

embarrassed/embarrassing

fascinated/fascinating

intimidated/intimidating

Grammar Talk: Present and Past Participles as Adjectives

Notice that the verbs in the sentences on the left are all "verbs of emotion." See how they change when they are turned into adjectives.

Galina was **excited** by the elections.	The elections were **exciting** to Galina.
She was **confused** by the proposal on the ballot.	The proposal on the ballot was **confusing**.

*The past participle of a verb (verb + -ed or irregular form) and the present participle (verb + -ing) can be used as adjectives. The past participle tells how someone feels: "I am **fascinated** by the American political process." Fascinated says how I feel about the American political process. "The American political process is **fascinating** to me." The present participle, fascinating, describes something that will make someone feel fascinated.*

What happens to the verb when the subject of the sentence experiences the emotion? What happens to the verb when the subject does not experience the emotion?

Activity A Class Chat Follow-Up With a partner, take turns reading sentences. Partner A reads sentence 1. Partner B makes a new sentence, changing the past participle (*-ed*) to the present participle (*-ing*). Then Partner B reads sentence 2, and Partner A changes the sentence.

1. Galina was embarrassed by her lack of knowledge.

   Galina's lack of knowledge was embarrassing to her.

2. José is very interested in the democratic process.
3. People were confused by the ballot.
4. Galina is fascinated by politics.

Select learners who scored 2 in any category and have them model the interaction for the rest of the class.

Grammar Talk

Follow the suggestions on p. 7 for introducing the grammar point. Add the participles in the Grammar Talk to the list posted during the Class Chat.

 Use Unit Master 55 (Grammar: Present and Past Participles as Adjectives) now or at any time during the rest of the unit.

Answers

When the subject of the sentence experiences the emotion, the verb takes *-ed* (past participle). When the subject is not having the experience, the verb takes *-ing* (present participle).

Activity A

Model the first sentence with a volunteer. Have learners use their Class Chat charts to create more sentences.

Answers

2. The democratic process is very interesting to José.
3. The ballot was confusing to people.
4. Politics is fascinating to Galina.

 Assign Workbook pp. 46–47.

Unit 7 *Lesson 1* **97**

Activity B

Direct learners to the most relevant information on the card by asking these questions:

- Who is the registered voter?
- Where does Galina go to vote?
- Is parking available?
- Is the polling place accessible for handicapped people?
- What is the number of Galina's congressional district?
- What other districts are listed?
- At what time do the polls open?
- What is the date of primary elections in Galina's state?
- What is the date of general elections?

Elicit these responses to the directions in the student book:

- She received this card as proof that she is registered to vote.
- She needs the card to know when and where to vote. She also needs it to know her districts so she can find out about the candidates.

Activity C

Make two signs, *Yes* and *No*. Post them in different areas of the room.

- Start with a show of hands for each alternative. Model the activity. Select one person from the *Yes* group and one person from the *No* group to read the examples in the text.
- Ask learners to move to the area of the room *(Yes or No)* that represents their opinion. The learners in each area will constitute a group for this activity.
- Have each group prepare a minimum of three arguments that support their opinion.
- Tell anyone who is undecided to walk around, listen in on the discussions, and take notes, but not participate.
- After group reporters have spoken, tell all those who have changed their minds to join the group that represents their new opinion.

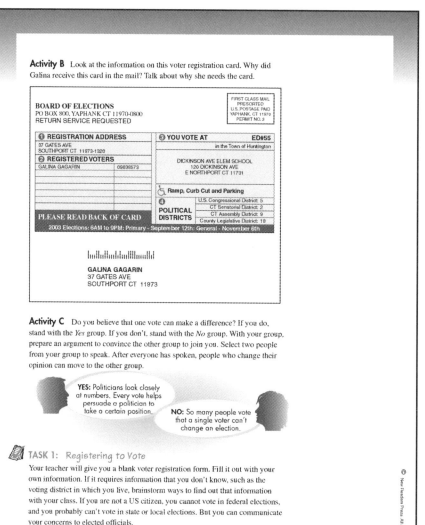

Activity B Look at the information on this voter registration card. Why did Galina receive this card in the mail? Talk about why she needs the card.

BOARD OF ELECTIONS
PO BOX 800, YAPHANK CT 11970-0800
RETURN SERVICE REQUESTED

FIRST CLASS MAIL
PRESORTED
U.S. POSTAGE PAID
YAPHANK, CT 11970
PERMIT NO.3

① **REGISTRATION ADDRESS**
37 GATES AVE
SOUTHPORT CT 11973-1320

② **REGISTERED VOTERS**
GALINA GAGARIN   09638573

PLEASE READ BACK OF CARD

③ **YOU VOTE AT** ED#55
in the Town of Huntington

DICKINSON AVE ELEM SCHOOL
120 DICKINSON AVE
E NORTHPORT CT 11731

Ramp, Curb Cut and Parking

④ **POLITICAL DISTRICTS**
| U.S. Congressional District: 5 |
| CT Senatorial District: 2 |
| CT Assembly District: 9 |
| County Legislative District: 18 |

2003 Elections: 6AM to 9PM; Primary - September 12th; General - November 6th

GALINA GAGARIN
37 GATES AVE
SOUTHPORT CT 11973

Activity C Do you believe that one vote can make a difference? If you do, stand with the *Yes* group. If you don't, stand with the *No* group. With your group, prepare an argument to convince the other group to join you. Select two people from your group to speak. After everyone has spoken, people who change their opinion can move to the other group.

YES: Politicians look closely at numbers. Every vote helps persuade a politician to take a certain position.

NO: So many people vote that a single voter can't change an election.

TASK 1: *Registering to Vote*
Your teacher will give you a blank voter registration form. Fill it out with your own information. If it requires information that you don't know, such as the voting district in which you live, brainstorm ways to find out that information with your class. If you are not a US citizen, you cannot vote in federal elections, and you probably can't vote in state or local elections. But you can communicate your concerns to elected officials.

98 Unit 7 Lesson 1

Task 1

If you choose to do this activity, you will need to obtain a voter registration form for each learner:

- Contact the board of elections in your area and ask for voter registration forms.
- Check the Federal Election Commission or your county, city, or state government web site for registration forms that can be downloaded. Also check your local library. In addition, some learners may have access to voter registration forms or be willing to get them for you.

- Write the word *SAMPLE* across the top of each form before distributing them to learners.
- While all learners should complete a form, make sure they understand that only US citizens can actually register to vote.

Lesson 2: Keeping Informed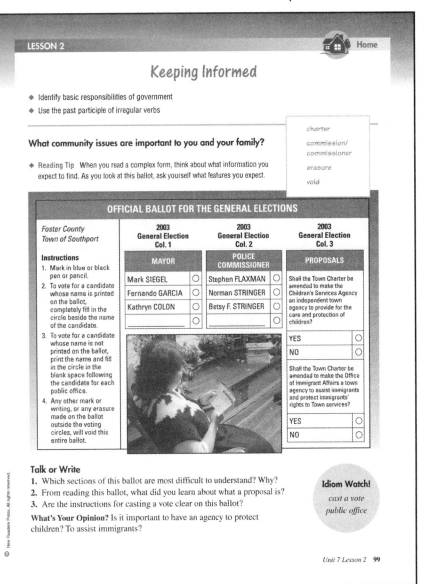

Read the title and point out the lesson objectives below it.

- Tell learners that in this lesson they will identify the basic responsibilities of government and ask a local representative to visit their class.
- Explain that the word *keeping* in the lesson title means *staying*. *Keeping informed* means *always knowing what is happening.*

Question

Read the question aloud to learners. Provide examples of typical community issues (e.g., potholes, garbage collection, neighborhood safety).

<u>One Step Up</u>

Have learners write in their notebooks about a specific issue for their community or neighborhood.

Reading Tip

Read the tip aloud; then follow these steps:

- Ask learners if they have seen a ballot before. If so, where? Do they know how to find out before going to vote what information will be on the ballot?
- Divide learners into small groups and tell them to find the following information on the ballot:

<u>Group 1</u>
1. The name of the second candidate for police commissioner
2. The column and line proposing an amendment to the Town Charter for protection of immigrants' rights
3. The name of a woman candidate for mayor

<u>Group 2</u>
1. The line giving instructions for entering a name on the ballot
2. The name of a woman candidate for police commissioner
3. The name of a proposed agency that would protect immigrants' rights

<u>Group 3</u>
1. The name of the first candidate for mayor
2. The line proposing a child-protection agency
3. The line stating what will void the ballot (i.e., make it invalid)

<u>Group 4</u>
1. The line stating which colors should be used on the ballot
2. The name of the third candidate for police commissioner
3. The line that tells how to vote for a candidate

If you have more than four groups, create more sets of clues, or give the same set of clues to more than one group. Have groups present their search results.

Talk or Write

This exercise engages learners in reading an election ballot.

Follow the suggestions on p. 5 for comprehension questions.

<u>Answers</u>
Answers will vary.

What's Your Opinion?

Stress that many communities already have organizations that protect children and assist immigrants. Why would a town want to create a separate government agency?

Vocabulary

Follow the suggestions on p. 6 for introducing and reinforcing vocabulary words.

- Write the words on the board or a transparency. Ask learners for the number of syllables in each word and write the number next to each.
- Pronounce each word several times. Ask which syllable is stressed. Write that syllable in capital letters on the board. Then write the other syllables.
- Choose words for individual learners to pronounce.

Group Chat

 Use Customizable Master 3 (3-Column Chart). Follow the suggestions on p. 7 for customizing and duplicating the master.

- Put learners in small groups. Give a copy of the master to each group.
- Appoint a recorder and reporter in each group. Have recorders list group members' names and responses to these questions:

  What have you done to keep informed so far?

  What other resources will you use to keep informed?

- Have group reporters share their responses. Make sure that learners' lists of resources are well developed and include formal and informal sources.

Grammar Talk

Follow the suggestions on p. 7 for introducing the grammar point. Then follow these steps:

- Tell learners that, when used with the auxiliary (or helping) verbs *have* or *had*, past participles form the *present perfect* or *past perfect* tense.
- When used with the verb *be*, past participles either become participial adjectives describing a state (e.g., *The voting machine is*

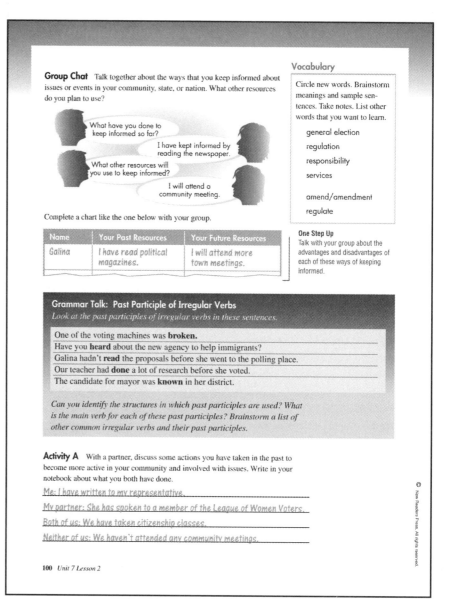

broken.) or form the passive voice (e.g., *The machine was broken by a voter.*).

Use the brainstorming activity as a review of irregular verbs:

- List learners' responses on a large sheet of paper and post it in the room for the remainder of this unit.
- Have learners identify similar types of participles (e.g., *blown, flown, written, bitten*). Compare them to the simple past forms.

 Use Unit Master 56 (Grammar: Past Participles with Regular and Irregular Verbs) now or at any time during the rest of the unit.

Activity A

 Provide each pair with a copy of Customizable Master 8 (Johari Window). Tell learners to use one window for each option in the student book.

- Remind learners that political action is only one kind of community involvement.
- When pairs have completed their organizers, ask volunteers to present their work.

 Assign Workbook pp. 48–49.

Activity B

One Step Down

Simplify this activity by preparing answers in advance.

- Copy each question in the student book onto an index card. Give one card to each of half the learners.
- Write the answers on another set of cards and distribute those to the other learners.
- Have learners find the person with the corresponding answer or question.

Technology Extra

If your learning center does not have computer access for learners, assign this research as homework.

Activity C

After learners have completed the exercise, discuss the sharing of responsibilities by various levels of government.

Answers

Note that items 2, 3, and 8 describe federal government responsibilities, but few or none of the other items have a single clearcut answer. For example

- Local governments set local traffic and parking rules; state governments set overall speed limits and other statewide rules of the road; and the federal government makes additional rules for traffic on US routes and interstate highways.
- Local governments regulate garbage disposal, but environmental and recycling rules made by state and federal governments also affect garbage handling.
- Schools are often funded by local taxes and run by local school boards, but the state and federal governments make many of the rules for schools and may provide additional money as school aid.

Take the opportunity to have a class discussion of how different levels

of government are involved in the areas listed in the activity.

- Encourage learners to share their knowledge and experience.
- You may want to do some research in advance so that you can provide specific information on how these governmental activities are accomplished in your area.

Task 2

If your representative cannot come, do one of the following:

- Invite an aide.
- Write the questions and send them in a letter.

- Ask the representative to speak to several classes or at a school assembly.
- Select one question of interest to the whole group and set up a phone call with an aide.

Activity B How much do you and your group members know about your state? Find out which group in your class is able to answer the most questions correctly:

One Step Up
Write one or more questions for other groups to answer.

1. What is the capital of your state?
2. Name several cities in your state.
3. Name some important mountains, lakes, or rivers in your state.
4. Who is your governor?
5. Who is one of your senators in Washington?
6. Who is one of the representatives for your area in Washington?
7. Who represents you in your state legislature?
8. When did your state become a state?
9. What is your state flower?
10. What is your state bird?

Technology Extra
If no one in your group knows an answer, find it on the Internet. Locate a state government web site.

Activity C National, state, and local governments have different responsibilities. The responsibilities of national and state government are defined by the US Constitution. Each state government defines the responsibilities of the local governments in that state. It may define several forms of local governments, such as city and county governments. With your group, decide which responsibilities are carried out by local, state, and federal government. Review the answers with your teacher.

declare war
disability insurance
unemployment
worker's compensation

local government responsibility	1. To make traffic and parking rules
_____	2. To set up laws for international trade
federal government responsibility	3. To regulate business between states
_____	4. To provide for the health and welfare of the citizens
state government responsibility	5. To make laws about unemployment, disability insurance, and worker's compensation
_____	6. To regulate garbage disposal
_____	7. To provide schools
_____	8. To declare war
_____	9. To make regulations for construction of buildings

TASK 2: Stay Informed
Invite a local representative to your program. With your group, prepare for the meeting. Make a list of questions for your representative about any issue that concerns you. Practice asking these questions and be ready to take notes.

Unit 7 Lesson 2 **101**

Lesson 3: Getting Involved

Read the title and point out the lesson objectives below it.

- Tell learners that in this lesson they will learn ways to be more active citizens.
- They will also write a letter to their local newspaper about an issue of their choice.

Questions

Read the introductory questions aloud. Encourage focused listening by asking follow-up questions about learners' answers.

Attention Box

This vocabulary should be understood, but learners should not be expected to produce the words at this point.

Photo

Ask learners questions like these:
- Where are they?
- What's going on?

Caption

Read the caption aloud to learners.

Ask if learners understand the term *low-income housing* (housing for people who cannot afford to rent apartments or buy houses in areas where housing is expensive).

Listening

Play the audio or read the listening script on pp. 140–141. Follow the suggestions on p. 5 for listening comprehension.

- Play the audio or read the script five times. Each time, ask learners to practice focused listening for the answer to one question. Talk about possible answers after each playing.
- Some learners may want to hear the script a few more times; others may be able to provide answers more quickly. Adjust the activity to learners' needs.

Getting Involved

- Learn how to be a more active community member
- Learn about the activities of community agencies and organizations

Have you ever attended a community meeting? If you have, why did you attend? If you haven't, why not?

- Listening Tip To understand a discussion, it helps to have background information. Read the caption below for background information before listening to this discussion. The listening script starts on page 138.

Galina has been reading and hearing a lot about the town's plan to build a new low-income housing project not too far from the local high school. Now she is at a community meeting. A representative of the town council is answering people's questions about the project.

Talk or Write

1. What was the main issue discussed at the meeting?
2. What concerns did people voice? What responses did the speaker offer?
3. Which answers surprised you?
4. What other questions would you ask?

102 *Unit 7 Lesson 3*

Talk or Write

In this exercise, learners listen for main ideas.

Clarify any questions about the listening. Then have learners write their answers.

Answers

1. The main issue was a town's plan to build low-income housing.
2. People were concerned about the possibility of overcrowding in the high school, falling property values, and increases in crime and drug activity. The speaker told people that the town council had taken these concerns into consideration in the planning stages. He said that the project would solve problems and not create them. He also said that the opposition had exaggerated and said untrue things about the project.
3. Answers will vary.
4. Answers will vary. (Write learners' suggestions on the board or an overhead transparency.)

Extension

Role-play the meeting in groups of six learners. One learner will be Mr. Schuler, and the other five will be town residents in the audience. In addition to a few questions from the listening script, have audience members ask several questions of concern to their own community.

Vocabulary

Follow the suggestions on p. 6 for introducing and reinforcing vocabulary words. Then play a word game:

- Write all the vocabulary words from this unit on the board or a transparency.
- Allow several minutes for learners to study the words and their placement.
- Ask learners to close their eyes as you erase one word. Draw a horizontal line in place of the word.
- Ask learners to guess which word is missing. Repeat until all words have been erased.
- Ask volunteers to come to the board and re-enter the words in the correct blanks.

To review all unit vocabulary, use Unit Master 57 (Vocabulary: Learner-to-Learner Dictation) now or at any time during the rest of the unit.

In the US

Elicit a definition for the word *grassroots*. One possible definition is "starting and growing with ordinary people, not with leaders or people in power." Brainstorm examples of grassroots organizations.

- Have learners read the passage silently. Then ask a volunteer to read it aloud.
- If the learner has problems with pronunciation, make minimal corrections.
- Read the passage again to the group. This time ask learners to pay attention to correct stress on words in sentences.

Compare Cultures

Read the questions in the student book. Then open a discussion about organizations in different countries.

- Organize the information in a two-column chart on the board or an overhead transparency.

- Write the name of the country in the left column. In the right column, name the organization and describe its activity.

One Step Up

Ask groups of learners from the same country to prepare a brief report about a grassroots organization in their home country.

The report should explain the purpose of the organization and whether or not it was successful. If it failed, the report should explain why.

Pronunciation Target

Play the audio or read the words and sentences. Have learners repeat the sentences after you.

Ask each learner to write three additional sentences with a disappearing *h* and read them to the class.

Activity A

Answers

1. It's <u>him</u>.
2. It's <u>her</u>.
3. You're <u>here</u>.
4. I live at <u>home</u>.
5. I need the verb <u>have</u>.
6. Movies are made in <u>Hollywood</u>.
7. It's <u>hard</u>.
8. It's <u>huge</u>.

 Assign Workbook pp. 50–51.

★ **In the US**   *Self-Reliance and Involvement Traditions*

Rather than wait for the government to solve problems, people in the US sometimes start grassroots organizations. Your community center's after-school program was probably started because a group of parents wanted activities for their children. Some local organizations develop into national movements. Such organizations address issues like health problems, environmental damage, hunger, and housing shortages. Many groups work for political action. A grassroots organization somewhere in the US is working on almost every community concern.

Vocabulary

Circle new words. Brainstorm meanings and sample sentences. Take notes. List other words that you want to learn.

- housing project
- shortage
- town council
- grassroots
- low-income
- overcrowded/overcrowding

☛ **Compare Cultures**

How are community problems resolved in your home country? What kind of grassroots organizations exist there? How are they similar to or different from grassroots organizations in the US? Have any groups grown into national or international movements?

Pronunciation Target • The Disappearing h

🎧 Listen to your teacher pronounce these words in two ways, stressed and unstressed. Can you hear the difference?

he her him   ee er im

Now, listen to your teacher pronounce each word in a phrase.

What organization **did he** join?
I've **seen her** at the polling place.
Have you **heard him** at the meeting?

Did you notice that the phrase sounds like one word? Say these sentences with a partner. Notice the position of your tongue and lips. Sometimes when the h is at the beginning of a word, it disappears and you hear only the vowel sound.

Activity A   Ask a partner these questions. The answer to each question must start with *h*. Listen carefully to the way your partner pronounces the answer. Then switch roles. Decide which answers have a disappearing *h* sound.

1. If it's not *her*, it's who? It's _____.
2. If it's not *him*, it's who? It's _____.
3. If you're not *there*, you're where? You're _____.
4. Where do you live? I live at _____.
5. What verb do you need for the present perfect tense? I need the verb _____.
6. In what city are many movies made? Movies are made in _____.
7. If it's not soft and easy, it's what? It's _____.
8. If it's very, very big, what is it? It's _____.

Unit 7 Lesson 3   103

Activity B

Remind learners that community involvement includes participation in ethnic centers and clubs.

Activity C

Ask a confident learner to lead this whole-class brainstorming activity.

- Brainstorm local issues that are important to learners and their community.
- Have learners write their ideas on the board or a transparency. Tell them not to worry about spelling errors and grammar; these will be corrected after all responses are listed.
- Put learners into groups by taking a simple tally: all those interested in a particular issue will form a group.
- If more than five learners declare the same interest, designate two groups for that issue. Then compare the two groups' concerns and questions.
- Provide each group with a large sheet of paper to draw an enlarged idea map like the one shown in the text.

Task 3

List the following steps on the board or a transparency for learners to follow as they complete this task:

- Find answers to your questions.
- Brainstorm solutions.
- Write solutions on your idea map.
- Present your issue to another group.
- Add their concerns and solutions to the map.
- Write a letter to the editor of your local newspaper with your concerns and solutions.

If possible, provide learners with some examples of letters to the editor. Otherwise, use this one:

Dear Editor:

We are very unhappy about the potholes in our streets.

Our cars get damaged, and our neighborhood streets are dangerous for bike riders. We want the people responsible for this problem to take action immediately before someone gets seriously injured.

What kind of pressure can we put on our elected officials to make them take action?

The Huntley Park Neighborhood Watch Group

Peer Assessment

Use Generic Assessment Master 15 (Peer Assessment Form for Projects and Tasks). Give a copy to each learner for use during the group presentations.

Follow the suggestions for peer assessment on p. 4.

Have learners complete and exchange the forms before writing their letters to the editor.

One Step Up

Ask groups who actually send their letters to report back in a later class about any response.

Review Unit Skills

See pp. 8–9 for suggestions on games and activities to review the unit vocabulary and grammar.

Activity B Are you active in your community? Do you want to be? Think about ways in which you have been able to make a difference. And think about things you wanted to do but couldn't or didn't. For example, have you ever helped people in your neighborhood? Did you volunteer your services with a community organization? Have you ever been a member of a neighborhood committee? Talk to a partner about your participation in your community.

> Have you ever helped out your neighbor?

> Yes, I've done some shopping for the elderly lady next door.

> Have you wanted to do more for your neighborhood?

> I've always wanted to organize a Neighborhood Watch group, but I don't know where to start.

Activity C With your class, identify some local issues that are important to you and your community. List the issues on the board. Decide which issue is most important to you. Work in a group with others who chose the same issue. Brainstorm specific concerns and questions about this issue. Make an idea map like the one below.

Streets in bad shape
- Cars get damaged
- Cost of repair?
- Neighborhood looks run-down
- Dangerous for bike riders
- Who is responsible for fixing?

If your group put questions on the map, decide how you could get answers. List possible sources of information and answers below your map.

✓ **TASK 3: Write about an issue**
In your group, work with the idea map from Activity C. Brainstorm possible solutions to the problem. Try to get answers to your questions and use that information in your discussion. Add the solutions to the map. Present your issue to another group. As you talk about your concerns, ask other groups for their ideas. List their concerns and solutions. Then in your group, write a letter to the editor of your local newspaper about the issue. Identify the concerns, and present one or more possible solutions.

One Step Up
Stay involved. Send the letter you wrote in Task 3 to your local government representative or to the government agency that is responsible for that issue. If possible, you may want to send the letter as an e-mail message.

104 *Unit 7 Lesson 3*

Unit 7 Challenge Reading 🌐

Reading Tip

Read the tip aloud with learners. Then ask, "How do you feel about becoming citizens?"

- Discuss the reading tip as a whole class.
- Sometimes learners—especially those whose home countries are in this hemisphere—say they plan to return home. Others who stay in the US remain noncitizens by choice, out of loyalty to or identification with their home countries or cultures. Their need to "belong" may not be as strong as that of the author of "Why I Became an American Citizen."
- In cases like these, you may wish to discuss the learners' feelings about being noncitizens in the US and what that means for their lives here.
- Avoid judgmental remarks and listen without interruption to what can be a stimulating discussion.
- This may be a good time to remind learners that being able to see several sides of an issue is considered a high-level thinking skill.

Challenge Reading

Have learners read the complete story silently and without interruption.

- Tell them to mark new words with a highlighter or pen or write them in their notebooks. Do not let them interrupt the reading with questions about words or with dictionary searches.
- Elicit the main point of the essay (i.e., becoming a US citizen does not mean losing your ethnic identity).
- Have learners work in small groups to identify the essay's subordinate ideas and find supporting details. Assign a recorder and a reporter in each group.

Use Customizable Master 9 (Main Idea and Supporting

UNIT 7 Challenge Reading

◆ **Reading Tip** Relating an article or story that you read to your past experiences can help you understand it better. Before you read this newspaper story, think of your own feelings about becoming a citizen.

Why I Became an American Citizen

By Christine Castro

When my mother became a US citizen in 1980, I asked her why her hair wasn't blond. I was 5 at the time. I don't remember it, but my mom tells me when she walked through the door after her swearing-in ceremony I just stared at her, puzzled.

I thought being American was having blond hair, eating at McDonald's, and watching fireworks on the Fourth of July. I thought being American must be the greatest thing in the world. I wanted to be an American.

Instead, I was a Filipino girl with brown skin, choppy black hair, and slanted eyes. Nobody looked at me and knew that I had been in this country since I was 9 months old. In grade school, children ran circles around me chiming, "ching, chang, chong," as if I were a strange foreigner. When I spoke to them in clear English, they were often startled.

My parents worked hard, paid their taxes, and abided by the laws. We held green cards. We had every right to be here. But when I traveled outside the country or applied for a job, I had to flash my green card. When I turned 18, I couldn't vote like my friends. I spoke English, pledged allegiance to the flag, and lived here, but I still wasn't American.

My mom wanted to come here as a young woman to study architecture at a graduate school. But she was the only girl in the family, and moving to another country at that time was unheard of. When she finally moved here, she says, she decided to take advantage of the privileges of citizenship. After all, this would be her home.

Had my dad, Tomás, become a citizen as well, my brothers and I would automatically have become naturalized. But he was not ready. There was martial law in the Philippines, and relinquishing his Filipino citizenship meant giving up his property rights. Besides, he said, he wanted the decision to be our own.

At last, my father, brother Ricky, and I applied for citizenship together in December, interviewed in April, and took our oaths in late June. My dad says it was the growing anti-immigrant sentiment that finally persuaded him to apply. Ricky wanted to be able to vote and travel easily. I couldn't wait for the day when I wouldn't have to show the green card to prove I belonged.

I kept telling myself I shouldn't be nervous, but I couldn't help it. I feared that though I had lived here my entire life, they would decide that

Glossary box:
abided
advantages
allegiance
mesmerized
privileges
puzzled
swearing-in ceremony

Unit 7 Challenge Reading **105**

Details). Give one copy to each group and have the recorders enter the ideas and details. When groups have finished their lists, ask reporters to read them to the class.

Learners' charts may include the following ideas and details:

- *Idea:* child's idea of what it means to be an American; *details:* blond, eat at McDonald's, watch fireworks
- *Idea:* a noncitizen status is seen as a reason for discrimination; *details:* being seen as a strange foreigner with brown skin, choppy black hair, and slanted eyes
- *Idea:* advantages of being a citizen;

details: travel easily with US passport and a right to vote

- *Idea:* confusing emotions; *details:* pride of being a US citizen and regret at giving up official ties to home country
- *Idea:* pride in being both a Filipina and an American; *details:* holding on to home values and traditions while fulfilling the responsibilities of an American citizen

Unit 7 *Challenge Reading* **105**

Talk or Write

Put learners into small groups. Have the reporters in each group read from their idea chart. Then, as a large group, compare all responses.

Possible Answers

1. The main idea is that she is proud to be an American. Although she now finally feels that she "belongs," she still keeps Filipino values and traditions.
2. Refer to the *ideas* above.
3. Refer to the *details* above.
4. Answers will vary.

Writing Task

Provide 10 minutes of quiet time for learners to reflect on one of the three topics given. If they prefer not to write a personal commentary, have them write a more general essay about becoming a citizen.

Use Generic Assessment Master 14 (Writing Checklist and Error Correction Symbols). After learners write a rough draft, give each a copy of the master.

- Tell learners to go back over their writing, revising it for organization and adding details if needed.
- Then have them go over their essays again for grammar and spelling corrections.
- When all revisions have been made, ask learners to write a final copy.

---

they didn't want me. And I was also frustrated. I knew that so many Americans did not know the answers to some of the questions I would be asked at my interview. And I didn't think it was fair that I could be discriminated against for that. But I passed the test and survived the interview.

From then on, I eagerly awaited my swearing-in ceremony invitation, circling the mailbox like a vulture. And when I did get the letter, I counted the days, telling everyone the big day was near. I'm not sure what I expected—a wave of inspiration to overcome me as I pronounced my oath, to walk out of that convention hall mesmerized. I would like to say when 4,000 people waved their plastic flags and the national anthem resounded, I was in awe. I want to say, "Yes, I am proud to be an American."

But I'd be lying if that was the only side of the story. My 10-year-old cousin in the Philippines wrote me and said she didn't understand why I became a US citizen. "Aren't you proud to be a Filipina?" she asked. The truth is, I'm proud to be both. I am still a Filipina, holding dearly the values and traditions with which I was raised. But I am now an American. I will do what I can to help this country as it has helped me. It is my duty as a citizen.

My naturalization certificate is tucked in a manila folder in a bookshelf in my dad's office. To me, it is just a piece of paper with my name and picture on it. It is what the certificate stands for that is very dear to me. I can say that I am an American. I do belong.

Talk or Write

1. What is the writer's main idea about becoming an American citizen?
2. What arguments does the writer use to prove her point?
3. What examples does she provide to make her point?
4. How are the writer's experiences similar to yours? How are they different?

Writing Task

Write a paragraph on one of these topics:
- why I want to become a US citizen
- why I do not want to become a US citizen
- why I became a US citizen

Unit 7 Project

Learners make a community resource guide.

Get Ready

Have learners work together or in small groups to complete all parts of the project.

<u>One Step Down</u>

Have learners work in groups of four. Divide the work between them as follows:

- One person creates the list of local, state, and national government officials.
- Another person focuses on the information for local, state, and national government agencies and organizations.
- A third assembles the guide.
- A fourth makes the presentation.

Do the Work

Make multiple copies of Unit Master 58 (Unit 7 Project: Make a Community Resource Guide). Have learners use the copies to prepare the pages of their guide. Information for each entry in the guide should be recorded on a separate copy.

- Tell learners to complete a chart for each official. Have them write not only the name of the official but also the official's title and agency or organization.
- Direct learners to prepare information about agencies on separate copies of the master.
- Finally, have them organize their pages by local, state, and national levels and, within each level, by nature of issue.
- Provide groups with colored paper or card stock for the cover and with clips or rings to hold the pages together.

Present

- Have a volunteer from each group explain why the group selected the particular agencies included in its guide.

- Ask the volunteer to also explain in what way each agency can help with the group's issues.
- Have each group name at least one official who can help solve a particular community problem.

Technology Extra

Assist learners in using a word-processing program.

Assign Workbook p. 52 (Check Your Progress).

Use Unit Master 59 (Unit Checkup/Review) whenever you complete this unit.

UNIT 7 Project

Make a Community Resource Guide

It's helpful to have the names, addresses, and phone numbers of your local, state, and national officials, as well as agencies and organizations that deal with issues that concern you. To keep that information available, make a community resource guide.

Get Ready

You will need
- a list of your local, state, and national government officials
- a list of agencies or organizations that you are interested in
- materials to make your guide: lined paper for the pages, card stock or colored paper for the cover, and clips or rings to hold the pages together

Do the Work

1. Group the names of the officials into three categories: local, state, and national. Start a new page for each category. Put information about agencies and organizations in a separate category.
2. Prepare an entry for each official. Write the person's name, job, address, phone number(s), and e-mail address. Next to each name, write the type of issues that the official could help you with. Do the same for agencies and organizations.
3. Prepare a cover for your guide. Put a title and your name on it.
4. Put together the cover and the pages of your guide with rings or removable clips (so that you can add new information and update information if necessary, particularly after an election).

Present

1. Show your guide to your teacher or someone else in your classroom. Ask for comments and suggestions. Make changes.
2. Share your information, including addresses and phone numbers, with other members of your class. Explain why you selected the agencies and organizations that you included.
3. Take notes, and include additional resources and contacts that other students who completed their presentations gave you.

One Step Up
Include any available web site addresses for the listings in your guide.

 Technology Extra
Type your information on a computer. Use special features, such as bold type, to make it easier to read. Print the pages for your guide. Save the file so you can make changes.

Unit 7 Project **107**

Unit 8: It's Never Too Late

Materials for the Unit

- Magazine pictures of people, young and old, reading and studying
- Catalog of continuing education classes at local colleges
- Index cards
- Poster board
- Customizable Masters 2, 3, 5
- Generic Assessment Masters 10, 14, 15
- Unit Masters 60–65

It's Never Too Late

Read the title and the unit goals listed below it.

- Ask learners how they feel about learning at their age. Ask if it is any different from learning at a younger age.
- Ask, "What are some advantages of both situations?"
- Tell learners that one goal of this unit is to find their personal learning style. Have them reflect on what their style might be.

Ask these questions:

- Do you like to study alone in a quiet place or with sounds in the background?
- Do you study in the evening or in the daytime?
- Do you read silently or aloud?
- How long can you study without getting tired?
- How do you remember new material?

Post magazine pictures of people reading and studying for the duration of the unit. Ask learners to add to the display by bringing in more pictures.

Photo

- Read the questions below the arrow. Briefly discuss learners' responses.
- Mention that public speaking is difficult for many people in their first language, and more difficult in a second.

UNIT 8
It's Never Too Late

Finding Your Learning Style

Community 1   Work/School 2   Home 3

- ◆ **Vocabulary** Words for giving a speech • Words about ways to learn
- ◆ **Language** Past continuous • Past perfect continuous
- ◆ **Pronunciation** Disappearing sounds and syllables
- ◆ **Culture** Learning at any age

Have you ever had to speak English in front of many people? How did you feel?

Willie's daughter is getting married. She and her parents are talking with a wedding planner. Willie's wife and daughter are excited, but he is worried. Willie came to the US from Poland 23 years ago. He has worked hard, and he owns a successful business. But he doesn't understand everything the wedding planner says, even when he checks his dictionary. She doesn't always understand him either. Willie wants to give a speech at the wedding. He wants to express his pride. But he thinks that his English may embarrass his family.

Think and Talk

1. What do you see in the picture? How do you think each person feels?
2. What's Willie's problem? Do you know anyone who had a similar problem? What did that person do?
3. If a friend asked you how to improve his or her English, what advice would you give?

108 *Unit 8*

- Put learners in pairs and ask them to look at the photo. Have them list each thing they see.

Guide the work by asking these questions:

- How many people do you see?
- Where are they? (Explain the meaning of *wedding planner's* office.)
- What are they looking at?
- What are they wearing?
- What else do you see?
- What is the man reading?

Caption

After learners read the caption silently, have volunteers read it aloud.

Think and Talk

Discuss the questions as a class or have small groups talk and report back.

Possible Answers

1. We see people at a wedding planner's office. Remainder of answer will vary.
2. Willie is worried about speaking at his daughter's wedding. Remainder of answer will vary.
3. Answers will vary and may include the following: spend lots of time with and listen closely to native English speakers, study grammar, listen to audio, listen to songs, study pronunciation rules.

Vocabulary

Follow the suggestions on p. 6 for introducing and reinforcing vocabulary words. Ask learners for other words in the word families of *improve, pride,* and *speech* (e.g., *improvement, proud, speak*).

Idiom Watch

Learners may know the verb *marry* and the adjective *married,* but may not be familiar with *get married.* Practice questions and answers for each of these forms.

Gather Your Thoughts

Distribute Customizable Master 5 (Idea Map). Follow the suggestions on p. 7 for customizing and duplicating the master. Make a copy for each pair of learners. Alternatively, provide each pair with a large sheet of paper and have them copy the map from the student book.

- Ask a volunteer to read the directions from the student book aloud.
- Ask pairs to share their idea map with the class. Have each partner read and talk about the content of one circle.

What's the Problem?

Follow the suggestions on p. 5 for identifying and analyzing problems.

Provide an example from your own experience. Use these questions to structure your example and learners' responses:

- What was the step you were afraid to take (e.g., a speech you had to make, a job interview)?
- How important was it?
- Do you wish you had taken that step?
- Was it really as frightening as you had imagined?

Give learners the option to reflect on these questions privately in their notebooks. Ask volunteers to read parts of their entries.

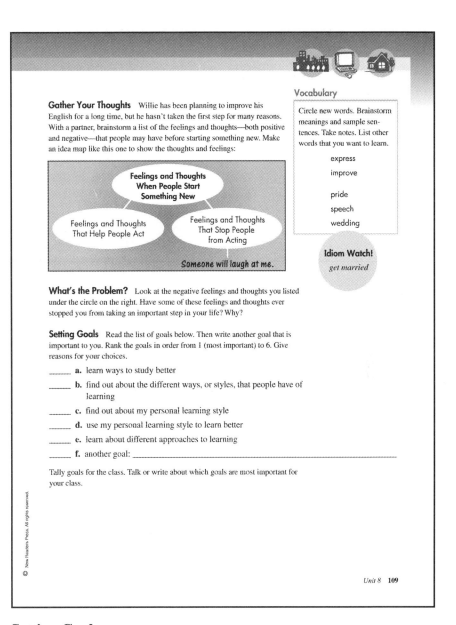

Gather Your Thoughts   Willie has been planning to improve his English for a long time, but he hasn't taken the first step for many reasons. With a partner, brainstorm a list of the feelings and thoughts—both positive and negative—that people may have before starting something new. Make an idea map like this one to show the thoughts and feelings:

Feelings and Thoughts When People Start Something New

Feelings and Thoughts That Help People Act

Feelings and Thoughts That Stop People from Acting

Someone will laugh at me.

Vocabulary

Circle new words. Brainstorm meanings and sample sentences. Take notes. List other words that you want to learn.

express
improve
pride
speech
wedding

Idiom Watch!
get married

What's the Problem?   Look at the negative feelings and thoughts you listed under the circle on the right. Have some of these feelings and thoughts ever stopped you from taking an important step in your life? Why?

Setting Goals   Read the list of goals below. Then write another goal that is important to you. Rank the goals in order from 1 (most important) to 6. Give reasons for your choices.

_____ **a.** learn ways to study better

_____ **b.** find out about the different ways, or styles, that people have of learning

_____ **c.** find out about my personal learning style

_____ **d.** use my personal learning style to learn better

_____ **e.** learn about different approaches to learning

_____ **f.** another goal: _____

Tally goals for the class. Talk or write about which goals are most important for your class.

Unit 8   **109**

Setting Goals

Follow the suggestions on p. 5 for setting goals.

- Read and talk about each goal with the whole class. Answer learners' questions and explain where necessary.
- Provide examples of learning styles (e.g., some people learn better by doing; some learn better by looking or observing; others learn better by listening).

Lesson 1: What Works Best for You? www

Read the title and point out the lesson objectives below it.

- Tell learners that in this lesson they will learn how to find the right schools for themselves.
- They will also make a guide to educational resources in their community.

Introduce Task 1 (p. 112) now.

- Read the directions for the task carefully together.
- Tell learners they need to begin looking for educational resources now and to bring in information about any they find.
- Allow several 15-minute sessions during this lesson for groups to share information and plan their resource guides.

Question

- Read the introductory question aloud. Then have learners complete this sentence in their notebooks:

  I learn best when ____.

- If learners have difficulty, refer back to the questions about study preferences at the beginning of this unit.

Photo

- Tell groups to analyze the photo for details and list the objects they see (e.g., office setting, plumbing supplies, phone book, pen in hand, reading glasses).
- Ask learners to describe the situation using the photo details.
- Point out Willie's facial expression and ask learners to guess how he feels and why.
- Talk about reasons people use yellow pages.

Reading Tip

Read the tip aloud.

- Tell learners to skim the phone listings to answer the question, "Do any schools look too good to be true?"

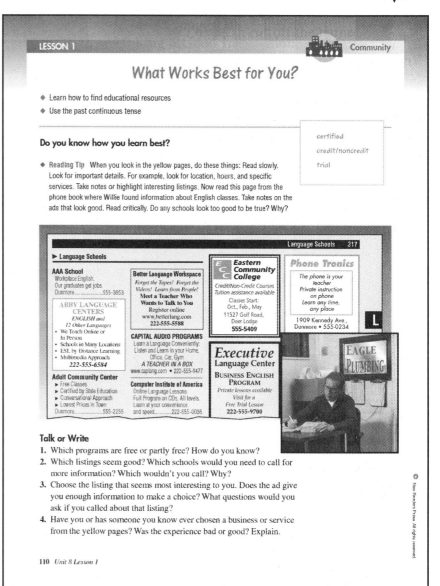

- Ask volunteers to explain their answers.

Talk or Write

This exercise helps learners read for details.

- Have learners dictate answers to you as you write them on the board or an overhead transparency.
- Tell them you will write what they tell you, including any errors.
- Ask learners to identify the errors, correct them, and write the corrected answers in their notebooks.

Answers

1. Adult Community Center offers free classes. Eastern Community College offers tuition assistance. Executive Language Center offers a free trial lesson. Their ads give this information.
2. Answers will vary.
3. Answers will vary. Questions to ask include the cost and location of the course; the length of the program; whether the course results in any certification or licensing; and whether the course includes citizenship preparation.
4. Answers will vary.

Vocabulary

Follow the suggestions on p. 6 for introducing and reinforcing vocabulary words.

Additional words may come from the Talk or Write discussion and answers. Ask learners if they heard any unfamiliar words they want to add to this list.

Class Chat

 Use Customizable Master 3 (3-Column Chart). Follow the suggestions on p. 7 for customizing and duplicating the master. Make a copy for each learner.

Allow 10 to 15 minutes for this activity. Each learner should talk to at least five others and write their responses.

- Draw the chart on the board or an overhead transparency.
- Have a volunteer model the first part of the chat (e.g., *I was studying English in this school last year. What were you doing then?*). You answer (e.g., *I was teaching English in another school in Chicago.*). Ask the volunteer to write your response on the chart.
- Learners should understand that their statement will stay the same throughout; only statements from other learners will change. Have learners rewrite their own statement each time; it will give them practice with the past continuous.
- Circulate; assist any learners having difficulty.
- Ask a few volunteers to read their statements and questions. Have someone who answered their question read the answer.
- Tell learners to save their completed charts for Activity A.

Grammar Talk

Follow the suggestions on p. 7 for introducing the grammar point. Then introduce the past continuous:

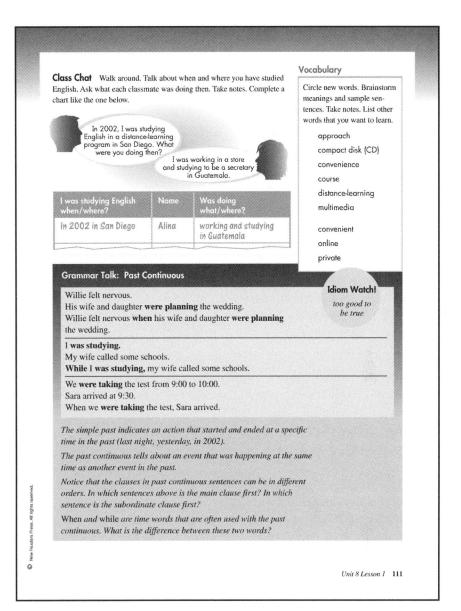

Unit 8 Lesson 1 111

- Ask learners to look carefully at the verb tenses as they read and compare the sentences.
- Allow learners a few minutes for silent reflection and analysis of the grammar point.
- Ask what words join the two clauses. *(while and when)*
- Review the meaning of *main* and *subordinate* clauses. Ask learners which clause contains the *past continuous* and which clause contains the *simple past.*

Answers

The *main clause* comes first in the first complex sentence. The *subordinate clause* comes first in the second and third complex sentences.

Both *when* and *while* can be used to mean *during the time that.* They suggest action that was continuing in the past (e.g. *While I was studying,* my wife called.). *When* can also be used to introduce an action that happened only once in the past (e.g., We were taking the test *when Sara arrived.*).

For more practice with the past continuous, use Unit Master 60 (Grammar: Question Game) now or at any time during the rest of the unit.

Assign Workbook pp. 53–54.

Activity A

- Model the activity using the example sentence in the student book.
- Clarify for learners that their own clause will be written again with each new statement from other learners.
- Remind learners that the order of the clauses can change. Have them write some or all of the sentences in reverse order as well.
- Invite volunteers to write sentences on the board.

Correct possible errors using Generic Assessment Master 14 (Writing Checklist and Error Correction Symbols).

Activity B

Extension
Expand this conversation practice by asking partners to create three additional questions.

Task 1

By now, learners should have been able to meet in groups several times to plan and organize their task.

- Ask learners which things they would like to know more about.
- Make a chart showing all the categories that interest learners across the top. Ask each learner to write his or her name on the chart under the preferred category.
- The four or five categories with the most names under them will be those used in the task, and the learners who signed under each will form a group.
- Learners who did not write their names under one of these categories can decide which remaining category interests them most and join that group.
- After learners have brought their information about resources to the groups, allow at least another hour for groups to assemble their guides.

Activity A Class Chat Follow-Up Use the information in your Class Chat chart to write sentences in your notebook about yourself and people in your class.

When I was studying English in San Diego in 2002, Alina was working and studying in Guatemala.

Activity B Look at the types of language schools in the listing on page 110. How many different language-learning approaches can you find? Make a list in your notebook. Then reread the list with a partner. If necessary, make changes to your list of language-learning approaches. Ask yourself the questions below, considering only language-learning approach. Don't consider cost or location.
- Which school would be your first choice? Why?
- Which school would be your last choice? Why?

Write your answers in a chart like this one. Talk about your answers with your group. Did everyone agree, or do different people prefer to learn in different ways? How could this information help you learn English better?

First-Choice School	Reason	Last-Choice School	Reason

TASK 1: *Make a Resource Guide*

What do you want to know more about? Cooking? Plumbing? Computers? Money management? Brainstorm and do research with a partner or a small group of classmates who want to learn similar things. Follow these suggestions:
- Talk with other students, friends, teachers, and neighbors to find educational resources in your community.
- Look in the yellow pages for schools that might teach that subject.
- Look for flyers, community newspapers, and supermarket bulletin boards.
- Check nearby community colleges, YMCAs, and community centers.
- Research new technologies: studying online, with CDs, with audiotapes, or with videos. Check the Internet for ideas.
- Make an alphabetical list of all the resources that you find. Include phone numbers, addresses, web site addresses, and your comments.
- Share your guide with other students in your class.
- Your class may want to combine the resource lists from all the groups into a learning resource guide to share with other classes in the school.

- In the group presentations, each group member should name, display, and describe at least three resources.

Lesson 2: Working Out the Details www

Read the title and the lesson objectives listed below it.

Tell learners that in this lesson they will hear about active listening. They will also practice it with a guest speaker.

Question

Read the question aloud with learners. Use it to start a discussion about telemarketing.

- Ask, "How do you feel about telemarketing calls? What do you say?"
- Balance the discussion by asking, "Does anyone know someone who has worked as a telemarketer? Why might someone take this job?"

Attention Box

Have learners categorize the words. What do they have in common?

This vocabulary should be understood, but learners should not be expected to produce the words at this point.

Photos

Ask these questions:

- What can you tell about Willie from the photo on the left?
- What are the people doing in the photo on the right? What do you think they are saying?

Caption

Have a learner read the caption aloud.

Listening Tip

Read the tip aloud. Then ask these questions:

- How can silence help you learn?
- Why do you think people rush to ask or answer questions? Why do they agree or disagree with a speaker before thinking?
- Have you ever used silence in conversations? What happened?

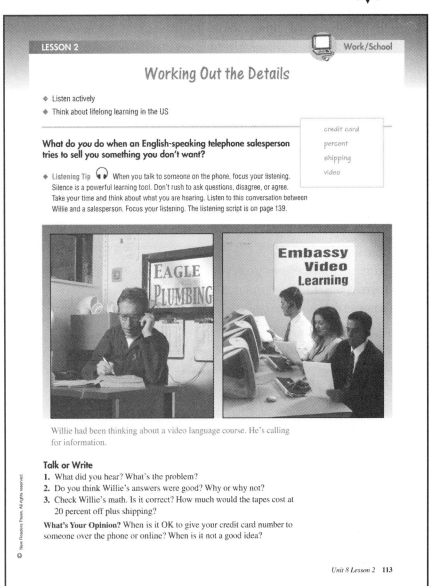

LESSON 2 — Work/School

Working Out the Details

- Listen actively
- Think about lifelong learning in the US

What do *you* do when an English-speaking telephone salesperson tries to sell you something you don't want?

credit card
percent
shipping
video

- Listening Tip 🎧 When you talk to someone on the phone, focus your listening. Silence is a powerful learning tool. Don't rush to ask questions, disagree, or agree. Take your time and think about what you are hearing. Listen to this conversation between Willie and a salesperson. Focus your listening. The listening script is on page 139.

EAGLE PLUMBING

Embassy Video Learning

Willie had been thinking about a video language course. He's calling for information.

Talk or Write

1. What did you hear? What's the problem?
2. Do you think Willie's answers were good? Why or why not?
3. Check Willie's math. Is it correct? How much would the tapes cost at 20 percent off plus shipping?

What's Your Opinion? When is it OK to give your credit card number to someone over the phone or online? When is it not a good idea?

Unit 8 Lesson 2 **113**

🎧 Play the audio or read the listening script on p. 141. Follow the suggestions on p. 5 for listening comprehension. Then ask these questions:

- What do you know about Willie from the conversation? Explain. (Elicit that Willie seems smart.)
- Is the salesman reading from a script or speaking normally? Why do you think so?

Talk or Write

This exercise helps learners practice focused listening.

Follow the suggestions on p. 6 for comprehension questions.

Possible Answers

1. First have learners tell only what they heard; then ask for opinions about what they heard.
2. Answers will vary.
3. Yes. [Cost of tapes ($223.40) less 20% ($44.68) = $178.72 plus shipping (12 tapes × $5 each or $60) = $238.72]

What's Your Opinion?

Be sure learners give reasons for their opinions.

Vocabulary

Follow the suggestions on p. 6 for introducing and reinforcing vocabulary words.

After copying the words in their notebooks, ask pairs to guess the part of speech of each word. Then appoint a team of three learners (one for each word cluster) and have them check the words in their cluster in a dictionary.

Idiom Watch

Ask, "Has anyone heard this idiom? Do you know similar expressions in other languages?"

In the US

Have learners read the passage silently. Then ask them to close their books. Do an oral fill-in-the-blank exercise by reading the passage aloud slowly and skipping key words. Ask learners to call out the word if they remember it.

Compare Cultures

Bring in catalogs of continuing education classes at local colleges. Read some of the class titles. Ask these questions:

- Are there similar classes in most countries?
- What kind of person would take this class? Why?

Elicit opinions on lifelong learning in different countries. Ask:

- Does anyone know a person who returned to school when he or she was older?
- What happened?

Use Customizable Master 2 (2-Column Chart). Follow the suggestions on p. 7 for customizing and duplicating the master. Make a copy for each group.

- Have learners discuss opinions about lifelong learning in their groups, using the text questions as a guide.

In the US   Lifelong Learning and Self-Improvement

Most Americans believe that it's never too late to learn. Research shows that people who continue to learn, continue to grow mentally. Adults bring life experience with them when they go back to school. Adults know *what* they want to learn, and they often understand better than young people *how* they want to learn. Lifelong learning, sometimes called *continuing education*, is popular among people of all ages. There are many ways to learn—in a classroom, online, through a mentor, and with television or video courses.

Self-improvement programs are especially popular with Americans. Many people read books or join groups that help them manage time or money better, do better at their jobs, have better health, and so on.

Compare Cultures

Lifelong learning is popular in the US, but not everywhere. In your group, talk about attitudes towards adult learning in other countries. Are there places in your home country where adults can take classes to improve their skills? If so, what are some popular things to study? What do you think about adult learning? Do you think that there is an age at which learning becomes difficult? If so, why do you think that happens? In your group, complete a chart like this one:

Positive Attitudes toward Lifelong Learning	Negative Attitudes toward Lifelong Learning

Vocabulary

Circle new words. Brainstorm meanings and sample sentences. Take notes. List other words that you want to learn.

misunderstand

outdo

preview

reconsider

continuing

fluent

insecure

lifelong

actively

mentally

Idiom Watch!
change your mind

Activity A With your class, find the meaning of the prefixes in the following words. Notice that prefixes can be added to nouns, verbs, or adjectives.

disrespect, **dis**miss	**micro**scope, **micro**wave	**out**do, **out**live	**re**live, **re**consider
inability, **in**secure	**mis**spell, **mis**understand	**pre**view, **pre**fix	**un**happy, **un**tie

Work with a partner to think of as many words as you can with these prefixes. Check your words in a dictionary or with an English speaker. By yourself, write a sentence using each word. Read your sentences to your partner. Then share your words and sentences with the class. Which pair of students has the most correct pairs of words and sentences?

One Step Up
Outside of class, listen and look for more words that have these prefixes. Report back to your group.

- As each learner gives an opinion, the group decides whether to record it under *negative attitudes* or *positive attitudes*.
- List group responses on the board or a transparency.

Activity A

Some prefixes will be known to learners, and some will be new.

- Write a prefix from the student book on the board or a transparency.
- Have learners guess the meaning by looking at the examples in the text.
- Appoint a learner to confirm the meaning in a dictionary.

Then do the following:

- Have learners work in pairs to find new words using the prefixes.
- Circulate to help or answer questions.
- After five minutes, have a learner in each pair read his or her sentences. Each time, ask learners, "Is the sentence correct?"
- Acknowledge the pair that creates the most correct sentences.

 Assign Workbook pp. 55–56.

Activity B

- Review the rules for active listening from the student book.
- Have learners select a topic from the book, or assign a topic.
- Tell pairs that one speaks for two minutes while the other listens.
- At the end of two minutes, call, "Time!" so partners can switch roles.

When partners have finished, ask these questions:

- How did it feel to listen silently and actively for two minutes?
- Was it difficult? Why or why not?
- How did it feel to have someone listen attentively to you?

One Step Up

Assign this activity for further practice in active listening.

Task 2

Follow these steps:

1. *Choose a speaker or speakers.* Make the selection of a speaker a class project.
   - Think creatively. A learner's friend or relative may be flattered to be a role model.
   - Consider teachers, employees, or volunteers at your learning center who may be taking professional or continuing education courses.
2. *Prepare for the speaker.*
   - Prepare a few questions ahead of time, e.g., "Where did you study? Why did you do it? Did you have any problems? How did your family react? Do you recommend continuing education?"
   - Agree on a time limit for the speech and stick to it.
3. *Prepare learners.*
   - Review active listening.
   - Encourage learners to ask questions after the speaker has finished.
   - Model active listening by being attentive.

Activity B Practice active listening. Read this list of questions with a partner. Each partner selects one question to talk about for two minutes.

- What is your personal experience with lifelong learning?
- Have you taken a continuing education class? What happened?
- Have you ever started to study something new and then stopped studying? What did you want to learn? Why didn't you continue?
- Do you believe that people grow mentally as they get older? Does mental growth depend on age or something else? What else?
- What has helped you grow mentally as an adult?

One Step Up

Outside of class, actively listen to a friend or family member talk, but don't tell the person what you are doing. First ask a question, and then really listen to the answer. Follow the rules for active listening. Report what happened to the class.

While one partner talks, the other listens actively. Follow these rules:

Rules for Active Listening

- Be silent for the whole two minutes.
- Look at the speaker.
- "Be there" mentally—thinking only about what the speaker is saying, *not* about other things.
- Ask the speaker at least one good question about what he or she said.

Talk about your experience with the class. How did it feel to really listen to someone? How did it feel to have someone give you his or her attention?

 TASK 2: Listening Actively to a Speaker

As a class, talk about people you know who are good models for lifelong learning—perhaps someone who learned a new skill or occupation later in life. Invite one or more of these people to be guest speakers in your class. Tell them when and for how long you want them to speak and what you want the speeches to be about. You can get some ideas from the questions in Activity B, or you can choose another aspect of lifelong learning.

When each person speaks, follow the rules for listening actively. At the end of the speech, ask questions. Record the speaker's answers in your notebook.

The next time you meet as a class, talk about each speech. What things did the speaker do well? What did you learn from the <u>content</u> (what the speaker said) and the <u>delivery</u> (how the speaker said it) of the speech?

Technology Extra

Use a computer to publish a short summary of each speech. Add some of the best questions your class asked and the answers that the speaker gave. Title each summary "____ (speaker's name): A Lifelong-Learning Model." You may want to share your class summary with another class or post it on the school bulletin board.

Unit 8 Lesson 2 **115**

---

4. *Review.*
   - In the next learning session, ask learners what they found most difficult about the speech.
   - Brainstorm strategies to improve active listening.
   - Ask, "How can active listening improve your English?"

Ongoing Assessment

During the speech, note how learners perform on these features:

a. General quality of listening
   0 = did not listen actively
   1 = actively listened part of the time
   2 = was attentive and interested throughout most of the speech

b. Appropriate questions
   0 = none or irrelevant questions
   1 = some problems asking relevant questions
   2 = clear, appropriate questions

c. General quality of body language
   0 = obviously inattentive
   1 = generally attentive with occasional distractions
   2 = indicated full attention

Technology Extra

Post the printed summaries in your room for learners to read.

Lesson 3: Showing Your Pride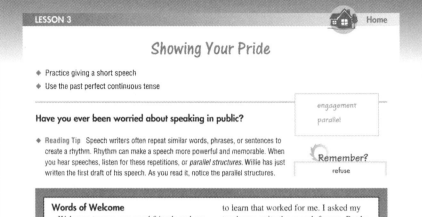

Read the title and point out the lesson objectives below it.

- Tell learners that in this lesson they will write and give a short speech.
- Follow the suggestions on p. 5 for talking about the title.

Learners' attitudes towards *showing pride* will vary. In many cultures, it is impolite to praise yourself. In some others, displays of pride are gendered. And in still others, if you are proud of yourself, you say so.

Question

Read the question aloud; then ask these questions:

- Have you ever given a speech?
- How did you feel before giving it? After giving it?

Photo

Ask these questions:

- What is each person doing?
- How is the woman feeling? The man? How do you know?
- What else can you tell about the people in the picture?

Reading Tip

Read the tip aloud with learners.

- If possible, give examples of repetition in a speech. Dr. Martin Luther King's famous "I Have a Dream" speech is a good choice.
- Ask learners to close their books while you read the speech aloud. Ask for first impressions: What is the occasion? Is the speech a good one for the occasion?
- Tell learners to scan the speech for repetition.
- Have learners read the speech aloud at least twice in their groups, with each learner reading a paragraph. Circulate to help with pronunciation.

Talk or Write

This exercise helps learners reflect on underlying meaning.

Showing Your Pride

- Practice giving a short speech
- Use the past perfect continuous tense

engagement

parallel

Remember?

refuse

Have you ever been worried about speaking in public?

- **Reading Tip** Speech writers often repeat similar words, phrases, or sentences to create a rhythm. Rhythm can make a speech more powerful and memorable. When you hear speeches, listen for these repetitions, or *parallel structures*. Willie has just written the first draft of his speech. As you read it, notice the parallel structures.

Words of Welcome

Welcome to you, my good friends and my dear family.

When Barbara and I came to this country, I thought I could not have been happier. But I was wrong.

When we had a beautiful daughter, an American daughter, I thought I could not have been happier. But I was wrong.

When Barbara and I became citizens, I thought I could not have been happier. But I was wrong.

When my daughter said she wanted to marry, I was happy. But when she asked me to give a speech at her wedding, I was also frightened. I wanted to say great things. But my English wasn't good. I had lots of problems communicating!

So I decided to go to Belmont Adult School to improve my English. They put me into the class of an excellent teacher. He knew that I had doubts about learning at my age. But he told me that we are never too old to learn. He showed me ways to learn that worked for me. I asked my teacher to write the speech for me. But he refused. He said I needed to express my own thoughts and feelings. I asked him to help me write a speech. But he refused. Instead he helped me find the English that I needed. Thanks to him, I found the way to say what is in my heart—and to say it in English.

This is the happiest day of my life. Life has been good to me. This country has been good to me. Now my daughter is getting married.

Barbara and I look forward to a new stage in our relationship with her, and to our new relationship with . . .

I wanted to say great things. But my English wasn't good.

Talk or Write
1. Give three reasons for Willie's happiness.
2. Have you ever made a speech on a special occasion? How did you feel?

Use these questions to expand learners' ability to "read between the lines."

Possible Answers

1. Willie is happy because he came to the US; he has a beautiful daughter; he and his wife are US citizens; his daughter is getting married. Although the book does not mention obstacles Willie had to overcome, ask learners to recall their own and imagine Willie's.

2. Answers will vary. Mention that a famous study found Americans are more afraid of speaking in public than of going to the dentist or even dying. Ask learners, "Do you feel that way?" Discuss ways to overcome speaker anxiety, e.g., make notes and practice; underline key points in your notes; remember your audience wants you to succeed; include humor.

Vocabulary

Follow the suggestions on p. 6 for introducing and reinforcing vocabulary words.

For further practice with the unit vocabulary, use Unit Master 61 (Vocabulary: Review) now or at any time during the rest of the unit.

Group Chat

Use Customizable Master 3 (3-Column Chart). Follow the suggestions on p. 7 for customizing the master. Make a copy for each learner.

- Model the activity by reading the dialogue in the speech bubbles. Read one part and have a learner read the other. Repeat the model a few times.
- Ask learners to save their completed charts for Activity A.

Grammar Talk

Follow the suggestions on p. 7 for introducing the grammar point.

Tell learners they have already used the past perfect continuous in the Group Chat.

- Write sentences from the Group Chat on the board (e.g., *Barbara had been wanting to learn to drive.*).
- Ask a learner to come to the board and underline the verbs in the sentence.
- With the class, write the pattern for the past perfect continuous: *had* + *been* + simple verb + *-ing*.

Use Unit Master 62 (Grammar: Practice Interview) now or at any time during the rest of the unit.

Pronunciation Target

The focus of this activity is listening for discrete sounds.

- Have learners close their books as you play the audio or pronounce the words naturally.

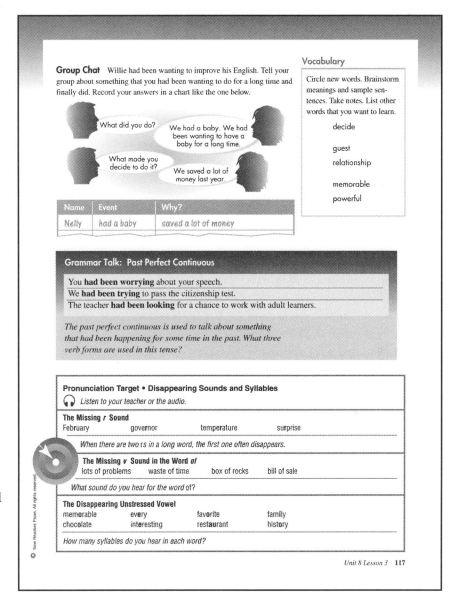

Group Chat Willie had been wanting to improve his English. Tell your group about something that you had been wanting to do for a long time and finally did. Record your answers in a chart like the one below.

What did you do?

We had a baby. We had been wanting to have a baby for a long time.

What made you decide to do it?

We saved a lot of money last year.

Name	Event	Why?
Nelly	had a baby	saved a lot of money

Vocabulary

Circle new words. Brainstorm meanings and sample sentences. Take notes. List other words that you want to learn.

decide

guest

relationship

memorable

powerful

Grammar Talk: Past Perfect Continuous

You **had been worrying** about your speech.
We **had been trying** to pass the citizenship test.
The teacher **had been looking** for a chance to work with adult learners.

The past perfect continuous is used to talk about something that had been happening for some time in the past. What three verb forms are used in this tense?

Pronunciation Target • Disappearing Sounds and Syllables

Listen to your teacher or the audio.

The Missing r Sound

| February | governor | temperature | surprise |

When there are two rs in a long word, the first one often disappears.

The Missing v Sound in the Word of

| lots of problems | waste of time | box of rocks | bill of sale |

What sound do you hear for the word of?

The Disappearing Unstressed Vowel

| memorable | every | favorite | family |
| chocolate | interesting | restaurant | history |

How many syllables do you hear in each word?

Unit 8 Lesson 3 **117**

- Ask learners to open their books and read the statements in italics.
- Pronounce the words or play the audio again. Ask learners to look carefully at the words in the book as they listen.
- Point out that in the second section, an unstressed *uh* has replaced *of*.

In the third section, an entire syllable is left out.

- As you read these words, clap out the syllables: *MEM ra ble*.
- After each word, ask how many syllables learners counted.

Tell learners they must be aware of dropped sounds to spell and understand well.

- Tell learners they can decide how they want to sound when speaking English.
- Explain that, while most educated people in the US pronounce in the shortened way, written English always uses the long forms.
- Be aware that some learners may think they communicate better if they articulate all the sounds.

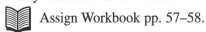 Assign Workbook pp. 57–58.

Activity A

Model a few sentences based on information in the Group Chat charts. Then assign pairs to write sentences using the past continuous. Ask each pair to write a sentence on the board.

Activity B

Possible Answers

1. No. Pronunciation varies with locale, degree of formality, and speaker's personality.
2. Yes. Americans pronounce words more carefully when speaking in public, on radio or TV, on the phone, in formal business situations, when they want to impress, or when they must be certain they are understood (e.g., making a 911 call).
3. Answers will vary. Some learners may see dropped sounds as sloppy pronunciation.

Activity C

* Synonyms that Willie used for *good* are *great* and *excellent.*
* Learners may include *dear* and *happy.* These words express positive feelings, but they are not synonyms for *good.*

Task 3

* Read the model speech aloud. Ask, "What is the occasion? Is this a good speech?"
* Brainstorm occasions for which a learner might need to give a speech (e.g., wedding, memorial service, baptism or christening, graduation, retirement party).
* List learner responses on the board or a transparency. Have each learner choose an occasion for his or her speech.
* Review the suggestions for writing a speech listed in the student book.
* Use learners' input to write a brief model speech on the board.

Activity A Group Chat Follow-Up Use your Group Chat chart to write sentences. Write about the people in your group. Use the past perfect continuous.

Nelly and her husband had been wanting to have a baby.

Activity B With a partner, write sentences using the words with disappearing sounds on page 117. Use one or more of the words in each sentence.

In a restaurant, he always orders his favorite food, chocolate cake.

When you finish, read your sentences to your partner. Answer these questions:

1. Do syllables and sounds *always* disappear in these words?
2. Do Americans sometimes pronounce words like these more carefully?
3. Which pronunciation do you prefer? Why?

Activity C In speaking and in writing, it's good to use *synonyms,* different words that have the same meaning. Look back at Willie's speech. How many synonyms can you find for the word *good?* Write them in your notebook. Write a sentence with each synonym. With your class, write the synonyms on the board. Then each student writes a sentence under each synonym. Read the sentences together.

 TASK 3: Write a Speech

Write a speech honoring someone on a special occasion. Use the speech on the right as a model for yours. Follow these rules:

* Greet the guests and name the event.
* Congratulate the guest of honor and say a few special things about that person.
* Mention any other special guests.
* Add a little humor or advice.
* Thank the guests for coming and tell them to enjoy themselves.
* Know when to stop. People want to have fun, not listen to a long speech.

Memorize your speech or use a few notes written on one index card. It's important to look at the audience, not at your notes, when you speak. Practice saying your speech to a partner. Then present it to your group. Finally, keep your speech in a safe place. You may need it for a celebration soon!

> Welcome, friends, family, and most of all, my dear grandmother. I'm so happy to be here at the one hundredth birthday celebration for my grandmother. I know she's happy to be here. Maybe she's surprised to be here too. I'm not surprised because I know she is strong and wonderful.
> At first she refused to come to her party. I know she did not want an elaborate celebration. She is modest. But she reconsidered, and here we all are at a simple party for her friends and family. As you can see, she has a lot of both. Happy birthday, dear grandmother.

118 *Unit 8 Lesson 3*

Provide each partner with a copy of Generic Assessment Master 15 (Peer Assessment Form for Projects and Tasks) to use in providing feedback.

* Give learners index cards to use for notes for their speeches. Tell learners to practice at home. Have them deliver their speeches in the next session.
* After they present, ask them how they felt as they gave the speech. Did the preparation help?

Assessment

Use Generic Assessment Master 10 (Oral Communication Rubric) to assess learners' speeches.

Use Unit Master 63 (Life Skill: Interview Checklist) now or at any time during the rest of this unit.

Review Unit Skills

See pp. 8–9 for suggestions on games and activities to review the unit vocabulary and grammar.

Unit 8 Challenge Reading www

Reading Tip

Read the tip aloud to learners. Then do the following:

- Have learners read the tip silently and then aloud to a partner.
- Ask partners to write the four steps in reading to get information.
- Review the four steps with the class: *Skim* for main points. Read slowly to *find examples and details. Summarize* by writing important points. *Evaluate* the points.

Tell learners to apply these steps for active learning as they read the passage silently.

- Allow several minutes for learners to skim the article silently, reading titles, words in boldface, and bulleted phrases.
- Have them close their books and ask volunteers to tell you what the article was about.
- Tell learners to read the article again, slowly. When they finish, ask them to give a more complete summary of the article by adding details and examples.
- After a third reading, have partners summarize the article aloud for each other. After actively listening, each partner adds details the other has left out.
- Together, partners write a summary of the article.
- Ask learners to write an evaluation of the article in their notebooks.
- Then have them share their ideas in small groups. Be sure they give reasons for their evaluations.

UNIT 8 Challenge Reading

◆ **Reading Tip** When you read an article or a section of a book to get information, follow these four steps to active learning.

1. First **skim** the article, looking for the main points.
2. Then read the article again more slowly to **find examples and details** to support those points.
3. Next, **summarize** the article for yourself by writing the points that seem most important.
4. Finally, **evaluate** the points for yourself. Ask yourself these questions: Does it make sense? Was any information new to me? Did anything in the article change the way I think about the topic?

Now follow the steps as you read this article about the most common ways that adults learn.

ADULT LEARNING STYLES

Learning makes your brain stronger. When you learn something new, whether it's how to use a new word, how to snowboard, how to make a terrific chocolate dessert, or how to do a geometry problem, your brain is creating new connections. Your brain is also storing the information so you can find it when you need it.

This happens to you if you are 2, 22, or 82 years old. In fact, the more you learn, the stronger your brain gets. And the stronger your brain gets, the more you can learn.

People start learning the moment they are born. They continue to learn throughout their lives. Learning is truly a lifelong experience.

But how do we learn? Many educators believe that we each learn best in one of three different ways, or learning styles: **visual** (by seeing); **auditory** (by hearing and talking); or **tactile/kinesthetic** (by touching, moving, and doing). Tactile and kinesthetic learning styles used to be thought of as separate, but educators now think that they are so similar that they can be considered to be one learning style.

We all use all these styles at different times, but most of us have one *dominant*, or main, learning style. You may already have some idea of your dominant learning style.

If your dominant style is **visual:**

- You like to see a person speaking while you listen.
- You like to draw pictures to help you remember.
- You may prefer to learn by watching videos or films.

If your dominant style is **auditory:**

- You like to read, but you may understand and remember better if you read aloud.
- You prefer to learn by listening to what other people say.
- You easily remember things that people say to you.
- You often have mental conversations with yourself.
- You repeat words or sentences to yourself while listening.

Here's an interesting question: Do you think that reading is visual? Not all educators agree with this idea. Some say that although we see the words, we actually get the information by hearing ourselves say the words in our heads. For that reason many educators say that people who prefer to learn by reading are **auditory** learners.

Unit 8 Challenge Reading **119**

A Learning Styles Quiz

- After learners read the directions silently, answer any questions. Read the directions again aloud.
- Tell learners to work quickly. Explain that in this kind of quiz, the first answer you think of is often the right one.
- Have learners skim the quiz to find unfamiliar words or phrases they do not understand. Answer any questions.
- Allow learners to work on their own. Set a time limit of about five minutes for the quiz.

Learners may benefit from this test-taking strategy:

- While learners are taking the quiz, watch for anyone struggling with one question. Encourage him or her to skip it, go on the next one, and come back to it at the end if there is time.
- Tell learners it is best to answer the questions they know first, and then go back to those they are not sure of.
- Tell them not to try to finish early but to use all the time they have to review their answers.

Talk or Write

Some learners will want to know the results of the quiz immediately. Tell them the Talk or Write exercise leads into the Unit Project, which interprets the quiz answers.

Alternatively, go to the Unit Project immediately after the quiz. Do the Talk or Write as a unit wrap-up or review.

- Have learners count off in twos. Tell the "ones" to answer the first question and the "twos" to answer the second question.
- Encourage learners to pair up or form small groups with others assigned the same number.
- Have the first person or group to finish answering question 1

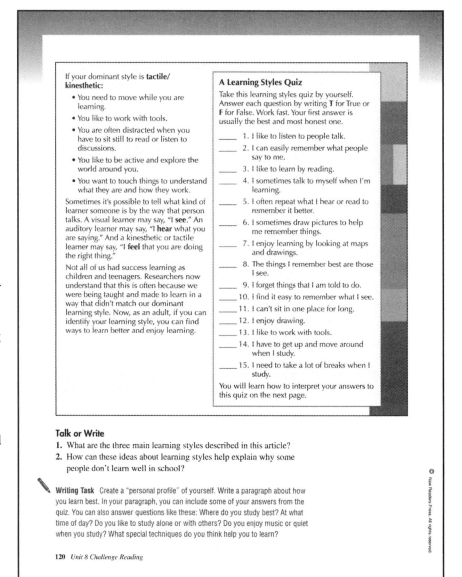

report to the large group. Ask if anyone has anything to add.
- Do the same with question 2.

Answers

1. The three main learning styles are visual, auditory, and tactile/kinesthetic.
2. Answers will vary but should include the idea that school is often oriented toward one style of learning, usually auditory. Those who learn best through another style are at a disadvantage in such a setting.

Writing Task

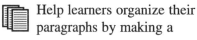 Help learners organize their paragraphs by making a

simple idea map or distributing copies of Customizable Master 5 (Idea Map).

- Tell them to write their name and the words *How I Learn Best* in the center circle.
- In the other circles, have them write activities that reflect their learning style (e.g., *quietly, moving around, looking at pictures, listening to music*).

Have learners use Generic Assessment Master 14 (Writing Checklist and Error Correction Symbols) to revise and edit their writing.

Unit 8 Project

Learners find their personal learning style.

Get Ready

- Make one sign for each of the three learning styles: *Visual, Auditory, Tactile/Kinesthetic.* Post them prominently in three different areas of the room.
- Have partners read the project instructions in the student book, listing questions or suggestions that might help them.

Do the Work

Tell learners to meet in the area designated for their learning style.

- Have groups choose a recorder, a reporter, a group leader (to read the question and keep the discussion focused), and a timekeeper.
- Tell the timekeepers to limit discussion to about 10 to 15 minutes per question. Each group member should have no more than a minute to talk about personal reactions to the Learning Styles Quiz.
- Circulate to focus discussion.

Model the steps in the student book:
1. **Talk.** Ask a learner the questions.
2. **Brainstorm.** Have recorders list suggestions or use an idea map. Use *Ways People with a ____ Learning Style Can Improve* as a head. Tell recorders to list their group's suggestions on the board or a large sheet of paper.
3. **Write.** Tell groups to expand their lists into suggestions for people with their learning style. Have them title this list *Suggestions for ____ Learners,* filling in the blank with the appropriate learning style. Provide these models for writing suggestions:

   You should ____.

   It would help to ____.

   You could try ____.

UNIT 8 Project

Find Your Personal Learning Style

Knowing your personal learning style can help you learn. It can also help your teacher work with you. Now you will analyze your learning style and talk with other students who have the same style. You will consider ways to make your learning style work for you.

Get Ready

Complete the learning styles quiz on page 120. Count the number of *True* answers you had in each of the following sections:

Questions 1–5 _____

Questions 6–10 _____

Questions 11–15 _____

If you had the most *True* answers in . . .
- questions 1–5, you probably are an **auditory** learner.
- questions 6–10, you probably are a **visual** learner.
- questions 12–15, you probably are a **tactile/kinesthetic** learner.

If you had the same number of *True* answers in more than one group, you may be comfortable in more than one learning style. However, you still may prefer one style to the others. This is your dominant learning style.

Do the Work

Make these signs and post them in three parts of the room: *Visual, Auditory, Tactile/Kinesthetic.* Go to your dominant learning style area and do the following activities with other students who prefer the same style:
1. **Talk.** Discuss how you felt about the learning styles quiz. Were you surprised at the results? Do you agree with them? Were they the same as the personal profile you had written? Why or why not?
2. **Brainstorm.** With your group, list ways that people with your learning style can improve the way they study and learn.
3. **Write.** As a group, write a short list of suggestions or tips for students who have your learning style.

Present
1. In your group, organize a presentation to share your information and tips with the class.
2. As a class, make a poster with the learning styles quiz, a scoring chart, and the tips each group created.

Unit 8 Project **121**

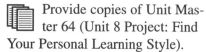 Provide copies of Unit Master 64 (Unit 8 Project: Find Your Personal Learning Style).

Present

- Tell each group to type its suggestions and illustrate them with clip art.
- As an alternative, ask a group member with clear handwriting to write the group's list on poster board. Have other group members illustrate the list with pictures from magazines.
- Have group reporters present their findings on learning styles to the large group or to another class, using the posters as visual aids. Ask them to include group members' personal experiences in the presentation.

Assessment

To assess learners' presentations, use Generic Assessment Master 10 (Oral Communication Rubric).

Assign Workbook p. 59 (Check Your Progress).

Use Unit Master 65 (Unit Checkup/Review) whenever you complete this unit.

Unit 9: Celebrating Success

Materials for the Unit

- Manila folders (for resume materials generated in tasks)
- Customizable Masters 1–3, 5
- Generic Assessment Masters 11–14
- Unit Masters 66–72

Celebrating Success

Read the title; then review the four groups of unit goals listed below it.

- Write *Getting the Job* on the board and ask learners to read it.
- Then complete the title by adding *You Want.* Ask learners what it means to get the job *you want.* How is it different from just *getting the job?*

Question

- Relate a personal anecdote in which you or someone you know convinced someone to hire you.
- Ask learners to tell how they got a job. Encourage them to describe successful job searches in other countries and the US.

Photo

As learners look at the photo, ask these questions:

- What can you tell about the woman on the left? Where is she? Why is she there? What kind of person is she? Why do you think so?
- What can you tell about the other woman? What kind of person is she? What do you think she is saying? What is her job? Do you think she is good at it? Why?

Caption

Have learners read the caption silently. Loss of status is a familiar theme to many immigrants. Ask, "Why is Martha worried? Do you think she has good reasons not to take the job?" Have learners explain their answers.

Think and Talk

Follow the suggestions on p. 6 for comprehension questions. If learners have already answered questions 1 and 2, ask them to add details to their answers.

Possible Answers

1. A woman is showing someone a flyer. They are in an office. Both women are wearing suits.
2. The sign says that the woman behind the desk is a job counselor. Also, there are job announcements on the bulletin board. The counselor is telling Martha about a job.

3. Answers will vary. Begin the discussion by asking for a definition of *overqualified.*
4. Answers will vary.

What's Your Opinion?

Opinions will vary but may include the following: any job is a good one if it helps you to become independent; Martha should continue her job search until she finds a better opportunity; Martha should take the job, continue her education or training, and then look for another job.

Vocabulary

Follow the suggestions on p. 6 for introducing and reinforcing vocabulary words.

Have partners ask and answer these questions:
- What personal characteristics help people make personal and career advancements?
- What obstacles to advancement have you overcome?
- How have you tried to advance?

Idiom Watch

Ask, "What does it mean to *make the most of yourself?*"

Gather Your Thoughts

- Describe your own personal characteristics and how you have used them successfully.
- Write on the board or a transparency *Employment skills = Personal characteristics and skills you need to get and keep a job.*

Distribute a copy of Customizable Master 5 (Idea Map) to each learner. Have learners complete the maps individually.
- Tell learners that if they cannot write a characteristic for each heading now, they may wait to get ideas from the discussion.
- Practice reaching consensus. Tell learners that everyone in the group must agree that a skill, characteristic, or experience is important to success before adding it to the list.
- When learners finish their discussions, ask what strategies they used to reach consensus (e.g., persuasion, debate, voting, negotiating, or compromise). Then ask these questions:
  Is working in a group a skill needed for success? Why?
  What have you learned here about working in a group?
  Have you used your group-work skills outside of class? Where?
  What happened?

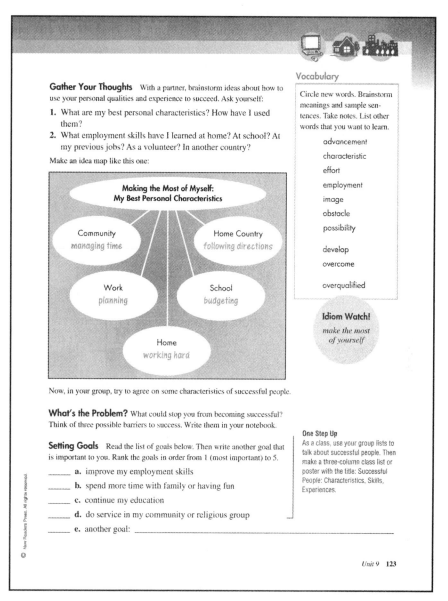

Gather Your Thoughts With a partner, brainstorm ideas about how to use your personal qualities and experience to succeed. Ask yourself:
1. What are my best personal characteristics? How have I used them?
2. What employment skills have I learned at home? At school? At my previous jobs? As a volunteer? In another country?

Make an idea map like this one:

Making the Most of Myself: My Best Personal Characteristics
- Community — *managing time*
- Home Country — *following directions*
- Work — *planning*
- School — *budgeting*
- Home — *working hard*

Now, in your group, try to agree on some characteristics of successful people.

What's the Problem? What could stop you from becoming successful? Think of three possible barriers to success. Write them in your notebook.

Setting Goals Read the list of goals below. Then write another goal that is important to you. Rank the goals in order from 1 (most important) to 5.
_____ **a.** improve my employment skills
_____ **b.** spend more time with family or having fun
_____ **c.** continue my education
_____ **d.** do service in my community or religious group
_____ **e.** another goal: _____

Vocabulary

Circle new words. Brainstorm meanings and sample sentences. Take notes. List other words that you want to learn.

advancement
characteristic
effort
employment
image
obstacle
possibility

develop

overcome

overqualified

Idiom Watch!
make the most of yourself

One Step Up
As a class, use your group lists to talk about successful people. Then make a three-column class list or poster with the title: Successful People: Characteristics, Skills, Experiences.

Unit 9 **123**

Extension
- In groups, have each learner say what he or she is most proud of (e.g., being a good parent, learning English, becoming a citizen, mechanical skills).
- Encourage learners to be specific (e.g., *I am proud that I helped my son with homework. Now he has graduated from high school.*).
- Have learners bring in pictures to illustrate their accomplishments. Ask them to write a sentence telling why they feel successful. Display the labeled pictures under the title *Successful People in Our Class.*

What's the Problem?

Follow the suggestions on p. 5 for identifying and analyzing problems. Barriers to success include low self-esteem, procrastination, fear of failure, poor language skills, lack of education or training, family obligations, health issues, or a weak job market.

Setting Goals

Follow the suggestions on p. 5 for setting goals.

Lesson 1: Making the Most of Yourself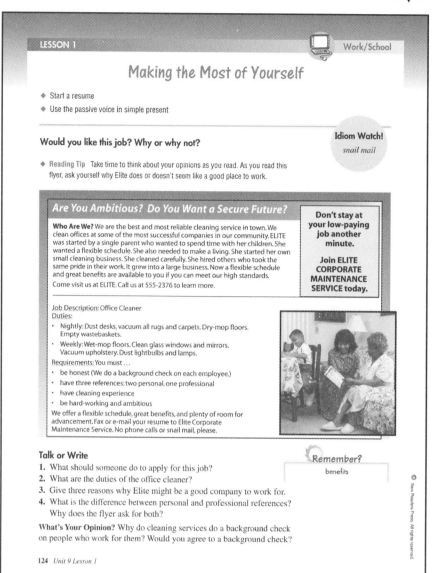

Read the title and point out the lesson objectives below it.

Tell learners that in this lesson they will begin a personal resume.

Questions

Read the questions aloud. Ask learners what the job is and whether they would like it.

Photo

Ask, "What are the people in the picture doing? Why is she trying to show the flyer to the other woman?"

Reading Tip

Read the tip aloud. Explain that good thinkers analyze and form opinions when they read.

- After learners read the flyer, ask, "Would you like this job?" List responses on the board. Ask if anyone has changed opinions after hearing others' ideas.
- Have learners read the flyer again. Then ask, "Did you find more reasons to like or dislike the job on your second reading?"

Talk or Write

This exercise builds analytical skills.

Follow the suggestions on p. 6 for comprehension questions.

Answers

1. Fax or e-mail a resume to Elite. (Ask learners what they could do if they had no fax machine or computer.)
2. Nightly: Dust desks, vacuum rugs and carpets, dry-mop floors, empty wastebaskets. Weekly: wet-mop floors, clean windows and mirrors, vacuum upholstery, dust bulbs and lamps.
3. Answers will vary but may include working for a reliable company, a flexible schedule, great benefits, room for advancement.

4. References give some indication of an applicant's skills, reliability, and personality. Learners may be confused by requests for references. Tell them a *personal reference* is someone who knows you and can speak about your character (e.g., a teacher, a friend, someone from your place of worship, a family doctor, or school principal). A *professional reference* is someone who can speak about your reliability and skills on the job. Former employers are best, but if you have no current work experience in this country, a person from an organization where you have done volunteer work is also good.

Tell learners to be sure to ask permission before giving people's names, addresses, and phone/fax numbers as references.

What's Your Opinion?

A background check is needed for security reasons. Usually applicants must tell where they have lived and worked for the past two years if they want to work in homes, stores, or business offices after closing time.

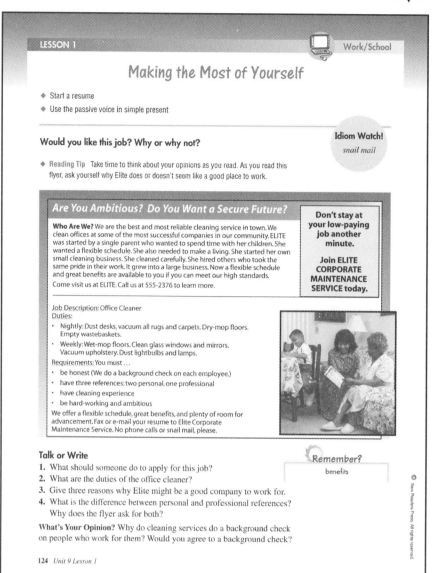

LESSON 1 Work/School

Making the Most of Yourself

- Start a resume
- Use the passive voice in simple present

Idiom Watch!
snail mail

Would you like this job? Why or why not?

- Reading Tip Take time to think about your opinions as you read. As you read this flyer, ask yourself why Elite does or doesn't seem like a good place to work.

Are You Ambitious? Do You Want a Secure Future?

Who Are We? We are the best and most reliable cleaning service in town. We clean offices at some of the most successful companies in our community. ELITE was started by a single parent who wanted to spend time with her children. She wanted a flexible schedule. She also needed to make a living. She started her own small cleaning business. She cleaned carefully. She hired others who took the same pride in their work. It grew into a large business. Now a flexible schedule and great benefits are available to you if you can meet our high standards. Come visit us at ELITE. Call us at 555-2376 to learn more.

Don't stay at your low-paying job another minute.

Join ELITE CORPORATE MAINTENANCE SERVICE today.

Job Description: Office Cleaner
Duties:
- Nightly: Dust desks, vacuum all rugs and carpets. Dry-mop floors. Empty wastebaskets.
- Weekly: Wet-mop floors. Clean glass windows and mirrors. Vacuum upholstery. Dust lightbulbs and lamps.
Requirements: You must . . .
- be honest (We do a background check on each employee.)
- have three references: two personal, one professional
- have cleaning experience
- be hard-working and ambitious
We offer a flexible schedule, great benefits, and plenty of room for advancement. Fax or e-mail your resume to Elite Corporate Maintenance Service. No phone calls or snail mail, please.

Talk or Write
1. What should someone do to apply for this job?
2. What are the duties of the office cleaner?
3. Give three reasons why Elite might be a good company to work for.
4. What is the difference between personal and professional references? Why does the flyer ask for both?

What's Your Opinion? Why do cleaning services do a background check on people who work for them? Would you agree to a background check?

Remember?
benefits

124 *Unit 9 Lesson 1*

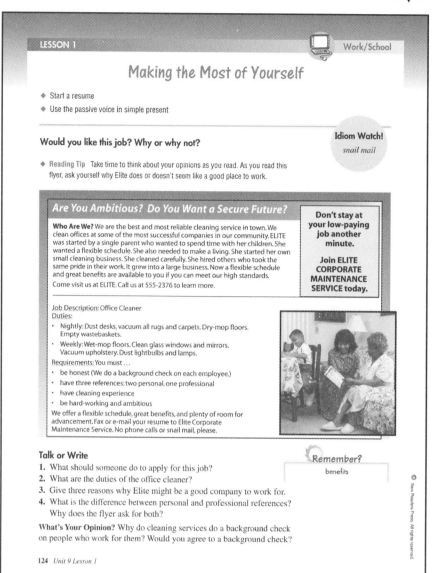

Vocabulary

Follow the suggestions on p. 6 for introducing and reinforcing vocabulary words.

- Tell learners that *background* is a compound word made up of two smaller words. Ask, "Can you guess the meaning?"
- Explain that these words are useful for job seeking. The second cluster includes characteristics often valued in the workforce.
- Ask, "Are you *ambitious?* Do you know someone who is? What are some characteristics of an *ambitious* person?" Repeat these questions with *flexible* and *reliable*.

Idiom Watch

Ask, "Is it difficult for a *single parent* to *make a living* in your home country? In the US?"

Group Chat

Clarify the differences between a job *title* and job *duties*. Explain that a cook *(title)* not only cooks but also plans menus and budgets, orders supplies, and supervises staff *(duties)*.

- Model the conversation with a learner. Have groups list every job group members have had.
- Have a group recorder list job titles on the board as the reporter reads them.
- After the first group reports, tell other recorders to write only new job titles.
- When everyone has reported, count the total number of job titles.

Extension

Do a minilesson on averages. Write on the board *Number of learners* divided by *Number of jobs* = *Average number of jobs per learner.*

Discuss the concept of *average.* Ask these questions:
- Who has had the most jobs?
- Who has had the fewest jobs?

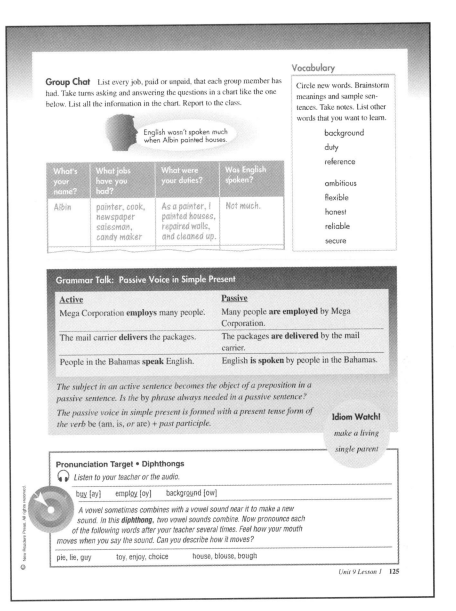

- Has anyone had the *average* number of jobs?

Grammar Talk

Follow the suggestions on p. 7 for introducing the grammar point.
- Ask, "How do we form the passive voice?" *(be* + past participle)
- Have pairs of learners make passive sentences using information from the Group Chat chart (e.g., *English is spoken at Raul's restaurant job*).

Answer

No, *by* is not always needed in a passive sentence.

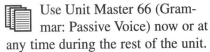 Use Unit Master 66 (Grammar: Passive Voice) now or at any time during the rest of the unit.

Pronunciation Target

Play the audio or read the words. Break the diphthongs into their component sounds:

buy = ah + e

employ = o + e

ground = ow + oo

For each diphthong, have learners say the two sounds slowly and then quickly so they blend together. Ask for other words that have these sounds and list them on the board.

 Assign Workbook pp. 60–61.

Activity A

- Have groups categorize the jobs. Tell them to add or change the headings if needed.
- Find out what kinds of jobs are available locally for English language learners. Are most employed in manufacturing or service jobs? (If learners are unfamiliar with the term *service job,* tell them it is "useful labor that does not produce a tangible product.") Do most use some English on the job? How much?
- Ask groups to create sentences about the kinds of jobs English learners have. Have recorders write them and reporters read them to the class.

Activity B

Explain that the *by* phrase is needed in the first sentence but not the second. Tell learners to use the *by* phrase when knowing who does the work is important.

Answers

3. The floors are mopped.
4. The desks and tables are dusted.
5. Windows are washed.
6. All cleaning jobs are checked by the supervisor.
7. Your house is cleaned until it shines.

One Step Up

- Have learners create a list of duties for each job in their Group Chat charts.
- When the lists are complete, demonstrate how to use strong, active verbs to describe job duties (e.g., Instead of saying, "I file, answer phones, and take messages," say, "I organize and maintain the filing system, direct calls, and take accurate messages.").

Activity A **Group Chat Follow-Up** Analyze the information from your Group Chat. With your class, think of ways to categorize the jobs that you and your classmates have had. Make a class chart like the one below. Put the initials of each classmate after the job that person had. If necessary, change or add headings to make the chart fit the kinds of jobs you and your classmates have had.

Health Services	Office Work	Food Services	Other:

When you have finished your chart, talk about these questions:
- What kinds of jobs did most class members have?
- Who do you think had the most unusual job?
- Who has had the most jobs?
- What did this categorizing activity tell you about your classmates or about jobs in the area where you live?

Activity B Change these sentences from active to passive. Write the new sentences in your notebook. If you think the *by* phrase is not necessary in a sentence, leave it out.

1. Elite cleans offices and homes. *Offices and homes are cleaned by Elite.*
2. Someone vacuums the rugs. *Rugs are vacuumed.*
3. Someone mops the floors.
4. Another person dusts the desks and tables.
5. Two people wash the windows.
6. The supervisor checks all cleaning jobs.
7. They clean your house until it shines.

As a class, talk about which sentences need the *by* phrase and which don't.

 TASK 1: *Prepare to Write a Resume*

Write about all jobs listed for you in the Group Chat. This can be paid or unpaid work, including housework, study, volunteering, working for relatives, caring for children, or looking for a job. In your notebook, write this information about each job:
- job title
- company and/or location
- job description and duties
- supervisor
- length of time on job
- skills used on job
- what you liked
- what you didn't like

Task 1

This task prepares learners to write their own resumes in subsequent lessons.

- Encourage learners to write as much information as possible about their jobs.
- Have each learner tell the class about one of their jobs. Have them use the bulleted list in the task as a guide.

Extension

Have each learner in the group use the list to write about every other group member's work experience.

- Invite some learners to report to the class on one job of another group member.
- Explain that this extra report will give them additional practice for their own job interviews, where they will need to talk fluently about their job experience.
- Give learners manila folders to hold the materials created in this lesson. They can refer to this folder as they develop their resumes through the rest of the unit.

Lesson 2: Making Your Work History Count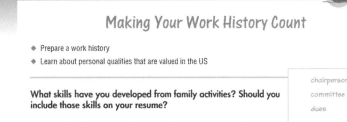

Read the title and point out the lesson objectives below it.

Tell learners that in this lesson they will start a work history.

Questions

Read the questions aloud.
- Have learners answer these questions in a journal entry to be written in learners' notebooks.
- This activity gives learners time to reflect on information they provided in the previous lesson and opportunity to write about valuable work experience they may not have considered before.

Photo

- Have pairs discuss the photo and speech bubble.
- Ask learners for the meaning of the phrase *make my experience count*. Ask, "What does Martha want to do? What is her plan?"

Reading Tip

Read the tip aloud. Repeat the final question to emphasize the reading objective.
- After silent reading, ask each group member to read one job description.
- Write the questions below on the board or a transparency, or prepare them as a handout for each group.
- Ask learners to focus on one job at a time, asking, answering, and explaining answers.

Job 1
- Was this a paid or volunteer job?
- What skills did she use in it?
- Did she need good English skills for this job?

Job 2
- What were her responsibilities?
- Where did she work?
- Why did she stop working there?

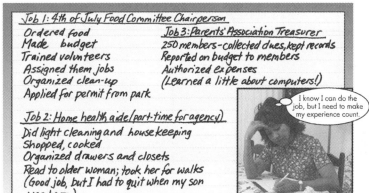

LESSON 2   🏠 Home

Making Your Work History Count

- ◆ Prepare a work history
- ◆ Learn about personal qualities that are valued in the US

chairperson
committee
dues

What skills have you developed from family activities? Should you include those skills on your resume?

◆ **Reading Tip** When you read information with many details, each detail may not tell you much, but you can put those details together to form a more complete picture. Read these notes that Martha wrote about her experience. Does this list of accomplishments tell you what kind of person Martha is?

> Job 1: 4th of July Food Committee Chairperson
> Ordered food
> Made budget
> Trained volunteers
> Assigned them jobs
> Organized clean-up
> Applied for permit from park
>
> Job 3: Parents' Association Treasurer
> 250 members - collected dues, kept records
> Reported on budget to members
> Authorized expenses
> (Learned a little about computers!)
>
> Job 2: Home health aide (part-time for agency)
> Did light cleaning and housekeeping
> Shopped, cooked
> Organized drawers and closets
> Read to older woman; took her for walks
> (Good job, but I had to quit when my son was born.)

> I know I can do the job, but I need to make my experience count.

Talk or Write
1. Which of Martha's jobs were paid and unpaid? Explain your answers.
2. What can you tell about Martha from reading her notes? What positive personal qualities does she seem to have?
3. Have you ever used home or volunteer experience to qualify for a paid job? If so, what was the experience? How did it help you? If not, can you think of unpaid experience that you could have used?

What's Your Opinion? Do you think it's OK to include unpaid work experience on your resume? Should you explain that it was unpaid?

Job 3
- Was she paid for this job?
- What math skills did she need?
- What experience did she gain?

Talk or Write

This exercise helps learners synthesize details as they read.
- Have partners discuss the questions and then help each other write answers in complete sentences in their notebooks.
- Spot-check learners' work. Note recurring errors to use as future grammar minilessons.

Possible Answers
1. The home health aide job was paid. We know because it was for an agency. The other jobs were unpaid volunteer jobs.
2. Martha is an organized person who is not afraid to try new things. She is responsible and can manage people and money.
3. Answers will vary.

What's Your Opinion?

Tally learners' answers. Ask, "Should all volunteer work be included on a resume? When is it appropriate?"

Vocabulary

Follow the suggestions on p. 6 for introducing and reinforcing vocabulary words.

After brainstorming meanings, play a modified Concentration game:

- Tell learners the object of the game is to remember as many words as possible and match them with appropriate people.
- Ask learners to select one word from the list that best describes them and to print it in large letters on loose-leaf paper.
- Have learners stand in a circle. Each takes a turn displaying the adjective and explaining his or her choice with this statement: *I am a/an ___ person because ___.*
- Start the game by modeling your own adjective (e.g., *organized*) and statement (e.g., *I am an organized person because I plan my lessons.*).
- After all learners have taken a turn, ask them to put their words away. Now each takes a turn at saying a name and remembering the corresponding adjective (e.g., *Donna is a hard-working person.*) If they are correct, they try again. Then the next person tries.
- The person with the most correct sentences wins.

Pronunciation Target

 Play the audio or read the listening script on p. 142.

Additional words include:

CONflict	conFLICT
PRESent	preSENT
DEfect	deFECT

- Have learners find similar pairs in a dictionary.
- Caution that some words have noun and verb forms with identical spellings, but stress does *not* change.

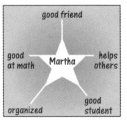

Pronunciation Target • Syllable Stress

The word permit *can be a noun or a verb depending on which syllable is stressed.* PerMIT *is a verb.* PERmit *is a noun. Listen to your teacher pronounce the two words. Repeat them. As a class, list other pairs of words whose stress changes in the same way.*

In the US   Personal Qualities That Americans Like

Americans like and admire certain qualities in people. American employers like to see those qualities in people who work for them. Look again at the words in the vocabulary box. The adjectives are all qualities that Americans admire. If your work history and resume show that you have these qualities, this can help you look good to companies. As a class, talk about the meanings of any words you don't know. Think or talk about how you can present your experience in a resume to show that you have many of these personal qualities.

Compare Cultures

Tell group members what success means for people in one country that you know about. Are the ways in which success is measured similar to or different from ways in the US? Do you agree with the measures of success in that country? Why or why not? What do you think are some good measures of success?

Activity A   On page 127, you listed some of Martha's personal qualities. Now think again, as you began to do on page 123, about your own good personal qualities. Are you ambitious? Hard-working? A good friend? A good teacher? What else?

Each person sits in the center of the class for one minute. The rest of the class tells that person about his or her personal qualities. Say good and true things about each of your classmates for one minute. Try to use some of the words in the vocabulary box. When it's your turn, enjoy hearing good things about yourself. Take notes about your personal qualities on a star-shaped idea map like the one on the right.

Discuss with your group: How did it feel to hear only good things about yourself for a minute? Were you surprised by any of the personal qualities that your classmates said you had?

Vocabulary

Circle new words. Brainstorm meanings and sample sentences. Take notes. List other words that you want to learn.

permit

assertive

eager to learn

hard-working

high-achieving

honest

optimistic

organized

persevering

self-reliant

Idiom Watch!
make something count

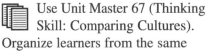

good friend

good at math   Martha   helps others

organized   good student

One Step Up
Make a list of your best personal qualities in your notebook.

In the US

Read the passage aloud. Ask if learners have noticed that employers and teachers like these qualities in workers and learners.

Compare Cultures

Discuss whether all of these personal qualities are positive in other countries and cultures.

Use Unit Master 67 (Thinking Skill: Comparing Cultures). Organize learners from the same country into pairs or groups of three.

- Have learners list the qualities considered positive in their home country in the left circle. In the right circle, tell them to list for the US all the qualities in the vocabulary box.
- In the overlapping section of the diagram, have them write any qualities that appear in both circles.
- Have reporters read from their group's chart.

Activity A

Tell learners to fill in a star-shaped idea map like the one in their book as they listen to other learners' compliments.

Activity B

- Elicit these words from the job description: *honest, experienced, hard-working, ambitious.*
- Have pairs list these words and then write words about Martha next to them. Tell them to circle words that are in both groups.
- Have partners take turns reading the open-ended sentences.

 Assign Workbook pp. 62–63.

Activity C

Extension

Play a Koosh Ball game. Learners stand in a circle tossing the ball to one another. The person who catches the ball says, "I want a job as a ____. I think I'm qualified for the job because I'm ____."

After everyone speaks, learners try to recall what was said. One throws the ball to another whose statement he or she recalls and says, "You want a job as a ____." If the information is incorrect, the second learner throws the ball back and the first one takes another turn.

Activity D

At the end of the activity, each group should have one paragraph for each learner. Learners who do not attend any meetings regularly can have the option of talking about learning sessions (e.g., *This class is attended by many students. The lessons are taught by a very dedicated teacher. Many questions are explained in clear language.*).

Task 2

- Remind learners to list action words in simple past.
- Explain that this activity will help learners complete the resume preparation form at the end of this unit.
- Make sure they put this work in their resume preparation folder.

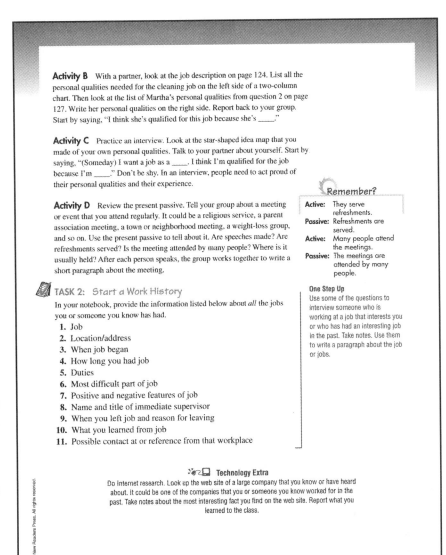

Activity B   With a partner, look at the job description on page 124. List all the personal qualities needed for the cleaning job on the left side of a two-column chart. Then look at the list of Martha's personal qualities from question 2 on page 127. Write her personal qualities on the right side. Report back to your group. Start by saying, "I think she's qualified for this job because she's ____."

Activity C   Practice an interview. Look at the star-shaped idea map that you made of your own personal qualities. Talk to your partner about yourself. Start by saying, "(Someday) I want a job as a ____. I think I'm qualified for the job because I'm ____." Don't be shy. In an interview, people need to act proud of their personal qualities and their experience.

Activity D   Review the present passive. Tell your group about a meeting or event that you attend regularly. It could be a religious service, a parent association meeting, a town or neighborhood meeting, a weight-loss group, and so on. Use the present passive to tell about it. Are speeches made? Are refreshments served? Is the meeting attended by many people? Where is it usually held? After each person speaks, the group works together to write a short paragraph about the meeting.

Remember?

Active:	They serve refreshments.
Passive:	Refreshments are served.
Active:	Many people attend the meetings.
Passive:	The meetings are attended by many people.

One Step Up
Use some of the questions to interview someone who is working at a job that interests you or who has had an interesting job in the past. Take notes. Use them to write a paragraph about the job or jobs.

TASK 2: Start a Work History
In your notebook, provide the information listed below about *all* the jobs you or someone you know has had.

1. Job
2. Location/address
3. When job began
4. How long you had job
5. Duties
6. Most difficult part of job
7. Positive and negative features of job
8. Name and title of immediate supervisor
9. When you left job and reason for leaving
10. What you learned from job
11. Possible contact at or reference from that workplace

Technology Extra
Do Internet research. Look up the web site of a large company that you know or have heard about. It could be one of the companies that you or someone you know worked for in the past. Take notes about the most interesting fact you find on the web site. Report what you learned to the class.

One Step Up

Help learners rehearse for the interview.

- Invite people from your learning site to be interviewed (e.g., maintenance people, security guards, the principal, the secretary).
- Discuss questions, such as salary and age, that are too personal and should not be asked.
- Give your guest the option of saying (as learners themselves may in a real interview), "I would rather not respond to that question."

Assessment

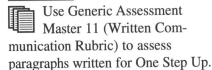 Use Generic Assessment Master 11 (Written Communication Rubric) to assess paragraphs written for One Step Up.

Lesson 3: Making a Good Impression 🔆

Read the title and point out the lesson objectives below it.

Tell learners that in this lesson they will prepare for a job interview.

Questions

Read the questions aloud. Elicit the following as steps needed to prepare for a good interview:

- Know the questions asked in a typical interview.
- Prepare and practice often.
- Learn unfamiliar vocabulary.
- Learn about the company and the work it does.

Photo

Follow the suggestions on pp. 4–5 for talking about the photo.

- Discuss the content of the photo with the class. Elicit comments about Martha's professional appearance and body language.
- Ask for evidence that shows Martha was prepared for this interview.

Listening Tip

Read the tip aloud with learners.

🎧 Play the audio or read the listening script on pp. 142–143. Follow the suggestions on p. 5 for listening comprehension. Then do the following:

- Have learners listen once and then write all the interview questions they can remember.
- Play the audio or read the script several times until all learners have listed at least five questions.
- Have learners read the questions back to you. Write each question, including any errors, on the board or an overhead transparency.
- Have pairs read the script of Martha's job interview (p. 140 in the student book), taking turns between Martha's and Ms. Koval's lines.

LESSON 3 Community

Making a Good Impression

- Prepare for a job interview
- Review verb tenses

administrative
belongings
clerical
conflict resolution
unfamiliar
valuable

Could you answer questions in an interview today? If not, what steps would you need to take first?

◆ Listening Tip 🎧 If you don't understand an interview question, it's fine to ask the interviewer to repeat or speak more slowly. Another way to understand interview questions better is to focus your listening. As you listen to Martha's interview, do some focused listening by concentrating on the questions that the interviewer asks. List at least some of those questions as you listen. The listening script is on page 140.

Your volunteer experience was clerical and administrative. Why have you applied to work as a cleaner?

Your ad said that you would train me. And I like the flexible schedule, benefits, and opportunities for advancement.

Martha is interviewing for a cleaning job.

MARTHA BERNARD
125 E. Amsterdam Ave.
Brooklyn, NY 11733
(718) 555-8713

Talk or Write
1. What kind of information does Martha have to provide?
2. Which questions were easy to understand? Which questions would you find most difficult to answer?
3. Would you change any answer made by Martha? How?
4. How would you prepare for this kind of interview? Explain.

130 *Unit 9 Lesson 3*

Talk or Write

This exercise develops focused listening.

Divide the class into four groups.
- Have each group dictate all four of their answers to a group recorder.
- Assign one question and answer to each group.
- Have the group reporters read their group's answer to the class.
- Ask other groups to compare the response with their own and comment on it.

Possible Answers
1. Answers will vary. Martha needs to provide a resume and information about her skills, her personal characteristics, and her plans for the future.
2. Answers will vary. Have learners explain their responses.
3. Answers will vary.
4. Answers will vary. List learners' responses on the board or a transparency.

Vocabulary

Follow the suggestions on p. 6 for introducing and reinforcing vocabulary words.

Ask learners for two related words in each category (i.e., two nouns, two verbs, or two adjectives).

Use Customizable Master 1 (Bingo) to play bingo using all the vocabulary words for this unit.

Group Chat

Use Customizable Master 2 (2-Column Chart). Follow the suggestions on p. 7 for customizing and duplicating the master. Make a copy for each group recorder.

Have learners refer back to Task 2 to describe their past job duties.

Activity A

Provide these additional examples of tense changing:

- Anna *has organized* a babysitting pool for the past few months.

  Anna *had organized* a babysitting pool in the past.

- Mark *has assisted* a teacher in class for a week now.

  Mark *had assisted* a teacher in class in his other school.

Task 3

Model the task, following the points in the student book. Use personal experience or the following example from an immigrant teacher:

Challenge: I wanted to get a job as a teacher, but I needed to be a citizen to get a permanent job.

Actions: I developed a plan of action. I studied for the citizenship test at my local library. I inquired about the application process at the immigration office. I filed my application, but I discovered that it takes five years to become a citizen.

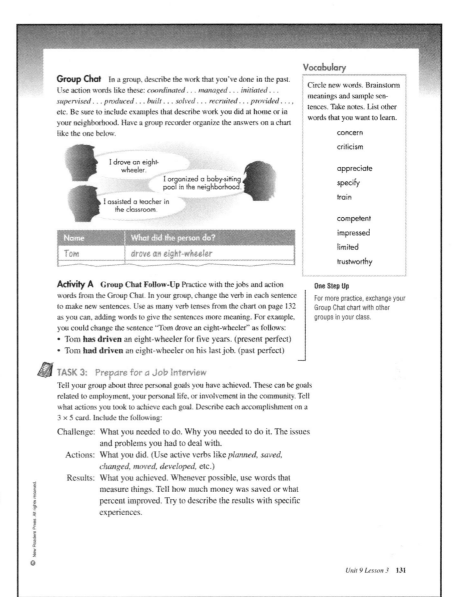

Results: At the immigration office I found out that I can be sworn in as a person intending to become a citizen. I promised under oath to become a citizen, and a little while later I became a teacher.

Learners often forget about their accomplishment of coming to and staying in the US.

- Talk about the steps and actions learners have already taken.
- Remind them of the strengths they needed and tell them to reference these as positive qualities they can talk about in job interviews.

Review Unit Skills

See pp. 8–9 for suggestions on games and activities to review the unit vocabulary and grammar.

Grammar Talk

Follow the suggestions on p. 7 for introducing the grammar point.

- As learners begin each row, demonstrate the tenses by taking a model sentence through the forms.
- Once you write the base sentence on the board or a transparency *(Martha is responsible.)*, you can make changes to it by erasing or adding words.

Present
Martha is responsible.
Martha is not responsible.
Is Martha responsible?

Present Progressive
Martha is being responsible.
Martha is not being responsible.
Is Martha being responsible?

Be + Going to + verb
Martha is going to be responsible.
Martha is not going to be responsible.
Is Martha going to be responsible?

Simple Past
Martha was responsible.
Martha was not responsible.
Was Martha responsible?

Future
Martha will be responsible.
Martha will not be responsible.
Will Martha be responsible?

Present Perfect
Martha has been responsible.
Martha has not been responsible.
Has Martha been responsible?

Past Perfect
Martha had been responsible.
Martha had not been responsible.
Had Martha been responsible?

 Distribute a copy of Unit Master 68 (Grammar: Verb Tense Sentences) to each learner. Have groups of learners complete the form with their own examples for each category.

Grammar Talk: Verb Tense Review
This chart reviews seven verb tenses that are often used.

	Affirmative Statement	**Negative Statement**	**Question**
Simple Present	I **am** concerned about it.	He **is not** trustworthy.	**Are** they competent?
	Martha **wants** a job.	Ana **doesn't like** criticism.	**Do** you **react** well to criticism?
Present Progressive	I**'m being** optimistic.	Ray **is not being** helpful.	**Are** you **being** assertive?
	We**'re looking** for a job.	Joe **is not talking** about his job.	**Are** they **preparing** a budget?
Be + Going to + verb	He**'s going to be** treasurer.	The effort **is not going to be** worth it.	**Are** there **going to be** obstacles?
	They**'re going to vote** for a chairperson.	He**'s not going to succeed.**	**Are** you **going to face** them?
Simple Past	Possibilities **were** good.	Lila **wasn't** overqualified.	**Was** your mother a single parent?
	He **developed** his best characteristics.	They **didn't offer** many benefits.	**Did** she **list** her references?
Future	I **will be** responsible for the duties.	She **will not be** an assertive candidate.	**Will** these children **be** optimistic and self-reliant?
	Now Tuan **will earn** a good living.	Their situation **will not help** them get more aid.	**Will** you **receive** the message by snail mail?
Present Perfect	As workers, they **have been** eager to learn.	I **haven't been** lonely here without you.	**Have** you **been** to this agency before?
	This year, I**'ve trained** six people in this company.	Carol **hasn't used** her car for weeks now.	**Have** you **stated** which kind of work you want?
Past Perfect	Amy **had been** sick.	Martha **hadn't been** optimistic about the job.	**Had** the personnel department **been** fair?
	I **had traveled** in South America during those years.	My parents **hadn't arrived** in the US in 1975.	**Had** the brothers **attained** high-level jobs?

What verb is in the first sentence in every pair? The second sentence in each pair has a regular verb. Notice that some sentences include long forms, while others include contractions. Take a few minutes to look at the chart again. Which tenses do you think you need most to review?

132   *Unit 9 Lesson 3*

 Use Unit Master 69 (Grammar: Review of Verb Tenses) now or at any time during the rest of the unit.

 Assign Workbook pp. 64–65.

Unit 9 Challenge Reading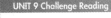

Reading Tip

Read the tip with learners. Talk about the meaning and function of a typical advice column.

Have groups generate a list of materials they read and their reasons for reading each. Begin by sharing examples such as these:

- I read mystery books for pleasure.
- I read newspapers for information on world politics and for sports.
- I read entertainment magazines for fun.
- I read computer manuals for my job.

Reflect on different writing styles in each reading source (e.g., computer manuals use technical language).

Challenge Reading

First, do a KWL activity. Distribute Customizable Master 3 (3-Column Chart) to each group of three or four learners. Have them write K (Already Know), W (Want to Know), and L (Learned) as the three column heads.

For the K column

- Have learners discuss everything they know about resumes.
- Be sure learners understand the purpose of a resume, the information needed, and the appropriate format, length, tone, and language.

For the W column

- Have groups discuss and record what else they want to know about resumes (e.g., Is one always necessary? Are there different kinds? How are resumes selected? What kind has a good chance of being accepted?).
- Have groups share their questions with the class. Explain that although not all answers can be found in the reading, the questions help to focus attention and improve comprehension.

UNIT 9 Challenge Reading

◆ **Reading Tip** Knowing the source of your reading may prepare you better for information introduced in the reading. The article below came from an advice column. Is the writer accurate and believable? Why? What do you think of Annabelle's writing style? What have you read that was written in a similar style?

Workplace Section

Ask Annabelle
Looking for a job? Can't find one?

Annabelle solves your most difficult career problems.

Dear Annabelle:

I have sent out over 100 resumes. I haven't gotten even one answer. What's going on?

How are interviewees chosen? How do they select people to interview? My friend told me that they throw the resumes into the air and read the first 10 that reach the floor. Is that true?

Jobless in Johnstown

Dear Jobless:

Yes, I have heard the one about throwing resumes in the air. It's just not true. If it were true, one of your 100 resumes might have gotten you a phone call by now. Your question is a good one. Just how are people chosen for jobs? I talked with personnel managers at 10 big companies about what makes a resume a "loser." Here are the things they do *not* want to see in a resume.

- **Messy.** Would you believe it? Coffee stains, whiteout, crossed-out words. Just plain ugly. Your resume is your introduction. You wouldn't wear a wrinkled shirt to an interview. Don't send a wrinkled resume.

---

accurate

conservative

down = sad

fasten your seatbelt = be prepared for an exciting experience

figure out = make sense of

fonts = styles of type

the one = the story, the joke

Unit 9 Challenge Reading **133**

- Have groups add the Talk or Write questions from p. 134 to the W column.

Allow 5 to 10 minutes for learners to read silently. If some finish ahead of others, ask them to list unknown words and expressions or to mark them with a pen or highlighter.

For the *L* Column

- First, have learners discuss the reading with their groups.
- Tell learners to complete this column with answers to the questions they wrote in the *W* column.
- Have them also add definitions for any unfamiliar words they listed or marked.
- If learners included the Talk or Write questions in the *W* column, they should add their answers to this section of the chart.

Circulate to answer any questions and to observe what learners say they learned.

Extension

Ask pairs of learners to read the parts of Annabelle and the two letter-writers. Encourage volunteers to perform for the class.

Talk or Write

Answers will vary.

Writing Task

Learners can use the *KWL* chart to answer the questions. They should use language and style appropriate for an advice column.

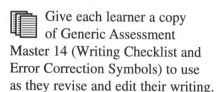 Give each learner a copy of Generic Assessment Master 14 (Writing Checklist and Error Correction Symbols) to use as they revise and edit their writing.

Workplace Section

...Ask Annabelle

- **Too long.** You may find the details of your life exciting, but a busy personnel manager wants the facts in a clear, simple form.
- **Too complicated.** Have a friend read your resume for you. If that person can't figure out what you've been doing for the past five years, you need to do some rewriting.
- **Not targeted for the job.** If the job description is for a lifeguard, don't emphasize your amazing computer experience. It's nice to tell companies that you have other skills and abilities, but stay focused on the job you're applying for.
- **Poor spelling and grammar.** They have to be perfect. If yours aren't, get a friend or teacher to check your draft.
- **Busy, busy, busy.** Yes, we are happy that you have lots of fonts on your computer, but this is not the time to use them all. No color, no pictures. White or beige paper. It's best to be conservative.

Annabelle

Dear Annabelle:

I had a friend read my resume and she said it was OK, but "flat." What does that mean? How can I fix a flat resume?

Down in Denver

Dear Down:

Your friend wasn't talking about the air in your tires. She was telling you, in a nice way, that your resume is boring, boring, boring. Don't worry. You can fix it with some strong, lively verbs. For example, which one of these phrases "sells" the writer and convinces the reader better— "Did filing" or "Developed an efficient filing system that saved the company time and money"?

Here are some strong verbs that you can use in your resume: *developed, created, planned, prepared, budgeted, advised, implemented.* Look them up in a dictionary if you don't know their meanings. Practice using them. Add one or two to your resume. When your friend reads it again, tell her to fasten her seatbelt.

Annabelle

P.S. Notice that the verbs are all in the past tense. If you're writing about your present job, use the present tense, but remember that all your past work experience is past, OK?

That's it for now. Don't forget to write to me if you need advice on job hunting. I'm here for you.

Annabelle Marti

Talk or Write

1. What do you think was the best advice Annabelle gave?
2. Do you think Annabelle's ideas are right? Give your reasons.
3. Were these letters easy to read? Why or why not?

Writing Task Write one of your own resume-related questions for a job-advice column. Then, as a class, put all the questions in a box. Each student chooses one to answer in the way that an advice columnist would. Write a serious answer using what you know, including the things you learned in this unit. Each student will read the question and his or her answer to the class. As a class, discuss the advice.

134 Unit 9 Challenge Reading

Unit 9 Project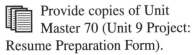

Learners use the work from this unit to prepare an up-to-date resume.

Get Ready

Provide copies of Unit Master 70 (Unit 9 Project: Resume Preparation Form).

Tell learners to review their work in Tasks 1 and 2. Remind them that both tasks prepared them to complete most of the work on this form.

Do the Work

- Make sure that learners use the resume language they learned in this unit to complete the form.
- This activity may be completed in sections, one section per learning session.

Technology Extra

Encourage learners to type their resumes on a computer. If possible, use the resume format found in a word-processing program.

Present

Have learners practice their presentations in pairs or small groups. For each job they have had, they should do the following:

- Describe the job in as much detail as possible.
- Tell when they started and stopped work.
- Provide basic information about the job responsibilities.
- Explain how this experience relates to a job they currently have or one they would like to have in the future.

Assessment

During the presentation, complete a copy of Unit Master 71 (Project Assessment Form) for each learner. The completed form will become part of each learner's portfolio.

Assign Workbook p. 66 (Check Your Progress).

Use Unit Master 72 (Unit Checkup/Review) whenever you complete this unit.

Self Assessment

Give each learner a copy of Generic Masters 12 (Speaking and Listening Self-Checks) and 13 (Writing and Reading Self-Checks) when they complete Unit 9. Go over the items together. The completed forms will become part of each learner's portfolio.

Complete Listening Scripts

This section contains scripts for the content of the audiotape and audio CD for *English—No Problem!* level 4. Pronunciation cues are indicated in square brackets.

Unit 1
Taking the First Step

Lesson 1, Page 12
Planning for Success
Listen to Patria and her grandmother talk about their dreams.

Grandmother: Your grandfather gave me this music box. I've listened to it play for the last fifty years. No matter where I've been, when I've heard this music, I've felt both happy and sad.
Patria: So are you glad that you came to the US?
Grandmother: I've had a wonderful life here, and the best part of it is knowing that your life will be even better than mine.
Patria: How do you know that? My friend Jack has always told me that making a better life takes planning and hard work, not just dreaming.
Grandmother: I've just always known it. Here, look at this. What is it?
Patria: It looks like a diploma. You never told me that you graduated from a special school.
Grandmother: It's for a course on natural medicines that I took a long time ago. I wanted to continue studying, but I couldn't. Still, I've taught myself much more about plants and herbs since then—how to use them to help people feel healthy.
Patria: So what else did you want to study?
Grandmother: I dreamed of being a nurse. I went to school for just a little while, met and married your grandfather, became a mother, and found a new dream in the US. I took a chance coming here, and I'm glad that I did. I'm not a nurse, but I've helped lots of people. And I've had many dreams come true. And what about you, Patria?
Patria: You've taught me everything you know about plants. You predicted that I would help people with my knowledge and maybe even become famous. That gave me a dream of my own.
Grandmother: Thank you, Patria. I . . . I guess I never realized that I'd helped you.
Patria: You really did. When I was in high school, I always dreamed of being a botanist. But, you know, I have to admit that working in the cafeteria at the Botanical Garden has been a dead-end job for me.

The people are nice, the work isn't hard, but I haven't been learning or growing. And for that reason, my dream began to seem so . . . so difficult. Sometimes I didn't even know how to begin. But I knew that I had to make it happen myself.
Grandmother: I know your dream will come true. I predict it.
Patria: Listen, sometimes your predictions come true and sometimes they don't, right? That's why I can't just dream. Some people can plan, but they never dream. Some people can dream, but they never plan. It's been good for me to dream, to see my long-term goals, but now I have to spend time planning carefully to make that dream come true. I've begun to think about all the steps I need to take. I've talked with other people and I've read some books. But to be successful, I need to keep on planning and working hard—working for years—until I finally reach my goal of being a botanist.
Grandmother: You'll find a way. But I don't want you to work as hard as I did. I want your life to be wonderful.
Patria: Working hard can be wonderful if you really love what you're working at. You'll see—sooner than you think.

Lesson 2, Page 16
*Pronunciation Target: Intonation with **Yes/No** Questions*
Listen for the intonation in these questions.
Have you ever been to a baseball ↑ game?
Have they arrived ↑ yet?

Lesson 3, Page 19
Pronunciation Target: Intonation with Statements
Listen for the intonation in these sentences.
If you don't know where you're ↑go↓ing, you'll probably never ↑get ↓there.
I like to visit the botanical ↑gar↓den.
Career counselors advise people on ca↑re↓ers.

Unit 2
Selling Your Skills

Lesson 1, Page 26
With a Little Help from My Friends
Listen to Hassam *[Hah-SUM]* and Masa *[MA-suh]* talk with their friend Peter.

Hassam and his wife, Masa, have invited a friend to their apartment to ask for advice. Hassam has an interview at an art gallery, and he wants to present himself and his work in the best way possible. Hassam's friend has a lot of experience interviewing.

Hassam: Peter, let's talk. You know, if my meeting with Ms. Patterson goes well tomorrow, she'll try to sell some of my work.
Peter: Do you have something to show her?
Hassam: If I had more time, I could make these photos of my work look more professional.
Peter: We never have enough time, Hassam. If you use what you have here, you'll do just fine.
Hassam: You're probably right. So do you think that if I added a little color to the photos, they would look better?
Peter: That's a good idea. Also, if I were you, I'd label each photo. You can make some nice labels and titles on your computer. By the way, these little cakes are delicious, Masa. You're so busy working in the bakery, how can you find time to bake at home?
Masa: They're good, but if I had the right ingredients, they would taste more like they do in Egypt. You know, you're right, Peter. I don't have much time for anything except my work. If Hassam sold some of his paintings, maybe we could take a vacation to see our families. We've both worked very hard these last two years.
Hassam: That's for sure. But let's get back to *my* problem. I really want to make a good impression tomorrow. I've prepared a resume. Any more suggestions, Peter?
Peter: Have you thought about what you're going to say to Ms. Patterson? You know, the way you present yourself is as important as your skills.
Hassam: I'm wondering what I should wear. Would I look too formal if I wore my new blue suit?
Peter: Good question. Let's talk about that.

Lesson 2, Page 30
Pronunciation Target: Sentence Stress
Listen for the stressed words in the sentences.
If I <u>needed</u> a <u>book</u>, I'd <u>go</u> to the <u>library</u>.
If I <u>wanted</u> a <u>job</u>, I'd <u>ask</u> my <u>brother</u> for <u>help</u>.

Lesson 3, Page 33
Pronunciation Target: Vowel Sounds in Say, Said, *and* Says
Listen for the sounds of the letter *a* in *say, says,* and *said.*

We say that we can help make a poster. Maria says that she can design web sites. Koji *[Ko-jee]* said that he could type.

Unit 3
Getting Help

Lesson 1, Page 40
Sharing Your Problems
Anna is talking with her co-workers about her daughter, Erin. Listen to their conversation.

Anna: Raising a teenager these days is very difficult.
Bob: I know. I sometimes feel like I'm losing control of my daughter. Everything I say is always wrong. Sometimes I just want to give up and let her do anything she wants. Then she'll learn her lesson!
Bonnie: I know how you feel, but we can't give up on them. They have to know we're there, paying attention to them.
Anna: Well, Erin stopped listening to me a long time ago. Since she met this boy, she's not the same person that she was. We used to talk about everything, but now she seems to be hiding something from me. And she's not paying attention to her schoolwork, so I'm worried.
Bonnie: Do you know this boy? Who is he?
Anna: I've met him a few times. He seems nice enough. He smiles and acts polite when he's in my home.
Bob: It's too bad we can't see how they act when they're *not* with us.
Anna: I don't trust that boy—maybe because he's *too* nice. Maybe he's trying to hide something. Once I thought that I smelled alcohol on his breath.
Bonnie: Well, what does Erin say?
Anna: Not much. When I asked her if he was drinking, she got very upset and started to yell at me.
Bob: Oh boy! She may be in a situation where you need to step in. If I were you I would stop her from going out with him.
Bonnie: That won't work. At her age, you can't just stop her. Be careful, she might keep seeing him just because you told her not to.
Anna: You know, I'm really scared for her. I suspect that sometimes he's violent. I think Erin is scared too, but I'm afraid to ask her.
Bonnie: Why do you say that he might be violent?
Anna: Well, I noticed some bruises on her arm yesterday. But she didn't want to talk about it.
Bonnie: You really should try to find help, Anna.

You probably need to go to the police to get protection for your daughter.

Bob: That doesn't always help. You really should get out of the neighborhood. Get out, as far as possible. This is no joke. It's serious business.

Anna: Oh! I don't know what to do. I really have to have a talk with Erin. I can't ignore this problem any longer.

Lesson 1, Page 41
Pronunciation Target: The Word of
Listen. What vowel sounds do you hear? *[For each pair, say the first phrase clearly and distinctly. Then follow with the colloquial pronunciation.]*

Lots of luck!	Lotsa luck!
in need of help	in nee duh velp
afraid of him	a fray duh vim
a friend of mine	a fren duh mine

Lesson 2, Page 44
Pronunciation Target: Holding Over Final Consonants
Listen. What sounds do you hear? *[For each pair, say the first phrase clearly and distinctly. Then follow with the colloquial pronunciation.]*

How are you?	How war you?
Look out!	Luh kout!
Come on!	Kum mon!
day or two	dae yor two

Unit 4
On Your Own

Lesson 2, Page 54
Becoming Your Own Boss
While waiting for the children to arrive, Donna and Sheba are watching a TV program about starting a business. Listen.

TV Interviewer: We've just been talking with Kimberly Corby Cooper, retired businesswoman and volunteer mentor for small businessmen and women who are just getting started. She told us a story about her career that was really inspiring. Kim, tell us, what advice do you have right now for a listener who wants to start his or her own business.

Kim: Ralph, I would say, "Go for it!" A man or woman who enjoys being creative and independent will enjoy having a small business. And actually the small business is not just a good way to become independent but also a good way to help other people. Did you know that most new jobs created in the US are in small businesses? Did you know that small businesses in the United States employ 51% of the workforce? The US Department of Commerce reported 9,907,000 self-employed people in 2001. Besides that, . . .

TV Interviewer: Wait a minute, Kim. This sounds too good. There must be some problems.

Kim: Oh, yes. In fact, according to the US Small Business Administration, over half of all new businesses fail within the first five years.

TV Interviewer: So this wouldn't be good for a person who needs a lot of security. Right?

Kim: No indeed. When my first company, which provided temporary secretaries, failed, I felt terrible. But I learned a lot. My second small business, which does office cleaning throughout the city, was very successful.

TV Interviewer: Do you have any advice for a person who wants to get started?

Kim: Yes, I do. Persistence pays, so don't give up. Learn from your mistakes and move on.

TV Interviewer: That's about all the time we have . . .

Donna: I can't listen to this anymore. Didn't you hear her say that over 50% of all small businesses fail? That's *half,* Sheba!

Sheba: I heard that 50% of all businesses succeed. *That's* half. I guess it depends on how you look at it. I thought her message was inspiring. Look at me, Donna. I'm a woman who came from Ethiopia. I did OK. I'll help you . . . *if* you really want to take the big step.

Donna: I want to, really.

Sheba: OK then. Let's get started.

Lesson 2, Page 58
Pronunciation Target: -tion [t-i-o-n] *Ending*
Listen for the stressed syllable.
coope<u>ra</u>tion
identifi<u>ca</u>tion
ope<u>ra</u>tion
pre<u>cau</u>tion

Lesson 2, Page 59
Pronunciation Target: **Could, Should,** *and* **Would** *with* **Have**
Listen for the reduction of the word *have.* *[For each pair, say the first sentence clearly and distinctly.*

Then follow with the colloquial pronunciation.]

Kim **would have** said where the center was located.
Kim **wooduv said** where the center was located.

I **could have** followed a sequence.
I **kooduv** followed a sequence.

My plan **should have** been more detailed.
My plan **shooduv** been more detailed.

Unit 5
Think before You Buy!

Lesson 1, Page 68
Shopping Smart

Bill is talking with his friends at school after class at the community college. Listen.

Bill: OK, guys, I need help. My old camera is broken and the warranty is expired. I spent a long time trying to figure out what to do with it, but I'm going to need to buy a new one, and, as usual, until I finish school and get a good job, I'm on a tight budget. Can you come up with ideas for how and where I could buy a new camera?
Keith: I've got an old camera. Want to buy it?
Bill: No, thanks! This time, I'd like to get a new, high-quality piece of equipment—but I want a good deal. Have any of you bought a camera lately? What do I need to know before I walk into a store?
Deborah: Well, you don't even need to walk into a store to make a purchase. You can find bargains on the web. There are also special product magazines that have good information and ads for cameras that you order through an 800 number or, again, through a web address. And, of course, there are the general consumer publications.
Bill: OK, but you know that I'm no expert on cameras. I don't want to read really technical explanations.
Keith: Well, one thing you need to think about is whether you want a traditional or a digital camera.
Bill: If I have a digital one, I can send pictures over the web, right? And I won't need to buy film. But that's actually really all I know.
Steve: Best thing you can do then, Bill, is to go to the library and read the latest issues of the consumer magazines. They'll tell you about the features and the advantages and disadvantages of each type of camera. They keep the explanations simple because they know the average reader is not a technical genius.

Deborah: Yeah, and they'll also rate different brands. It's a really good and easy way to do research when you want to buy a new product.
Keith: Also, sometimes they tell you which products are the best bargains—or the best buy for the money.
Bill: So once I research the possibilities and choose the camera I want, where do you think I can get the best price?
Deborah: Sometimes online prices are better than prices in stores. But big discount stores can have really good prices too. You can check prices at comparison-shopping web sites. You might try doing a computer search for words like *shopper, shopping,* and then maybe the combination *camera* and *shopping.*
Bill: I see I've got some work to do. Thanks for all your help!

Lesson 2, Page 72
Pronunciation Target: Stress in Compound Nouns and Common Phrases

<u>class</u>mates
<u>day</u>dreams
<u>camera</u> store
<u>picture</u> frame

Unit 6
Protecting Your Rights

Lesson 2, Page 85
Taking Legal Action

During coffee break at work, Mrs. Wu is calling Small Claims Court for information. Listen to the recorded message that she hears.

Welcome to the City Small Claims Court information line. To listen to this message in English, press *one.* For Spanish, press *two.* To listen to this message in other languages, press *three.* If you do not have a Touch-Tone phone or if you need to talk to an operator, press zero or stay on the line, and someone will help you.
[Electronic beep]
Listen to the following information before filing a claim. Press the pound key to have the message repeated.
Before filing a claim, you must contact the other person to discuss and try to resolve the problem. You must make sure the person knows you are going to sue.
Filing a claim: You can file a claim in this court if

the amount in dispute is five thousand dollars or less. The filing fee is twenty dollars. You can get claims forms at the Municipal Building.

Small Claims Court works quickly and will schedule your case within forty days.

Typical cases filed in Small Claims Court are auto accidents, property damage, landlord/tenant disputes, and collecting money owed.

A Small Claims Court judge will hear your case. Bring to court any papers, photos, contracts, or other things that support your case. You may also bring witnesses. You—the plaintiff, or the person suing—speak first. The defendant, or the person you are suing, can also present evidence. It's up to you to prove your case.

The judge may decide the case immediately or may mail the decision to you later.

Press the pound key to hear this message again.

Lesson 2, Page 86
Pronunciation Target: Initial Consonant Blends

Listen.

claim, class
pray, pride, product
plaintiff, plan, please
property, pressure
small
speak, spend, spring
stay, stare, state
try

Unit 7
Participating in Your Community

Lesson 3, Page 102
Getting Involved

Galina is at an open community meeting, where a representative of the town council is answering people's questions about a new low-income housing project. Listen to their discussion.

Mr. Schuler: Ladies and gentlemen, as you know, we are completing plans to build a new low-income housing project in the area between Clark and Elwood Streets. We have contracted our local builders already, and the work will begin this summer. I know that many of you are concerned about this project. I will try to answer your questions this evening. I know that members of our opposition have made you worry and fear what may happen.

But I promise you that this project will solve many of the problems this community has faced for years. It will *not,* I repeat, *not,* create more problems. *[brief pause]* I will take your questions now.

Audience Member 1: Mr. Schuler, how do you plan to solve the problem of our high school, which is already overcrowded? Won't the student population increase when the families move into the housing project?

Mr. Schuler: Those families are already here in our neighborhood, and their children already attend our schools. The conditions they live in are terrible. The new houses will improve these conditions. But the student population will not increase much more than what we already expected, based on higher elementary school and middle school enrollments. To make room for more students, we have already begun to move the school district headquarters out of the high school and into a new location. This will create more classroom space for all our children.

Audience Member 2: I am very concerned about the value of my home. I'm worried that it will go down because of the project. I've seen many FOR SALE signs near the high school. People are already running away.

Mr. Schuler: Unfortunately, our opposition has said many exaggerated and untrue things about this project. This has caused a small number of individuals to leave our community. But this town has a wonderful history of tolerance. It is a town that cares! We have grown successfully over the years, and we will continue to do so in the future!

Audience Member 3: How do you respond to the person who said that some town council members sold their own homes as soon as the proposal for this project was approved?

Mr. Schuler: One council member did sell her house. I'm sorry she couldn't be here tonight to answer your question, but she and I have talked about this ridiculous comment. The timing of her sale was merely a coincidence. She put her house up for sale as soon as her children had all started college, just at the time this project was approved.

Audience Member 4: Mr. Schuler, as parents we are very concerned about a possible rise in crime around the high school. We have seen that the overcrowded conditions in projects in neighboring towns have created an environment where drug activity and other types of crime have gotten out of control.

Mr. Schuler: When we planned our project, we paid special attention to the mistakes made by our neighbors. For one thing, we have taken steps to prevent overcrowding in this project. We have provided more plot space for each house. Every house will have a front and a back yard, and there will be good space between the houses. The project will look like a small village, not a typical city project.

Audience Member 5: What about the people who will live in these houses? I've seen lots of beautiful housing ruined in a year by the people who moved in.

Mr. Schuler: When we say low-income, we mean just that. These people *have* income. They are hard-working, just like you and me. They struggle, just as you and I do. They are young people, old people, people who normally wouldn't be able to afford a new house because of high costs at this time. They are good people, like you and me, who need a chance to make a good life for their families. *[pause]* Are there other questions? No? If not, I want to thank you for coming and for your interest in our community. Thank you very much, my friends.

Lesson 3, Page 103
Pronunciation Target: The Disappearing h
Listen to the stresses.

he, her, him
ee, er, im

What organization <u>did he</u> *[diddy]* join?
I've <u>seen her</u> *[seener]* at the polling place.
Have you <u>heard him</u> *[her-dim]* at the meeting?

Unit 8
It's Never Too Late

Lesson 2, Page 113
Working Out the Details
Willie is speaking with a salesperson about a video language course. Listen to their telephone conversation.

Salesman: Hello. You've reached Embassy Video Learning. Were you thinking about improving your English? Well, we have a program that can outdo any competitor's—only twelve tapes to fluent English. How can I help you?

Willie: I want to improve my English pronunciation and grammar.

Salesman: Let me tell you that you've called the right place at the right time. Give me your name,

address, and credit card number. In three days you will receive the twelve tapes, and, believe me, you'll never feel insecure about your English again. You can preview the tapes for thirty days and . . .

Willie: Excuse me. I have some questions.

Salesman: Of course you do. Tape One of the video learning program will help you ask those questions in perfect English. Just give me your name, address, and credit card number and you will receive the first tape, "Asking and Answering Questions in the Present Tense."

Willie: How much is it?

Salesman: Just three-ninety-five plus shipping.

Willie: That's a good price for twelve tapes.

Salesman: Three-ninety-five is for the first tape. The others are nineteen-ninety-five each.

Willie: Hmmm. I misunderstood. Well—eleven times nineteen-ninety-five is . . . let me see . . . two hundred nineteen dollars and forty-five cents, plus three ninety-five for the first one makes it two hundred twenty-three dollars and forty cents. How much is the shipping?

Salesman: It depends on where you live. Usually about five dollars a tape.

Willie: So each tape is . . . just a minute, uh . . . twenty-four ninety-five.

Salesman: I can see you don't need Tape Six, "Learning English for Math Problems."

Willie: I have my own business, and I need to be good at numbers. I'd been thinking about studying at home with videos. But I changed my mind. It's too expensive. Thank you. Goodbye.

Salesman: Wait. What day is it?

Willie: It's Tuesday.

Salesman: It's Super Tuesday for our company, and I can offer you a Super Tuesday special price.

Willie: No, really. Thank you very much. Goodbye.

Salesman: Wait. Take a minute to reconsider. Didn't you say that you were wanting to find a good course? Well, here it is, and now it's twenty percent off if you order immediately.

Willie: Goodbye.

Lesson 3, Page 117
Pronunciation Target: Disappearing Sounds and Syllables
Listen.
[Say the words in an everyday fashion so that the noted sounds disappear.]

The Missing *r* Sound
February *[feb-you-ary]*
governor *[guvva-ner]*
temperature *[tempa-ture]*
surprise *[sa-prize]*

The Missing *v* Sound in the Word *of*
lots of problems *[lotsa problems]*
waste of time *[wasta time]*
box of rocks *[boxa rox]*
bill of sale *[billa sale]*

The Disappearing Unstressed Vowel
[The underlined vowel should disappear.]
mem<u>o</u>rable *[mem-rable]*
choc<u>o</u>late *[choc-lit]*
ev<u>e</u>ry *[ev-ry]*
int<u>e</u>resting *[in-tres-ting]*
fav<u>o</u>rite *[fav-rit]*
rest<u>au</u>rant *[rest-rant]*
fam<u>i</u>ly *[fam-ly]*
hist<u>o</u>ry *[his-try]*

Unit 9
Celebrating Success

Lesson 1, Page 125
Pronunciation Target: Diphthongs
Listen.
buy
employ
background

Listen and repeat.
pie
lie
guy
toy
enjoy
choice
house
blouse
bough

Lesson 2, Page 128
Pronunciation Target: Syllable Stress
Listen and repeat.
<u>per</u>mit
per<u>mit</u>

Lesson 3, page 130
Making a Good Impression
Ms. Koval is interviewing Martha for a cleaning job. Listen to their conversation.

In this interview, Martha Bernard tries to focus on her skills, personal qualities that American employers want to see, and previous successes.

Ms. Koval: Hello Ms. Bernard. My name is Helena Koval. Please . . . sit down.
Martha: Thank you, Ms. Koval. Here's my resume.
Ms. Koval: So, Ms. Bernard. What can you tell me about yourself? I see here that you've had no paid work experience as a cleaner.
Martha: Yes, that was my biggest concern when I decided to apply for this job. However, the responsibilities listed in your ad are exactly the same as ones I perform regularly in my home and also performed in a previous job when I worked as a home health aide.
Ms. Koval: Hmmm. I see. However, cleaning an office requires a lot more than vacuuming a small carpet. You might have some difficulties operating a heavy-duty commercial cleaner.
Martha: I know that there will be new things to learn on the job. But I'm a very fast learner. And I'm eager to develop new skills. As you can see from my resume, I have done volunteer jobs. I was required to learn new and unfamiliar skills.
Ms. Koval: Interesting. I must say that I was impressed by your resume, even though it is limited. I'm curious. Your volunteer experience was clerical and administrative. Why have you applied to work as a cleaner?
Martha: Your ad said that you would train me. And I like the flexible schedule, benefits, and opportunities for advancement.
Ms. Koval: Let me ask you some questions regarding your personal qualities. As you know from our ad, we want an honest worker. Can you tell me why that is important for someone who cleans offices and homes?
Martha: Well, when you clean somebody's office space, you may find personal belongings or important documents that should be left untouched. You may even find valuables that the employees have left around. I am completely trustworthy, and people and agencies have trusted me in the past. For example, I handled quite a lot money as treasurer of my Parent's Association.

Ms. Koval: You've told me about your strengths. Now let's talk about your weaknesses.

Martha: People told me that as a volunteer I worked too hard. Sometimes that makes other workers look bad in front of their supervisors.

Ms. Koval: I know that problem from personal experience. OK . . . how would you handle a conflict with your colleagues at work?

Martha: I'd like to say that I'm quite competent at conflict resolution. I needed those skills in my position as Parent's Association treasurer. And, of course, being a parent has provided me with plenty of opportunities to practice conflict resolution. I believe that one way to stop a problem is to prevent it from starting. Being sensitive to my co-workers' needs, for example, may prevent unnecessary misunderstandings.

Ms. Koval: How do you react to criticism?

Martha: I try to learn from it. I believe that there is always something I can learn from both my superiors and my co-workers.

Ms. Koval: You've mentioned your child. Will your family responsibilities affect your work? We have a flexible schedule, but there *are* schedule demands, just like in any job.

Martha: I've planned my child care prior to this interview. I've also arranged for help in case of an emergency. Quite honestly, I don't expect to be absent from my job. You know, one feature of this job that appealed to me was the benefits it offers. I am sure that my family would do better if I had this job.

Ms. Koval: The fact that you have not worked with a supervisor worries me a little. I'm not sure how you would handle criticism and orders.

Martha: Of course, even as a volunteer, I had to follow orders. Even if I felt that things could be done differently, I respected the decisions of the organizers and worked cooperatively.

Ms. Koval: What do you see yourself doing five years from now?

Martha: I see myself working in a company like this, using my organizing skills as a supervisor of cleaners. I'd also like to learn sales skills. I'm good at that.

Ms. Koval: I can believe that. Frankly, I'm sold on your potential. You represent yourself very well. Of course, I need to check your references. What will they tell me about you?

Martha: That I'm a trustworthy person and a reliable one. Any job I start gets done.

Ms. Koval: Ms. Bernard, it was a pleasure interviewing you. I imagine that you'll hear from us within the next few days.

Martha: Thank you, Ms. Koval. I appreciate the time you've given me. I hope to hear from you soon. I know I'm a good worker, and I know that I can do good things at Elite.

Ms. Koval: Goodbye, Ms. Bernard.

Martha: Goodbye, Ms. Koval. Have a nice day now.

Working with Maps

Use the maps in this section for those opportunities when learners initiate topics about their home countries or items in the news.

US Map

Use the US map to show learners where their state and city are located. Ask them what state they live in, what other states they know about, and in what states they have friends or relatives.

Learners can write a paragraph about a state they think they might like to live in, giving reasons why, or a persuasive paragraph to convince someone to move to a certain state. Other learners could add to the paragraph in a chaining exercise. Here are some other activities you can do with the map:

- Use the map when appropriate to show where the characters in the student book live or where learners think they live.
- Addresses are referred to throughout the student book and workbook in the stories, forms, and elsewhere. Refer learners to the US map at each of these points to find the city or state.
- Have learners draw conclusions about life in different states based on the location of the state, e.g., north or south, near an ocean or not. Have them write short, descriptive paragraphs about life in a certain state.
- Show learners what states are considered parts of a region (the West, the Southwest, the South, the East Coast, the Pacific Coast, etc.).
- Have learners estimate distances between major cities.

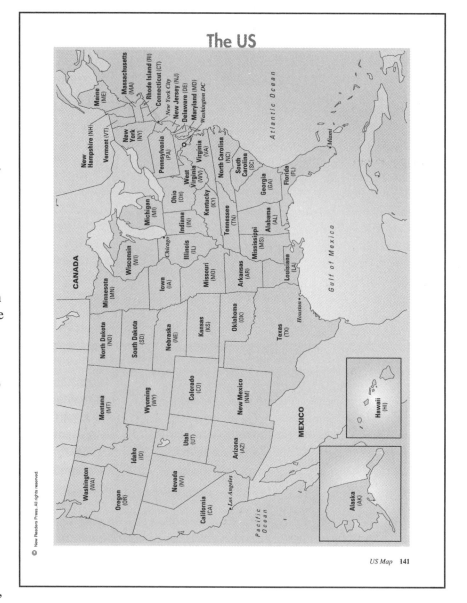

The US

US Map 141

World Map

Use a world map as a way to welcome new learners into your class.

- Post a wall map of the world on a bulletin board in your room. Have learners point to where they came from and where they are now.

- Take a Polaroid picture of each learner. Learners can write their names at the bottom of their pictures. Using a piece of yarn, pin one end of the yarn to the town they live in now and the other end to the town they came from, along with the picture of the learner. As new learners join your class, add their pictures to the map in the same way.

Refer learners to the world map in the student book when presenting the Compare Cultures portion of each unit.

As a quick review of adjectives, quiz learners with these kinds of questions:

- What language do they speak in Russia? (Russian)

- What are people who live in Canada called? (Canadians)

Invite learners to draw conclusions about life in different countries based on the location of the country. Then have them write short, descriptive paragraphs about life in a certain country.

Invite learners to bring to class an object or a picture that represents a country and have classmates guess what that country could be.

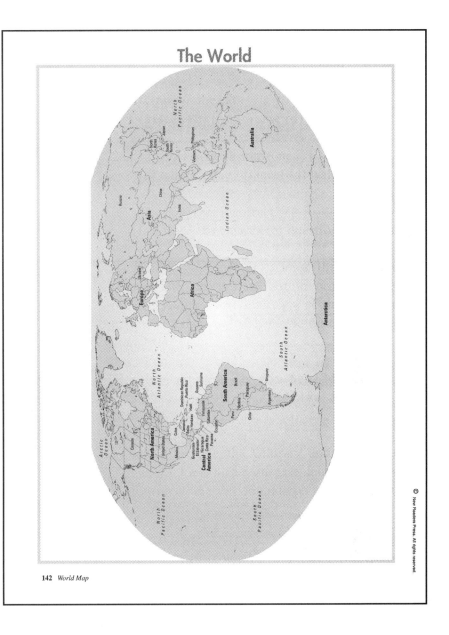

The World

142 *World Map*

Topics

Grammar and Pronunciation

A

adjective clauses with *who, which,* and *that,* 55

adverbs of time in past perfect, 83

articles, 89

C

complex sentences, 61, 83

compound nouns, pronunciation 72

compound sentences, 61

conditional contrary to fact, 27

connecting ideas with *so, because,* and *although,* 61

could, should, and *would,* pronunciation with *have,* 59

D

disappearing /h/, 103

disappearing sounds and syllables, 117

E

embedded questions, 72

F

final consonants followed by a vowel, pronunciation, 44

G

gerunds, 89

I

indirect speech, 33

infinitives, 89

intonation
in statements, 19
with *yes/no* questions, 16

O

objects of prepositions, 41

of after a word ending in a consonant, pronunciation, 41

P

passive voice in simple present, 125

past continuous, 111

past participles, 69, 97
of irregular verbs, 100

past perfect, 16
compared with present perfect, 16
adverbs of time in past perfect, 83

past perfect continuous, 117

past tense, 13
compared with present perfect, 13

prepositional phrases, 41, 44

prepositions of time *(on, in, at),* 89

present and past participles used as adjectives, 69, 97

present participles, 69, 97

present perfect, 13, 16
compared with simple past, 13
compared with past perfect, 16

R

reductions
could, should, and *would* with *have,* 59
of after a word ending in a consonant, 41

S

sounds
of *a* in *say, says, said,* 33
of consonant blends, 86
of diphthongs, 125

stress
in compound nouns, 72
in sentences, 30
of syllables affecting word meaning, 128

T

-tion ending, pronunciation 58

V

verb tense review, 132

W

who, which, and *that* in adjective clauses, 55